RELATIONSHIPS

Nothing, But The Truth!

Tracy McNeil

TRACYMAC
Publishing
A Division of Peace Place, LLC

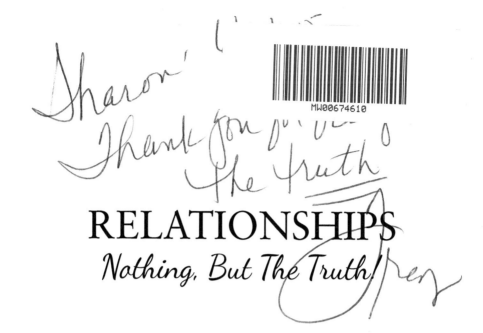

TracyMac Publishing
A Division of Peace Place LLC
P.O. Box 767
Knightdale, North Carolina 27545

Distributed by the Ingram Content Group

The author and those who have been interviewed have provided written consent and have tried to recreate events locales, and conversations based on their memories, reflecting a portion of their life experiences. In order to maintain anonymity, in some cases, the author has changed or excluded names of individuals and places and may have changed some identifying characteristics and details.

The information is not intended to replace professional medical or psychological advice. The author does not offer medical advice or prescribe the use of any technique as a form of treatment for physical or mental disorders without the advice of a physician, directly or indirectly. In the event you use any of this information for yourself, the author and publisher assume no responsibility for your actions and are in no way liable for misuse of the material.

Front Cover Design: Jessica Tilles – TWA Solutions (www.twasolutions.com)
Back Cover Design: Owen McNeil – Another McNeil Creation – A Division of Peace Place LLC
Back Cover Photos of Kisha Lee, Frandrea Madden, Robin White and Diane Hamilton: Purpose Productions and Photography (www.purposeproductionsandphotography.com)

ISBN—13: 978-0-9891013-0-1 (Paperback)
ISBN – 10: 9891013-0-45

Library of Congress Control Number: 2014915915

McNeil, Tracy A.
Relationships: nothing but the truth / Tracy A. McNeil

First Edition

Printed in the United States of America

Dedication

Dedicated to the memory of
My maternal grandparents
Joel Evance Rawls and Annie Cornelia Lash Rawls

My paternal grandparents
Johnnie Jones and Mabel Brinkley Jones

To them and all my ancestors who have paved the way, thank you for your shoulders on which I stand so that others may stand on mine.

Acknowledgements

I thank God.

I thank MacFamily2–Owen and Jayda of MacFamily3, for your undying and ever evolving love, mutual support, laughter and understanding and our faith in God as one another. What we have is real. I thank my parents Walter E. Jones and Thomasine Pleasant Rawls Jones and I am absolutely grateful for every relationship I was allowed to write about in this book. To each of you who gave me entrance into your life, permission to write about your incredible story and give the world access to your truth, I AM in so love with you and our relationships.

I thank my siblings, aunts, uncles, cousins, nieces, nephews, in-laws, "framily", friends and colleagues, because of you, I love you and I love relationships. To every reader, book club, discussion group and church gathering—thank you in advance for your willingness to start conversations that ignite action and set positive change ablaze. I thank Trice Hickman and Jessica Tilles for the trail they have blazed that lit my path within the literary world. Your friendships and professional relationships prove it is possible to mix business with pleasure. Linda Randolph, I appreciate you for professionally transcribing some of the initial interviews. For every relationship that has deliberately coached my life, be it through mentoring, spiritual connection, formal coaching and those incredible souls who inspire and coach me from a distance, I appreciate you! To relationships past, present and future, thank you.

Who is... TracyMac?

*"Truth is not something outside to be discovered,
it is something inside to be realized."*
—Osho

Did you know you were in this book? You are! You are in a relationship with people, places and things. You live a truth. What are your relationships truths? Who's truth? In all of its nuances, *Truth* is a comprehensive term that implies accuracy and honesty. Relationships and truths have been around long before history had a story. We have relationships with everything. Be it yours or someone else's, sometimes you may not know someone's truth until you hear their story. We communicate our stories through listening, speaking and writing. Listening to someone's life is like having access to a live, personal diary. Hearing their unique truths through relationships somehow has a way of illuminating and acknowledging your own.

As a professional, certified life coach, Tracy McNeil (affectionately known as TracyMac, "The Relationship Broker") has been a self-discovery, relationship, and personal development coach since 2004. But, like you, she's dealt with relationships all her life. In this relationship project, she shares real world stories, experiences and lessons learned, with a lively feel about relationships that are positively identifiable. You will read stories, conversations and events written candidly, honestly and even humorously about her life, along with some of her most cherished relationships with family, friends, clients and colleagues, who are all sharing and showing the honest realities of their personal and professional lives. As India.Arie sings, "Truth is—every relationship is a lesson."

These realities hail from people very much like you who have intriguing and diverse relationships with God, self, church, family, traditional marriage, sexuality, friendships to various forms of abuse and infidelities. Relationships can also take on the form of experiences and characteristics, such as the relationships we have with love, communication, sex, money, health and wellness, business, marriage, divorce and even social media. There is nothing dead or alive that is or is not expressed through relationships. Everyone has a different perspective and has had their share of ups and downs, as there is no hierarchy to pleasure or pain.

TracyMac has written and is sharing with the evidence of a skilled, relationship change agent. This is not simply another book about relationships that suggests steps, 1-2-3s or how to's and what to do's that may not be practical for your unique life. But, you will see the range of experiences and be encouraged to:

- ❖ Unapologetically embrace your truth about relationships, as you see others openly share theirs
- ❖ See yourself within and through the lives of others, without feeling exposed or condemned, but more connected and accepted
- ❖ Allow yourself to disagree with someone else's truth, without ignorance or hate, in order to cherish an even sweeter expression of your own
- ❖ No longer be embarrassed by the hell you may have gone through or are now ready to end
- ❖ Cease being ashamed of your journey, if its ordinary or crazy as hell
- ❖ Appreciate the relationship you have with yourself and celebrate it
- ❖ See the value of your unique story and appreciate seeing the similarities and differences shared by others
- ❖ Build and maintain more harmonious and strategic, personal and professional relationships

This book is an invitation into the reality of genuine relationships, while offering a greater sense of purpose, hope, direction, success, laughter, peace and love. Relationships are a life exchange, and only within relationships can you enjoy the privilege of your life being read, and help write and even turn the pages of the most fascinating lives. Enjoy a unique experience and journey through *Relationships: Nothing, But The Truth.*

Table of Contents

Introduction

In the beginning, there were relationships. Some relationships are without form, filled with dissatisfaction and feel void, indeed. There are relationships that thrive, facilitate discovery, development, celebrate individualism, build character, enjoy copious amounts of laughter, promote growth and sustain betterment. By listening, there are many things I know and understand about relationships, and many more things I have yet to discover. Individuals and relationships have a story, and relationships are how we interpret, exchange and communicate with one another. Relationships can flow from form to formless, and be shaped by almost any person, place or thing.

We have an individual relationship with ourselves that is a single thread, and we are interwoven into one cloth with other people, places, experiences, spirits, attributes, characteristics and things. The dynamics of our relationships vary and sometimes peace within a relationship can seem boring, while drama appears attractive and exciting. Yet, contrary to popular belief, drama is dysfunction's playhouse and is overrated. It can destroy the best dreams, visions and intentions. There are many experiencing very functional and viable relationships, including the one they have with themselves. But, where are those people? If we take cues from the news, social media, some of radio's "Top 10" and reality TV, it may seem the end of meaningful relationships would be imminent. The reality of most of our relationships look nothing like reality TV, *if* that's what you want to call it. But, it may feel as if it's morphing that way.

Behaviorally speaking, its human nature to imitate and accept what we see. Where are the examples of good relationships and relationships with what, or whom? Some who have good or even great relationships aren't given the spotlight or don't choose to tell their story because it's not entertaining, dysfunctional or dramatic enough. But everyone has a story! You have a story! Some of us don't meet negative statistics, fall into racial, gender, religious or geographical stereotypes, or don't have a hell to heaven testimony. Even though some of our testimony has some "straight from hell" experiences sprinkled in it, we haven't taken the stage because our life story may never impress the crowd. Others have survived the flames of a living hell and don't smell of smoke.

When I saw stories of those incredible lives, I used to look at my own story and thought, *I don't have a John Brown thing to say.* I mean, whose attention is my story going to hold? What proof do I have of resilience, persistence and the ability to overcome? Who is going to listen to my seemingly ordinary and be motivated to be or do better? I began to question my ability to be an effective example. I shrank my story smaller than it already was. Other times, and around folks who had *Lifetime* movie-worthy stories, I added to my story sometimes, and a few times I outright lied. I wanted the sensation of attention or the superSHEro cape of being a strong-ass Black woman. Truth be told, I didn't want to feel guilty for being who I was or having what I worked to have and overcome. I didn't realize my story didn't seem sensational because I lived with it. It had become so familiar that I didn't see its worth. So like many others, I shrugged, kept quiet and kept it moving. I wasn't ashamed and felt very deserving, but it seemed more acceptable to flow through life, play it safe and not say a word; applaud "them" and sit comfortably on my hands when it came to me and mine. Until one day...

I watched my daughter as she was playing. There was a rush of all my emotions, dreams and desires of wanting her to be loved beyond me, be happy and fulfilled. I wanted Jayda to have a relationship with God that lived outside religion, have healthy relationships with family and have great friends. I wanted her to know the joy of being in love, with herself and a lover. I wanted her to be musically inclined. After all, my mom's family is packed with very talented musicians, and my dad's family is filled with artists and musicians, too. I could sing all right, but did not play an instrument, so I knew she would have to grow with and beyond me through relationships.

My husband, Owen, and I had an old Yamaha keyboard. Neither of us could play it, but I bought it to plunk out chords for lyrics I'd write, or to break down vocal parts when I used to direct choirs and do vocal coaching. Since I was no longer using it, and I wanted to introduce Jayda to music, he put it in her room. We didn't want her to get hurt, so Owen set it on the floor instead of on the keyboard stand. She was not quite two years old then, and she loved to play the pre-recorded tracks and would *walk* on the keys. She also loved to dance to Kirk Franklin's song "Whatcha Looking 4?" You couldn't tell her and her pacifier they weren't setting it off! She would play with her toys by herself and dance while the music was playing. When the music would stop, she would give her pacifier a moment of relief and sweetly demand, "Mo peeze!" She eventually learned which button to push to put the CD on repeat. As I sat on the floor to play with her with blocks and puzzles that day, I looked at her, and thoughts raced through my mind at warp speed, making time halt.

I wondered what kind of life she would have. What kind of examples would she have other than Bible characters because church was almost all I knew? Deborah, Ruth and the two Marys were the best yet, and then there was Jezebel, but there had to be women in between. I knew there were incredible women in Black history, but I didn't want to have to go way back for her to look at black and white pictures or PBS documentaries. There was Oprah, but she didn't know us. It wasn't that I didn't want to have examples of white women or any men, I simply wanted her to see and have a pattern of what success and the value of relationships could look like in her skin. What current examples would she have about good relationships now?

I had been so conditioned by testimony services in the church. Some folks I knew, who were championed, were more respected and received attention because of their stories of hardship that turned triumphant. I read about women and men of all races who were celebrated and presented in history books, and who 'bout had to die to live. Because of those experiences, I thought you had to go to hell and back to have a story worth telling. Now, I had some stories all right, but not like those, and I did NOT want one. God knows I didn't want Jayda to have to have one either. But I did want her to be aware of their triumphant experiences so she could learn from them without having to experience them that way, as I did. I learned that if you did this that would happen. So, I didn't do it because I knew what would happen. I wasn't going to need to prove I had to have the same lesson when I was taught by the lessons of others. I wanted her to know those people and be appreciative of how incredible their lives were and had become. But where were they? Would they be willing to tell the truth? Would I be able to tell the truth and was my truth good enough? What could I do? Who could I be to her? Was my life salty enough to season hers? I wanted her to know about them. Where were these voices, these stories and these relationships?

I knew they were out there because I was out there. I knew I wasn't alone. I wanted Jayda to see those stories and hear those people, too. I could not predict her life or all her life's decisions, but I wanted her to see and listen to the lives of people; regular people who used their "regular" to be extraordinary so she could be equipped by example to write her own. I wanted her to experience functional, consistently sustaining and loving relationships with herself, life, family, friends, time, career, money and her lover. But I didn't want my protection to become suffocation because learning some things from experience can be the best teacher. I looked around, took inventory of my life and not only did I discover I was one of those people, but I knew all of those people. When it comes to the relationships in my personal and professional life, I hit the jackpot! So have they! (Aww, c'mon, it's a sad cow that can't ring its own bell!)

My wanting to hear from these brilliant voices wasn't all about Jayda. I wanted people I had relationships with to know about one another! See, I have this uncanny knack of being a relationship bridge builder—it's a gift, actually (ring-a-ling!). I have constructed bridges of friendship and relationship for people who would have never connected. It's effortless for me to build a similarity or commonality bridge, using the tools of purpose, mission, truth and humor. Their backgrounds and personalities are so different that on the surface they are extreme opposites, but in their heart of hearts they are kindred. I wanted them to hear and be aware of one another so they could see and hear themselves without my forcing the connection. I simply create the space, the opportunity and facilitate it—should they choose the way of the relationship bridge. Knowing how to have relationships determines how well we function within our community. I wanted Jayda to have an example. I wanted you and me to have examples. I wanted to be an example and share examples for anyone else who chose to see me and us as one. I also wanted to express my love and acceptance for those who don't. Love anyway!

Special Note: To maintain the authenticity of each participant's voice, interview responses were lightly edited.

Foreword

Margaret Packer
Executive Manager to Lisa Nichols
Motivating the Masses, Inc.

Relationships: Nothing But The Truth is an eye opening, soul stirring read that will transform humdrum thinking to conscious living and loving relationships on purpose. This collection of amazing stories will have you laughing and examining your truth, while expanding your emotional framework and causing you to be an active participant in your own life. This book is for mature audiences only, meaning those of you who take responsibility for your life and your relationships. This is not just another great read, this is an experience. I believe that where energy goes, energy grows and I want to have the best relationships I can so I came to the expert, Tracy (TracyMac) McNeil. I believe a seed must be sown into the ground in order for there to be a harvest. There are so many great seeds in this book, so as you read...plant and water and expect your harvest.

You may have picked up this book because it was given to you as a gift, or purchased it because you were intrigued with the title, or you simply wanted to know more about relationships.

Whatever the reason, it is by divine appointment that you have this book in your hands. In it are exposed treasures that are waiting for you to find them. Joseph Campbell said, "The cave you fear to enter holds the treasure you seek." Be courageous to keep turning the pages and let the coaches, teachers, stories and valuable lessons leap off the pages and enter your eyes, heart, and DNA. As you read each chapter, you may have a private breakthrough. With that being said, stop and celebrate and be ready to step into your new awareness.

If you're living and breathing you have relationships and by reading this book you will clearly identify where you are in many areas of your life. This is your opportunity to privately acknowledge and up level your relationships that could literally be non-existent, mediocre, or good at best, and transform them into life giving, transparent, powerful relationships, adding value to your life and those around you, leaving an amazing legacy.

As you read this book, take your time as you read each chapter. Make sure you make time to take immediate action—implement your own instructions. Now, I want to share with you something my grandfather taught me at a young age. "Chew the meat and spit the bones," which simply means: Read, absorb and use what is good and has value that you can digest and put into action. This would be the meat, so chew on that. The bones would be that which you are not ready for, doesn't feel right or you don't gravitate to, so simply "Spit the bones" and leave in the book for another season. Just keep on living because a season may come where you need this wisdom. This book of insightful wisdom and knowledge collected with hundreds of years of experience is a must read. If you are ready for an honest awakening with yourself, through your own action, you will be able to produce a powerful transformation. Or, you can simply be a voyeur to see what it looks like for other successful relationships as they expose what it looks like behind the black curtain, where they share their breakdowns and how they have turned them into breakthroughs. Please feel free to use their examples only as a blueprint as you create, re-establish, and fortify your own relationships. It has been said that the robber of joy is comparison, so this is not for you to compare your life to theirs. It's simply a guide for what is possible.

Relationships are tender, delicate and fragile and yet somehow tough, resilient and strong. By truly understanding ourselves and having a relationship with ourselves we can have a better relationship with others. Since you are the first example by which others will treat you it is your responsibility to give them a good and healthy example by which others will follow.

This book challenged my own thoughts in many areas and particularly about what a healthy marriage looks like, and what my own marriage looks like. As I read the chapter about marriage, pondered about it, re-read the chapter, I took a good look at what my expectations were of myself, of my husband, of what society says and took a good look and asked, "How did I come to these conclusions?" As a result of reading and self-introspection, I asked myself, "How do I feel about my marriage?" After examining my answer, I asked myself, "Am I willing to experience a love I've never given or received?" I prayed about it, and re-evaluated what I wanted my relationship to look like. Because I was willing to embrace these words that were challenging my mindset, stretching me out of my comfort zone and stirring my soul, I had a breakthrough that broke me open to more compassion, grace and love for myself and for the love of my life. This book has changed the trajectory of our marriage, of our relationship for which I am eternally grateful. My prayer is that you will eagerly read this book and allow all that is good to penetrate your being so that you can have breathtaking relationships on purpose and by design and not by chance.

It's a great privilege to recommend this work of TracyMac as she has stepped into her brilliance with knitting her own experiences, teaching, coaching, and breakthroughs along with other brilliant spirits to break the chains of mediocre thinking and living with this roadmap of tools to help you be liberated to live your best life ever. You are responsible for your relationships and you have the power to make them better. This requires thoughtful and mindful reading. Read with an open mind and heart, taking responsibility for what is and where you want to be. Finally, take action by being ready to expand and contract where needed, as you influence your relationships forever. I invite you to step into the next best season of your relationships.

Reading Tips

"Today you are you! That is truer than true! There is no one alive who is you-er than you!"

— Dr. Seuss

- Keep an open mind.
- Be honest with yourself.
- Do the "Implementation Guides" and take your time, but don't procrastinate like you do when it's time to pay your taxes.
- Keep a reader's journal to write down truths about yourself as you read. Don't judge your words, but make them responsible and empowering.
- Use *Relationships: Nothing But The Truth* to help you have some of those conversations you may have found difficult, awkward, controversial or challenging.
- Create or become a part of a book club or discussion group.
- If someone featured truth identifies with yours, feel free to reach out to them. See *References*.
- If you disagree with someone's truth, remember that their truth is as much truth to them as yours is to you. Just because you can't eat it doesn't mean you have the right to kill and bury it! Love anyway!

Chapter One

Goodness Sake, My Weight

"It takes more than just a good looking body. You've got to have the heart and soul to go with it."
—Epictetus

I may as well address the obvious relationship issue first. Oh for goodness sake, my weight, my weight, my weight! This relationship reminds me of the chorus of the song "It's A Thin Line Between Love and Hate." I've used weight to my advantage as comfort and camouflage, and other times it's been uncomfortable and exposed my undisciplined areas of life. Weight and I have always seemed to have an issue. Either I didn't have enough of it, or I had too much—way more of the latter, of course. This extra weight relationship is loyal and definitely sticks closer than a brother.

I am far from the smallest I've ever been, but I thank God because after years of being on different medications, eleven surgeries, and being misdiagnosed with cancer and lupus, I can proudly say I am now the healthiest I've ever been in my adult life! I'd better be after all that! There was also a time in my life, not too long ago, when I would have migraine and cluster headaches so badly, I would experience temporary paralysis on the right side of my face. I looked like I was having a stroke. Every single time, I was more scared that my face wouldn't return to normal than I feared the longevity of the excruciating pain. A few days ago, test results are still showing my blood work is a little wonky, so we'll see about that, but I am no longer on any medication and I feel great. I went years not being able to say that. Thank God!

I am healthy now and being overweight is still present and accounted for—every-single-size-18-pound-of-it. Whenever I used to read a book or weight- related article, watch a television program or engage in conversation about it, it was assumed that all fat, obese or morbidly obese people were feeding a problem or lazy. I did some serious reflection and soul searching. At one time I'd gotten up to a size 26 and I decided to get a Lap-Band in 2009. If I couldn't stop eating too much of the wrong foods on my own, maybe something else could help me. I kept having complications with the band due to reoccurring hiatal hernias and band blockage, and all the fluid was removed from the band in 2011, making it completely ineffective. It did help me lose forty-five pounds. So, there I was with a band that didn't work and I had gained the weight back. I decided to do it without surgical intervention. Eat less. Move more. So don't trip about the size 18s, I left the 26s. So where did this weight issue come from?

I knew I had a few issues growing up and in my adult life, but they weren't hungry and I wasn't feeding them. I was a skinny little kid. When I was at my lowest weight as an adult, around one hundred twenty-five pounds, I had an addiction to Pepsi that would rival any illegal drug on the street. I'd buy five, two liters for the week, put them in the freezer at night, take one out in the morning, pour my doses in my cup with crushed ice, take the bottle with me and sip on my straw-drip all day. What? I went walking and running at night so that fixed it, right? I was in a size 5. My food choices were unhealthy, but because I wasn't overweight then it wasn't a problem. I would run two or three miles, three to four days per week, and after injuring my knee, I pretty much stopped cold turkey. That's when I started to gain weight. No running, how about Tae Bo?

TAE BO

Remember those videos? I fondly remember the time my friend Annie Wardington and I decided we were going to take on Tae Bo. I bought the VHS set (a long time ago, eh?!) and we planned for her to come over so we could do the workout together. Well, she came over, we warmed up with Billy Blanks, and then my phone rang. I answered and after I ended the very short telephone conversation, she and I started talking about the video. I offered her some tea and well…what started out as us drinking water and warming up had progressed to sweet tea, her homemade turkey salad, chips, snacks and sitting down. All we did was *watch* Billy and the crew. We warmed up and cooled down all at the same time. We didn't implement a thing and it showed! Have you ever been so out of shape that your clothes get frustrated? Frustrated clothes roll up, gap, gather, pinch and pull! I mean, it's a terrible thing to have your girdle and knee highs roll down at the same time. It'll change your walk and have you walking sideways. Well, our ill-fitting clothes were so frustrated with us and we were frustrated with ourselves. We wore our frustrated Sunday suits, but were thankful that our expanding frames would be hidden underneath our choir robes. We evolved into a life of elastic waistbands or as she said, "Rubber in the waist." We had the workout clothes, TV, VCR, the video, time and space, but we didn't use it. Poor Billy was trying to help us, but instead we helped ourselves to talking, eating and drinking, which allowed us to need plenty of rubber in the waist. We knew, but we didn't do. We did not implement. I never did workout right to those tapes. Just writing this is causing me to reminisce about great times we had at Annie's house or James and Tina Watkins' house, and all of "the crew" would come together, have some good times laughing and eating back in the day. True friends for life!

I had no consistent implementation with working out, and some reasons were justifiable—after fracturing my ankle now having a little "arthr" in one knee and a whole lot of "itis" in the other, I don't run like I'd used to. But the elliptical has taken away that excuse. But every pound I weigh is because of me. Me. I know more about what's healthiest for my body and I exercise and eat much better. One of the reasons for my being overweight is lack of *consistent* exercise and being fond of the unhealthiest foods—cake, cookies, pie and chips. A slow and picky eater, what

I did like, I ate often. What I did eat, I ate all that was on my plate. Aren't you supposed to? I was a part of the Clean Plate Club. How about you?

Being a part of the Clean Plate Club should not have been a requirement to keep from getting a spanking or going outside. Being a member of the Clean Plate Club was a sign of love and appreciation. A clean plate was a sign of obedience and gratitude. How else were you supposed to show your parents, grandparents, relatives and church folk you appreciated the hard work they did to put food on the table that they spent all day cooking? It was pleasing to them for you to eat all of your food. It was a culture. It's still hard for me to throw food away once I put it on my plate, so I just don't put as much on my plate. But let me tell you how this Clean Plate Club business used to go down with me, the little girl named Tracy.

THE CLEAN PLATE CLUB

Here she was again, sitting at the dinner table alone, staring at five empty chairs, four of which were once occupied, but had become vacant because her family had finished their dinner and passed the Clean Plate Club. The dishes had been washed; the only light on in the kitchen was the one from the stove and sunlight coming in from the window. The sun was still out and the streetlights hadn't come on, so there was still time to play! The only thing holding her back from walking through that screened door was finishing the cold food on her plate. It started out smelling good and piping hot, but time and taste had made hunger wax cold, literally. She counts the twenty-two green peas—some were still plump and some were starting to look like mini, wet, green raisins. Separating them one by one, thinking, *If I don't like them, surely they don't like each other*. It's also her ever-failing master plan to spread the food out so it would appear that some had been eaten. The homemade hamburger seemed to be alive, as charred spots showed signs of abuse, the bell peppers looked like its arms and legs and the onions were its eyes. She swore she could see them blinking. The gravy looked like a pool of mud, swimming with rice, or as she saw it, maggots. The longer she looked at the food the longer it stared back at her.

Turning around, she looked through the screen door, startled by laughter and the sound of bouncing balls, as voices debated about cheating while playing stick ball. She knew her play time was doomed by these enemy creatures on her plate and that dreaded piano. So she pushed having to practice the piano out of her mind and she decided to play a game of stickball with these creatures on her plate. They had nothing better to do than to be up for a game of stickball. They had time to be her playmates, or at least let her act like it. She had a creative burst of excitement! The gravy could become the field, scattered peas clumped together to become the bases, the rice, which she was convinced were the same maggots she'd seen in the garbage can, become fans and that big ol' piece of blinking meat would get fork split into several pieces to become the players. They were all Black, ya know? All of them were stationery except the batter... And IT (no gender assigned) hits a homerun! Crack! Right out of "Maggot Park" and the maggots were already standing! "Black Burger" circled all the bases, several times off one hit, matching the sound of activity going on outside. That inning lasted a little while before she realized the mess she had made on the plate and now it looked even grosser. What was worse than this plate of mess, sitting alone, not being able to play outside, still hungry and having to practice piano was the house rule: "Tracy, if you don't eat it for dinner, you will see it again for breakfast!" Oh my Lord!

Now you have to know, back then around 1974, there were no microwaves. Well if it were, there wasn't one for miles from Tracy's house. So, the thought of this baseball field of mess—on a 1974 "kitchen appliance green" plate—was going to have to be reheated in the oven was enough to blow chunks! She couldn't bear having her mom catching her at it again, and raking all the food together and sometimes feeding it to her. *What can I do?* she thought. She looked around for her brother because sometimes, if her food wasn't too cold, he'd do a drive by and eat it for her. But he was *way* outside. She swallowed in thought, now realizing her throat was a little dry because she was thirsty. That's Part B of the dinner rule: No drinking until you have eaten. But that red Kool-Aid was just an arm's reach away; her dad had moved it to the middle of the kitchen table as a deterrent. She reached her praying mantis-looking arm over to the orange Tupperware cup, but drew back quickly, thinking she heard someone coming. No, it was her dad walking down the hallway. She knew he wasn't coming in her direction because she heard the sound of the wooden parquet flooring pop. It always made that sound when someone walked past the bathroom.

With the coast clear, she took a quick sip, and put the cup right back, exactly on the water circle that had been made on the table. Her thirst slightly quenched, but disappointed because the ice had melted and it tasted like water that was only thinking about having a little flavor. She couldn't see the Kool-Aid, but she knew it was red because she saw her sister pour everyone a cupful. Who cares if it was strawberry, cherry, black cherry or fruit punch flavored? All she remembered was that it was red. "Aha!" she almost said it out loud, "If I can't see inside the cup, they can't see inside the cup." Rubbing her little boney fingers and hands together, her big—no HUGE—bright eyes quickly shifted from left to right, and smiling wide (no matter the missing and varying sizes of her first grade teeth), she had instantly conspired a new, foolproof master plan. And this one HAD to work. It was a matter of life and dying of food poisoning if she had to eat this homemade mess of a stickball game, all scrapped together. Checking all entrances, she grabbed the cup, guzzled down the red Kool-Aid as it got sweeter and sweeter with each swallow. As she had seen her mom, and sometimes her dad do, Tracy raked all of her food together, and slid it all to one side of the square, plastic plate. With her fork in her left hand and using her crowded fingers on her right hand, she began to shovel the stickball field, bases, players, crowd and batter into the cup, which had now become their dugout. But she was too smart to keep it ALL in the cup, so she scooped out a few players, fans, onion eyes and bases, and slid them around the smaller field of mud she left on the plate.

Man! If she could pull off this caper and get through her piano lessons without crying, this plan would work for the rest of her life! With her heart beating fast, her smile gone, but her eyes still bucked with nervous excitement, she heard, "Tracy! Tracy! *Tracaaaaay!*"

Not quite ready to answer, but too scared not to, her mousy voice quivered, "Yes."

"Are you finished with that food? I'm coming to see," said her mom.

"Almost…" said Tracy, trying to get the evidence off her fingers and from around the mouth and the sides of the cup. She was forensic smart thirty years before CSI.

"Almost?! Let me see, here I come!" her mom yelled from down the hallway. "And it bet-not be in the trash can." The best thing her mom could have done was gift her with that announcement because her mom had this uncanny, miracle-working knack of showing up stealth and Tracy's butt learned the lesson from a belt months prior—not to ever try the trash can trick again, not ever! Especially if she didn't stuff it down the sides and put a paper towel over it.

Implementation Guide: What's on your plate? What is your relationship like with your weight? How's your health? What's your relationship with food? What's your healthiest size or weight?

Chapter Two

Meet the Parents

"Truth is, by nature, self-evident. As soon as you remove the cobwebs of ignorance that surround it, it shines clear."

—Mahatma Gandhi

ME & MRS. JONES

Tracy had time to prepare. With the crime scene cleared, in comes her mom, the most beautiful woman she'd ever seen, rocking the best curly Afro in life, hip hugging, bell-bottom jeans, wooden platform shoes with brown leather straps, white buttoned down shirt tied at the waist, 1970's thin, with full breasts, light skinned, doe-shaped eyes, just a touch of makeup and frosted lipstick. She could pull a drag on her cigarette and exhale smoke that looked like it was doing a sexy belly dance, without touching it. With one slightly squinted eye from the smoke and a quick "what's up" head toss, she resembled Thelma from *Good Times*. Tracy couldn't remember the first time she saw her mom, but the first time she does remember was her mom getting dressed to go to the Marine Corps ball. She remembered watching her mom put on her silver platform shoes and makeup that evening, and she wore a lavender gown with an exaggerated keyhole neckline. She was so pretty. Knowing that wasn't the first time she'd met her mom, that's her first memory. They'd met for the first time in February 1969, or had they?

But every time she saw her mom, Mrs. Thomasine Pleasant Rawls Jones, she looked like she was going somewhere picture worthy and was picture ready, even first thing the morning. She could dress her little "a" has two "s's" off! And the first thing she donned was her smile. It was bright and exciting, yet it wasn't goofy because it was balanced with a slight frown that was embedded between her full, but plucked eyebrows. Her smile was beautiful, not just because of her teeth, but because she smiled with her eyes. She was nice, clean and took care of her husband and three children. She always looked good and smelled even better, but this sister didn't play.

Standing at a whopping five feet tall, when it came to spankings—no, beating time—she morphed into a super ninja or Captain Caveman's sister, who lived in give-you-something-to-cry-about city. She could dance, not just dance, but win dance contests—hand dancing, the turtle, the bump and anything else that came down the Soul Train line. Yet, she was regal and classy with it and everything else she did. She had to be this and only this to be equally paired with and married to this man Tracy called Dad. He wasn't mean, but he seemed too strong and serious to be questioned, or second guessed.

THE MARINE

Walter Earl Jones Sr. was a Marine's Marine. He was as squared away and as sharp as possible. His "gig line" was always straight, the name tag on his fatigues read: JONES. The letters looked high definition against that dollar bill green uniform. With precision, he faithfully pressed creases into the blouse and trousers until they appeared to be thin, white, chalked lines. He was so dedicated to the look of his poster-ready uniform that Tracy thought he was a little crazy. He'd wash his matching cover, or hat, in some kind of white stuff, set it on this silver ring to form it and put it in the oven. The oven! You the mean the same hot box her left over plates of food had to be reheated in? Then, he'd rub the belt buckle with Brasso, and when other people simply polished their boots, he seemed to massage them and shine them up as if he was doing it for a contest or to make money.

You see, she never heard her dad say too much in those days. He went to work Marine-Corps early and returned hardworking late. He always seemed to be calmly preoccupied about something else, but he had a way of seeming focused at whatever was at hand, at the same time. Almost like some Jedi mind trick stuff before Jedi's could do mind tricks. Between the jingle of his keys and a crisp whistle, Tracy always knew when he came home. His whistle was clear—high pitched and had a vibrato—but she could never identify the song he was whistling. She wondered if he even knew or was it just a random musical announcement. And even though he was approachable, it didn't seem like he would welcome immature interruptions. He was serious, yet content. But sometimes, especially when he went in that little cabinet he had that was filled with different kinds of bottles of what Tracy thought to be rotten and sour smelling Kool-Aid—red, brown and clear—he would play, laugh more and sing. Though her mom had recently started going to a new church, he didn't, but every time he had a taste of his Kool-Aid, he sang the best blues, church and quartet songs ever! He seemed happier, but never out of control, sloppy or foolish. His seriousness was cuddled with humility, maybe because of his shadow, Tracy thought, or at least that's what her five or six-year-old vocabulary compared it to. One day, she asked him if she could touch his shadow.

He would leave the bathroom door opened when he shaved because his shaving cream smelled hazmat toxic. He'd mix this powder called Magic Shave with water to make shaving cream and it stunk to high heaven. It smelled like garbage mixed with paint, any poisonous chemical from the storage shed, and a futuristic carcinogen had all been boiled in the same pot. Tracy would pinch her nose and hold her breath, but she liked to see him lather on the white creamy foam and with neat strokes, gradually revealing his hairless, brown skin again. Tracy observed her parents and siblings a lot, doing the simplest tasks, most times without questions. Because either she felt like she was in the way, they didn't notice she was there or her presence posed no threat to interrupt their activity. But this particular day, she saw him seeing his own reflection in the mirror and it made the "shadow" on his face stand out for some reason. It was as if she could see it when looking at him, but that day she realized he could see it, too, by looking at himself.

She was a little afraid and almost embarrassed for him, but encouraged by her childhood innocence and curiosity, she said, "Dad, what's that on your face?"

He almost chuckled. "It's my birthmark," he said, and leaned down and turned toward her.

"Does it hurt?"

"No, it feels like the rest of my skin."

"Can I touch it?" she asked, almost surprising herself.

"Yeah!"

It felt no different than the rest of the skin on his face and forehead, but because it was darker than the other side of his forehead, she imagined the texture was just as timid as she was, so it had to be softer. It was his birthmark that was almost half-heart shaped and covered half of his forehead and narrowed as it covered the side of his face and neck. When she touched it, she was surprised it didn't hurt him. It wasn't scary at all. In fact, it seemed to be a bonding moment, the assurance and agreement that would remind him and her to be accepting of others who may be marked in other ways. But when she walked out of the bathroom, she looked at her hand to make sure she hadn't rubbed any off and even though she didn't see anything on her fingers, she rubbed her hand on her shorts just in case. If he saw her, he didn't let on. Maybe because he had already barred the brunt of stares, questions and childhood jokes. Plus, he wasn't the kind of man to say much more about it. Because Tracy heard him chuckle a little after she was a few steps down the hallway, maybe he heard the parquet floor pop, too.

Like her mom, he dressed nice, but Tracy didn't see him too often out of uniform. When he did wear street clothes, he wore dress shirts and slacks and maintained them just as crisp and neat as his uniform, shoes too. He smelled good, too—Aqua Velva or Old Spice. He was handsome and had some "Pomp and Circumstance" about him. He had a contagious smile, nice teeth and he had a way of leaning back when he laughed, but never too loudly. And like his clean shaven face, being meticulous about his appearance, it didn't stop with his personal appearance; Mr. Jones required a clean house and no cutting corners. He could smell a stain and see a smell a mile away. He was serious about cleanliness, period! Who needed a white glove when he could use his brown finger! The house was so clean, whenever they had to move, passing military housing inspections was always a breeze. He may have had stock in bleach and that little bottle of brown Lysol with the red label and yellow cap.

Yep, the house was military ready for company coming over all the time. Who has white velvet furniture in their living room with three school-aged children? Yes, white! Three chirren! The living room was very well decorated, much like the rest of the home, but it was the "ooh ahh" room. He made them Joneses a clean tribe. The Joneses didn't have a lot of money, but he made it a point that cleanliness would make up for what money couldn't buy and no one would know the difference. The living room was decked out in blue velvet, oversized couch and loveseat and an oversized white velvet chair and ottoman. No plastic. Tracy's grandparents had enough plastic covering their furniture for a small city. So no sticky thighs and sweaty backs here in the Jones's house. Coffee table, end tables, lamps, drapes, ashtrays and whatnots were the epitome of '70's décor. Yeah there were several ashtrays in every room, because Earl Jones smoked, too—Newport.

The living room wasn't frequented until company came over. Well, *they* didn't frequent it, but Tracy did! Tracy was a latchkey kid. Yes, at five years old and she walked about three blocks home from school, most times alone. Now days, a five-year-old girl being outside alone is dangerous, and though Tracy walking alone may not have been the best decision to make, it was seen as the only option. She made it home or to the neighbor's house safely every day. And, on days she didn't want to be alone, she would lock herself out so she could go hang out with the neighbors. She would go in the house, tiptoe to the kitchen to see if her mom left a good snack on the counter. If the snack was good enough, after eating she'd beeline to that white ottoman as if she were stealing bags of unmarked cash. Sitting right in the middle of that plush white chair, she would stretch one of her boney, little legs across the side and lay back on the chair. She felt if she had to be in that big ol' scary house by herself, she would enjoy the best of it. She'd sneak into her brother's room and look at the scary KISS albums he had hidden or she'd stand tall on her sister's side of the room, walking up and down that side that was so interesting, only because it was forbidden. Empowering! And in forensic style she covered her tracks. Yes, vacuum tracks!

Implementation Guide: What is the earliest memory you have of yourself? How are you different from when you were a child? How are you the same? What do you know about your parents? What was your relationship like with whoever raised you? What positive memories do you have of them?

Chapter Three

The Five-Year-Old Girl

"Are you making sure that your story is going to be a good tell? There is a power in standing in your truth!"
—Lisa Nichols

THE TRUTH ACCORDING TO DIANE HAMILTON

I remember being a latchkey kid and walking home safely from school at five years old. At five years old, Diane walked home from school one day by herself, too. Unlike me, that wasn't normal for her to do. But this day, her mother wasn't there to pick her up. Diane lived in The Bronx, New York, and that day her walk home was much different.

TracyMac: Diane, tell us a little bit about you and we'll go from there. I love hearing you speak with your strong accent… straight from the Bronx.

Diane: Okay. My name is Diane Hamilton and I'm originally from New York City. I have been in North Carolina now for almost twenty years. I am a mother of three wonderful boys. I'm a wife, and I'm also a grandmother of three wonderful boys. I am working now as an accountant and I'm currently in the process of getting my life coach certification. I want to coach to offer women greater hope, happiness, and many other positive things I have become. That's me. That's me!

TracyMac: How did we meet?

Diane: Oh, I first met Tracy, there was a lady, a mutual friend of ours, was having, if I'm right, it was tea and conversation or…

TracyMac: I can't remember the title. Something like Tea and Talk or something like that.

Diane: Yeah, something like that, Tea and Talk. Well, we introduced ourselves, but only spoke briefly. It was nice meeting you at that event. I came there with my life coach at the time. Then I met you again at an event with another colleague of ours. That was a wonderful connection there and it seemed like the connection got stronger.

TracyMac: Yes, yes. You know, Diane, I still have that picture. I'm going to have to send it to you.

Diane: Oh okay! Wonderful. I bought your book, *The Book of Purpose,* and you autographed it for me that day. And then later, I saw your post on my news feed on Facebook, or something, and it was about you having a group coaching session. God just touched me. I had been looking to get my life coach certification. I didn't know if you certified life coaches, but God said, "She is the one!" So I called you. We had a great conversation, and the rest is history.

TracyMac: It is. Diane, you have a wonderful story. And I know you don't have time to go into a lot of detail about it, but tell those who are reading about Diane.

Diane: One of my speaking engagements was at a church and they gave me the topic, "Recovering Pieces of Me," and oh how that fit my story so well. My peace in my life was broken at the age of five years old. I was violated. From that one incident it just, I don't know if I want to say it went downhill because I was only five years old, but I didn't know that would play a huge role in the choices that I made.

TracyMac: Tell us what the violation was, was it sexual abuse?

Diane: I was sexually violated at the age of five years old by someone that I knew. Coming from school, my mother wasn't home, and he told me he would take me to where my mother was. I said okay because I knew him. And he took me across the street and he took me into a building and that's where everything happened. He sexually violated me. When I went back home I wasn't gonna tell my mother. I told my cousin and my cousin told me, "You need to tell." I told my mother. I remember going to the police, so he did get locked up. But what else happened? No one ever asked me if I was okay. No one took care of Diane. A piece of me left at five years old because no one asked me or checked in on me. I guessed they assumed I was okay. No one reassured me that it wasn't my fault. No one told me it would be okay. Someone took a piece from me; my peace, too.

TracyMac: Maybe him being locked up, they figured that ended it. He got what he deserved, he's locked up. But they didn't check on five-year-old Diane, that little girl.

CHOICES

Diane: They never did. They left that alone, me alone. And I went on with my life; I mean at five years old, you know, I grew up. I did kid things. I thought everything was okay. I was normal. I didn't ever think of anything other than just growing up, playing. As I got older it showed up as my making bad choices in relationships, even friendships.

TracyMac: What kind of choices did you find yourself making, Diane?

Diane: The kind of choices that I started making showed up as my wanting to be loved, I wanted attention. I wanted to be accepted. I wanted to be loved because a piece of me was missing and I didn't know how to love myself because that piece was missing. That piece needed to be nourished. So I tried to fill; it's like trying to fill up a hole. I was trying to fill the hole and the missing piece. When it came to friends, I would try to buy my friends. "Come on, let's go shopping! If you go with me I will buy you something!" Or if I was in a relationship I would do everything, even give up myself, so a man would stay. I thought him being with me would fill my void. But nothing did. When I look back, nothing was comfortable for me. I even had issues with my mother. I love my mother dearly, and she was an alcoholic. It was only so much she could offer me. Later on in life, I realized that a piece of her life was missing, too. I don't know what happened, but I know something happened. I went on through life looking, looking for great relationships and never found them and looking for that right person. Not finding the person, I started trying drugs for fun. I was going out, hanging out with my friends, thinking that was having a good time, but my drug of choice was coke, sniffing cocaine. Then I started noticing when I felt empty, I got high. I was what they call a functioning addict because I went to work every day. I dressed every day. If you saw me you wouldn't know it. Some people are functioning alcoholics; you go to work all the time, and no one knows. When the weekends came that's when I did my thing. If it rained outside I wanted to get high. If I wasn't feeling good I wanted to get high because I thought that was filling my void. But eventually I wasn't filling it, it was tearing me down.

TracyMac: Diane, when did you notice? What happened to cause you to say this isn't working anymore? Was there a particular moment to say this just is not working? What was that moment and what did you have to do?

Diane: Well, when it came to the drugs, God showed me that if you keep doing this your kids are going to be taken away from you. And not that I was living a life, and this might sound a little crazy, I wasn't in the street. I wasn't in places I shouldn't have been with my kids. I was living in a nice home, but God just showed me that and I said, "You've got to get it together!" And that's what I did. Once I got it together, I never looked back, I never touched drugs again. I haven't had a desire since. Wouldn't do it. That's it!

TracyMac: Was getting it together an immediate getting it together or was it a process? Did it happen like overnight, few weeks, from what you recall? What was getting it together? What did that mean to you? What do you want other people to know about how you did that?

Diane: I want them to know, I went to AA, I went to NA, and that was the process for me. I went to an NA meeting every day. That helped me with the drugs, but guess what? It didn't help me change my behavior. So I stopped getting high, but I was still trying to feel the void I was missing, I was still missing me, the little girl. A piece and peace was still missing. I was great with not getting high, but I still was filling that void with unhealthy relationships with men. I allowed them to take advantage of me because I wanted to be loved. I was like, here I am. I want you to be with me. I'll cook you dinner, take care of you....

TracyMac: So Diane, you were giving yourself literally, not so much as just out there, but in those relationships you chose to have, you were giving but what were you getting? Even though it was temporary, what were you getting?

Diane: I have to say that I was getting, at least I thought I was getting someone who loved me. To me, it was love. I thought when I gave of myself I thought it was love and attention, he loves me; he wants to be with me. When he got what he wanted he was on his way. You know, he'd stay for a little while and when I say a little while, it was around a month, a few months, whatever, and then I became needy. It became too much, because of the void I kept trying to fill. It was something missing, and I was tugging, thinking "you gotta be here". I was so needy, it was overwhelming. I wasn't loving myself and I looked outside myself looking for love. If I had the money I probably would have tried to buy the love at the love store! Because when I think about it, Tracy, that love thing, oh my god, that love thing! When we don't love ourselves it takes us down dark alleys leads us to ugly places. And that's what I needed. I needed me to love me. I did some things that were right. I took my kids out of the Bronx, New York, I moved to North Carolina, I got saved, went to church all the time, very spiritual, but I couldn't connect that thing. I didn't know how to just turn within instead of looking outside of me. It took a long time. And when I came here I still had that same behavior. It wasn't the drugs, but I still was looking for someone else to fulfill me and fill that void.

TRANSITIONS, PROCESS AND PROGRESS

TracyMac: And you still had that yearning and that desire.

Diane: Yeah, I had that yearning and that desire. But when I was in my forties I got it.

TracyMac: What did you get? What did you get!? Do tell! Do tell!

Diane: I prayed and I cried, and this is after having a child at forty-two years old. I prayed and I cried. And God just showed me myself. First thing I had to do was I had to accept, because I was very angry at my mother. I was angry because she wasn't there for me. And I was like, ooooh, she's an alcoholic! I will never be like that! The thing is, God took a mirror, not literally, but He took a mirror and put the mirror in front of my face. And when I looked at the mirror I saw my mother. And I said wait a minute, what's going on? That's my mother, that ain't me. What's going on? And God said, yes, it is you. You are her. You are her! Her choice was alcohol and your choice was cocaine. It's the same. It's one and the same. But I separated it, and I separated the drugs and I separated the alcohol. So when I separated that I separated me from my mother. I'm not like her because I didn't do *that*. I didn't do what *she* did. But, I did do it.

TracyMac: You know what, Diane, isn't it something how we forget that our parents are people? They are people who were here before we were. They are people who have struggled, people who had situations happen. And, we're so busy looking at what we think parenting should be, what we hope, what society says it should be, and sometimes we forget our parents are people first. Our mothers are women who went through struggles, some more extreme than others. But they went through situations with men, they went through financial issues, and then they wind up being our mother, and those things don't just turn off because they became parents. So that was a wonderful experience, even though the process didn't feel good, the recognition is excellent! Because a lot of people, grown folks, still don't realize that thing. Parents are held accountable for so many things they may not have done right in our lives, and we don't realize. That is a wonderful realization you had.

Diane: Yes, that set me free! When I was able to forgive my mother I was able to forgive myself, and then I was able to love myself. And then I was able to get the five-year-old and just love all over her and tell her it was not her fault and that it's okay. It's okay, Diane!

TracyMac: And what was that process like? How were you able to go from seeing that reflection of being so much like your mother was, but just having a different drug of choice and relationships filling the void you had? You recognized that that five-year-old girl needed you, but you couldn't just stop living and being a mom and working and doing things yourself. What process did you use to reconnect with her? Just tell us about that for a little bit.

Diane: I had to go back and think about the situation. I had to go back and think about the incident and see what happened. Not only to see what happened, but I had to actually go through the steps in a way, but look at it differently, because now I'm on the outside. I had to forgive him. I had to forgive him, so I was able to forgive myself for all the things I'd taken myself through and not loving myself. Then I was able to say, you know, this is what was missing in my life.

TracyMac: Did you do all of this alone? Were you alone in this process?

Diane: At first, I was alone but I did eventually get a life coach. When I say alone physically alone, yes I was, but God guided me through this. At that time I had a life coach. But I had to go back and I had to deal with that situation myself, and I had to forgive him.

TracyMac: So what did dealing with it look like? As we say in coaching you have to do your work. What did that look like on a daily basis?

Diane: I had to accept that it wasn't my fault, it was something that happened. It was something that happened to me. It was *not* me. I could no longer let it hold me back or define me. I couldn't let it keep me from loving myself. I couldn't keep hurting from that. I couldn't do that any longer; I had to set myself free.

TracyMac: So how did that look? How did it look in your relationships? How did it look in how you cared for your children? What differences, what behavior changes did you make?

Diane: I changed my behavior. I started loving myself and showing myself love. My process started before life coaching too. I started making different choices in relationships.

TracyMac: How so?

Diane: If I met a guy and I know what kind of relationship I wanted and he wasn't giving that, I wasn't giving myself to him physically anymore. I was holding out because I knew I deserved the best. If he wasn't giving me what I needed, I could let go because I know I am worthy of the best. So I was able to slow everything down and just take my time to get to know that person. I wasn't so needy for somebody else. If I was needy, I needed me, not me needing someone else. And I spent time with self and I went out and I took myself to dinner and I went to the movies, or I just stayed home and watched TV or you know writing in the journal. I was able to do that by myself opposed to needing to be in a relationship with somebody.

TracyMac: How was coaching beneficial to you? Before we even starting doing your coach certification and connecting on another level of relationship, tell me the initial experience you had with life coaching and how it benefitted your change and growth. How did it change your life and what you believed about yourself?

Diane: WOOOO! WHAAHOO!!!! Oh, man, have you ever been in church and you just want to shout?? It was a life-changing experience. Today, I live outside the box. I color outside the lines and I color beautifully! My voids are filled. I am revitalized! There's nothing that I can say that I regret today about way that I lived my life. I was able to face my fears. I was able to deal with I might consider short-comings in my life. Through coaching, I was able to stand up tall and strong in knowing who I am. I know without life coaching I could not have done that! I needed someone to help me and hold me accountable to change my behavior. I couldn't wait for my coaching session days to come. I was excited, like a little school girl in school. I was ready. I had my homework. I had my paper. I was ready. I was dedicated because she made me feel like I mattered. My life mattered. I recommend life coaching to everybody because it can help anybody.

Diane's life coach is an extremely effective life coach and was instrumental in Diane having that make-ya-wanna-shout experience! Her experience was excellent. (I'm not sure if everyone is carrying out their titles of professional coaches with the same level of authenticity and excellence that we all strive for). When Diane was being coached by her, she decided she wanted to become a coach and transitioned wonderfully into my coach certification program. Diane would connect with me on a different level because she told me she wanted to become what she once needed. She needed to help other women recover their pieces and peace; live revitalized and grow from "I can't" to "I did!" She did a lot of her own work prior to ever being coached, but she felt there was more. Once she had that effective and positive coaching experience, it helped her to see how much she mattered. She reconnected to the little girl who mattered. Her life coach helped her through the process to reconnect with that little girl...to look back, but not go back.

Sometimes through therapy and different forms of counseling you're taken back to that girl or boy or situation that changed your life in so many ways. In some cases, you are taken there and get stuck there. But coaching says, "Okay, that happened, but now, but God, what are we gonna do? What are we going to build better and profit from because of this?"

REVITALIZED

TracyMac: Diane, what now? Looking at your relationships now, what is your strongest belief about yourself and your relationships?

Diane: I have a lot to offer. The experiences that I have gone through, I'm so ever grateful and that might sound a little crazy, but God chose to take me through what I went through to be able to help somebody else. I help women become revitalized, where they can live their greatest life, and they don't have to be a prisoner of their past or feel empty and lost because of it. That they can pull out and explore all the greatness that lies within them. Because sometimes we can feel like that because we've been through these things, no one wants to listen to us. We carry it on our backs, but I no longer carry it at all. I share what I've gone through but I don't relive it. I see it, but I don't relive it. I know today that I am truly a life coach and I am getting my life coach certification with TracyMac Life Coach Services.

TracyMac: And one beautiful thing: you said, "I am a life coach." You are, and while earning a coaching certification, we don't wait until we finish the certification before we start coaching. We coach in the process. We've been excited since day one. You jumped in saying, "This is what I want! This is who I am! This is what I'm going to do, and you're gonna help me do it!" It put me on notice. Even though I trained and certified before, you came in with such energy and vibrancy, which is one of the reasons why I want you to tell people, you are Coach Diane Hamilton…

Diane: I am Coach Diane Hamilton of Revitalizing Coaching Systems. I am the revitalizer!

TracyMac: Yes! So with that process, what are you looking forward to doing as a coach? And what type of person are you looking forward to helping revitalize?

Diane: My ideal clients are women who are over thirty-five that have been successful and have been through various forms of abuse. I serve them well. Those women, who go to work every day, go to church every week, and we step out and we're looking good. We look outstanding, on the outside and things seem to be just great. But on the inside there's someone trying to fight to get out who wants to recover and be fulfilled. I help get that person out so they too, can color outside the lines like I do and they can live outside their box. What box? Those are the women that I want to revitalize and help, through my coaching practice, *Revitalize Coaching Systems. "Going from I can't to, I did!"*

TracyMac: Wow! And let me ask you this, why do you feel the need to do it as a coach and not just do it as somebody who may need a friend, or an acquaintance and just tell your story and offer encouragement? Why do you feel like coaching is the way to go for you?

Diane: Because it's different. When I come as a coach I show up as a blank page. No judging. It's different than when you come as a friend because as friends we come with random advice.

A coach helps get specific and gets results! We help you see and make your own big decisions. We expose you to your greatness. We help put you where you say you want to be. We're not telling you what to do at all. So for me, it's a different from me being a friend. A friend is with you and a coach is for you. I help people who may have lost pieces of themselves along the way. Helping people as a friend won't have the same results, the techniques and the tools that I have as a certified life coach. I get results! As a certified life coach I have some useful tools in my pocket. As a friend, I'm just comparing life experience, but that could not touch the tools that you have given me. TracyMac, I don't even think that you know what you have already equipped me with. I am listening! You are outstanding at what you do!

TracyMac: Wow. Diane, thank you so much for saying that. That is worth more than anything. This is one of those moments where words mean everything. And I am so grateful to hear you say it, and I receive it. I do. It's amazing that you would trust me through this coaching relationship and for it to grow into friendship and not only that but partnership because of the things we are and will be doing together. Because as a coach I don't know everything. As a coach I have not had every experience. And these women who are over thirty-five, who are professional going to work every day that need to be revitalized, learn how to color outside the lines and live outside the box. There are some tools that I have that are not precise enough for them, that I trust you to use yours skillfully. I've seen the evidence. I've seen your work in progress. I've seen the end results and the solutions. I'm just grateful to be connected to you in such a wonderful way that goes beyond what we had asked or thought. I'm grateful. You came in ready and willing and able. This whole part for me is great. I thank you. I thank you for even wanting to be a part of this "Relationships: Nothing But the Truth" project because I knew that that's how you operate. Nothing but the truth.

Diane: You know what? That's all we can bring. That's all people ask for. That's all we truly ask for in relationships…the truth. That's all, we just want the truth. One thing that I have truly loved is that there are many women out there that have been through what I've gone through. They are looking for someone to help them come out the box. I am fifty-two years old, living my life on purpose. I am more than excited. I really am. I just want to tell you thank you. I'm just preparing and making myself ready and qualified to answer their call. That's all. I am here! Thank you, Tracy. Thank you for allowing me to be a part of your life. This is beyond what I think you could ever imagine what it's doing for me.

Implementation Guide: What pieces may be missing in your life? What behaviors can you change? How can you color outside the line and lose the box? What will it take? Who can help you and who can you help? How can your life be revitalized? What "I can't" can become "I did"?

Chapter Four

Who Am I? Why Am I Here?

"If you don't know who you are, how will everyone else know who they are getting?"

—TracyMac

THE SECRET: SHE WON'T TELL

For almost eight years of my life, I didn't know whose child I was. The questions: "Who am I?" and "Why am I here?" weren't questions I came up with to write my first book. They weren't buzz words or something initiated by self-discovery, a different level of spirituality or purpose. They were questions I asked myself, or should I say, Tracy had been asking since she was a little girl. She didn't talk a lot but when she did she had some serious tattletale tendencies. When it came to telling, she told the truth, the whole truth! She wanted to hang around her siblings, but for the most part, they were not going to be bothered with a tattletale. Who would? They were five and four years older and it seemed, every time she came into a room where they were, they would leave, stop talking or start whispering. She begged and aggravated them constantly to tell the secrets too. There were probably no real secrets; they just didn't want her tattling. So one day, she worried them silly about seeing a picture of Dr. J's (Julius Erving) Colgate ad. She nagged and they'd had enough. Tracy's crocodile tears ceased when they asked her, "You wanna know a big secret? It's a big one and you have to promise to never tell anyone." Now Tracy was around five or six years old, making her siblings around nine and ten. Tracy, turning off the water works, nodded her head and said, "I won't tell."

"You promise you won't tell?"

"Yes, I promise. I won't tell it!"

"Cross your heart, hope to die, stick a needled in your eye?"

With the motions Tracy said, "Cross my heart, hope to die, stick a needle in my eye!"

This was serious. She had never been trusted with a big kid's secret before. Her heart was beating a little faster and she was so excited, she held her own hand. She sat down on the red and black couch in their den, and waited for them to come back and tell her this big kid's secret.

"Promise you won't tell nobody?"

"I promise."

"Mom and Dad don't want you to know, but you were adopted."

"Oooh, what's that?!"

"That means they are not your real parents. They are your play-play parents. We are their real kids."

They showed her a paper that looked much like the one kid's would get for participating in field day back then, but Tracy couldn't read.

"See, this is your adoption certificate."

"Ohhh!" Tracy said with pride and excitement. She knew a secret and had a certificate!

"Promise not to tell?"

"I promise!"

Tracy felt like a big girl. She now knew a secret. The value of knowing a secret overrode the content of the information. It didn't matter what it was, as long as it was a big kid's secret. And she definitely wasn't going to tell it, because she wanted to prove she could be trusted with more secrets. Her sister and brother left the room and Tracy thought, *If they are my play-play parents and these are my play-play sister and brother, where are the real ones?* As if a blessing from God, she immediately felt grateful that this family had taken her in. The mind of a child, eh?

THE DAY SHE FOUND OUT

As with any child, as Tracy grew up, things changed, but one thing that didn't change was Tracy hanging out with Mrs. Jones. They went everywhere together, especially to church. They listened to music together, sang together. Tracy felt close, and every now and then she'd watch Mrs. Jones and wonder why she hadn't told her she was adopted. She figured she'd never know the answer. Plus, since there were so many changes happening in her family, that was the least of her concerns. They had recently moved, her dad had started a church in their home, and their family had grown by two—her nephews. She felt all "grown up" about being an aunt! Tracy was taken out of public school and attended a Christian school called Community Christian Fellowship. It was a big adjustment for Tracy. The school was small; she was the only Black female, middle school aged student. Tracy decided to try out for cheerleading to make some friends. Not only that, she wanted to do something different besides go to school, church and home.

After making the team the cheerleading coach told her, "Make sure you bring your birth certificate because we'll need that in order to fill out the insurance papers for you to travel on the bus with the team." Now that request would make any other person say, "Okay," but that hit Tracy like a ton of bricks. She thought, *My birth certificate…* So much time had passed, she didn't think about being adopted much anymore, but thinking about her birth certificate made those bricks heavier. The adoption, the birth certificate and those bricks sat on Tracy's mind for two weeks. She would soon have to find out the truth from her parents. She didn't ask the first week and the day before the team was supposed to travel, the cheerleading coach said, "Tracy, if we don't get your birth certificate tomorrow you won't be able to travel to the game."

Tracy said, "Okay, I'll bring it." Her desperation to be a part of the team and break the mundane cycle of church, home and school gave her the nerve. You have to understand, her dad had started a church in their home and now going to a Christian school right down the street from their home, didn't allow her to travel more than a mile radius. The fear of asking for her birth certificate wasn't as great as needing to kick out of that rut. She procrastinated as long as she could.

On the morning of the game, she couldn't eat, didn't sleep well the night before and got up the nerve. "Mom, I need to take my birth certificate to school because they need it just to be able to fill out insurance information from you to travel with the team to the game."

"Don't you lose that birth certificate, Tracy! You give it to whomever needs it and you get it back. I am not calling the state of Virginia to get another one!"

Nerves, hunger, sleeplessness and fear made Tracy feel like she was in a tunnel.

"Do you hear me?" Mrs. Jones said.

"Yes," Tracy muttered. In her mind she shouted, *Okay, is this lady for real?* She and Tracy were the only ones at home. Mr. Jones…no, Pastor Jones had gone to his usual 5:00 a.m. prayer with the Marines, her sister was at work and her brother had taken his freedom to Virginia. Tracy thought, *I just blew her cover and all she says is 'Don't lose it?' First of all, I don't even know where it is.*

That instant, as if she could read her mind, Mrs. Jones said, "Go down to my room, and look under the bed, there is a lock box—open the box and yours is the green one!"

How cruel, this lady is going to let me find out by myself. She's not even going to tell me herself that I'm adopted or maybe she's waiting for my play-play dad to come home.

Tracy said, "Okay."

Now the house was small and the walk from the kitchen to their bedroom was all of fifteen paces. But that day, Tracy's feet felt like cinderblocks walking on fresh tar. The hallway seemed like a walk across the desert. The more steps she took the heavier those cinder blocks got and the stickier the tar. The more steps she took, the longer the hallway got. She had become a triathlete and finally made it into her parents' bedroom. She drug the cinderblocks through the thick tar and made it around to the side of the bed where her mom instructed her to find the lockbox. She bent down to reach under the bed, but she couldn't feel the box, so she had to get on her knees. Already feeling heavy, now on her knees, she lifted the bed skirt, and slid the box out across the hardwood floor. She just looked at it for a couple of seconds, knowing that she finally was coming face-to-face with a secret that she had held for eight years. For eight years, this secret was held in a little, fire proof, lock box and it wasn't even locked!

As if she was opening a treasure chest that had been buried under water for one thousand years, she heard tiny hinges screech as she opened it. Startled by her mom's voice, she jumped and the lid shut. "Yours is the green one!"

She opened the lid, hearing the screech again. Already feeling even more the oddball, she noticed there was only one green paper in the box. Most of the other papers that she could see were white, shades of light blue or manila. *Mine would be green*, she thought. Why was her birth certificate the only green one? Because she was the only one who was adopted. Tracy thumbed through the papers as if she didn't see the green birth certificate. She could have gone right to it, but she was looking for something, anything else to be green. She knew the truth was imminent. Her heart raced and she blinked to wet her wide, dry eyes. Taking the green birth certificate out of the box she turned it over and unfolded the paper. Tracy read:

> *Child: Tracy Anita Jones – February 27, 1969*
> *Mother: Thomasine Pleasant Jones*
> *Father: Walter Earl Jones, Sr.*

Tracy's fear turned into, "Oh no they didn't!" *Not only did they keep this a secret, they had the audacity to change the names on MY birth certificate to theirs?!* It was already bad enough that Tracy's real parents didn't know where she was because she'd moved so often with this family. It was already bad enough she had to ask to see her birth certificate. It was already bad enough she was in that room, by herself, on her knees. Now she had to read a forged document? For the first time ever, she became an indignant thirteen-year-old. She was going to demand that she at least know her real parents' names. This was supposed to be her moment and day of reckoning! Tracy stood quickly, not even pushing the box back under the bed, not feeling the cinderblocks on her feet, not feeling the stickiness of the tar or the desert in the hallway. What felt like miles moments ago now felt like inches, as Tracy arrived in the kitchen immediately, like the *Matrix*, before the movie came out!

Hand trembling, she held the paper up to her mom "Why did you change the names on my birth certificate?"

Her mom continued ironing, and without even looking up said, "What you talking about, Tracy?"

Tracy didn't quiet her tone, she raised it. "I said why did you change the names on my birth certificate?"

"What are you talking about, Tray-seh?!" Mrs. Jones said in a sassy, almost aggravated way, as she slowly looked up at Tracy, biting her bottom lip, as if she was ready to give Tracy a tongue-lashing. Both of them were in shock! Tracy never raised her voice to Mrs. Jones, she knew better. She looked sternly at Tracy and sat the iron upright on the ironing board as the the black and white cord from the iron swung back and forth.

With a flood of instant tears and an avalanche of words that had been bound by secrecy, Tracy shouted, "They already told me when we lived on Hyde Road that I was adopted and I promised never to say anything and y'all never told me!"

"What? What are you talking about?"

For the first time ever, in complete disrespect and with tears streaming down her face and neck she said, "I said, I know I'm adopted!"

"You ain't no adopted!" shouted Mrs. Jones. "That's just crazy, I know I had you! Where in the world did that mess come from? You ain't no adopted, Tray-seh!"

There were so many emotions that the only thing that kept Tracy sane was feeling the warmth of her own tears and watching its black and white cord swing back and forth. She didn't even want to look at the birth certificate anymore. She didn't want to see it anymore.

Tears poured out of Tracy's eyes and ran down her face, chin and neck like wild waterfalls. Her nose burned on the inside, she had a single-file line of lumps in her throat. Every emotion ran as fast as her tears: confusion, happiness, sadness, relief, perplexed and stupidity. She had so many questions, but one cycled the fastest in her mind: *How could I believe this?* She felt like she was in a time machine, going back to the day of being told the "big girl" secret.

She felt so stupid. She realized immediately that the prank ended with her brother and sister the same day or week that it was played. But Tracy wasn't angry with them. She was angry with herself for being stupid. Forgetting all about the walk she was to make to school, she dropped her head, left the tear-stained birth certificate on the kitchen counter, and went into her room to cry in shame. Her mom followed behind her.

"Now, Tracy I know you didn't believe you were adopted. I know you didn't believe that all this time. Don't you see you look just like your daddy? Why would you believe you were adopted?"

Her mom touched her back and what should have been a moment of comfort, turned into her mom being the first person to ever use speed dial on a rotary phone. She called her brother's number in Virginia and whoever answered the phone said he wasn't there. Her sister was at work and wouldn't you know she used speed dial rotary style again and called her there. She worked at Hardee's. Only hearing her mom's side of the conversation, it was obvious her sister was just as confused as Tracy felt. All she kept hearing was her mom repeating the same two questions: "Did y'all tell Tracy she was adopted? Why would y'all tell her that?" It was probably the breakfast rush and her sister couldn't carry on a conversation at work, especially that one. Besides, she didn't remember that old prank anyway. She heard her mom say, Tracy you were not adopted," before she hung up the phone. Mrs. Jones sounded sad this time. "I don't know why you believe that all these years."

Feeling hurt and embarrassed, Tracy sat up on the side of her bed. Her family wasn't all that affectionate, but her mom hugged her tightly. Tracy barely hugged her back. The hug wasn't the norm, yet it wasn't odd, it was befitting. Her mom gave her another hug and a kiss on her forehead. She went into the bathroom to wash her face. Shc was too embarrassed to stay there. She was going to walk to school and didn't want to be late. She had a game to go to after school. That's what caused all of this anyway. Tracy put her Bible and her books in her book bag, grabbed the birth certificate off the counter in the kitchen and walked to school. Why did she believe that? Why didn't she ever ask or at least hint around? And why didn't they remember?

Tracy cheered at the game that night and when she returned home, her dad said, "How could you believe you were adopted all these years?" Of course her mom told him. He hugged her and said, "You're my child. Can't you see you look like me? Can't you see you act like me? Don't you know you're smart like me?"

Tracy just nodded and went into her room and got the best sleep ever. Tracy never blamed anyone but herself for never questioning the prank, and years later she stopped doing that, too. As a matter of fact, she saw the movies *Annie* and *Oliver Twist,* and during the years she thought she had been adopted, she felt grateful to think this family had chosen her out of all the other orphans, and she loved them for that. The gratitude of feeling "chosen" made it okay. There was a sense of feeling different that kept her from typical teenage menacing. There was nothing to "get over" per se, accept her creative ideas of not belonging and learning the lessons: ask questions and the difference between secrecy and confidentiality.

Implementation Guide: What secrets are you keeping? What questions do you need to ask yourself? What questions have you been afraid to ask yourself? How can you find gratitude in something that wasn't so great? Who are you here to be? What are you here to do?

Chapter Five

Feeling Different? Upgrade to Wisdom Through Self-Discovery!

"Purpose is when you know and understand what you were born to accomplish. Vision is when you see it in your mind and begin to imagine it."
—Myles Monroe

THE TRUTH ACCORDING TO UNDRAI FIZER

Dr. Undrai Fizer is as unique as the spelling of his name. I have never met someone who is different from who I am, yet so much like who I am. He describes himself as a man on a mission. Undrai is one of my life coaches. I will proudly say he has been my most influential to date. I will tell you, his wisdom is earthly brilliant and heavenly guided. He has been a thought partner with me and to me, and I don't believe I would have ever leapt into full-time coaching and being self-employed when I did had it not been for our relationship and his awesome coaching. He'll tell you that we coach one another, but I still think I win with him coaching me. I first met Undrai, and the power of his mind and wisdom-filled words on Facebook in 2009 before I ever heard his voice or saw him face to face. Thank you social media!

During our first conversation, typing in messenger, Undrai said, "You get me, eh?!" and I responded, "Ehhhh," because I felt the same way. Relief! We instantly realized we had met ourselves expressed as one another. I didn't have to say something and then dumb it down for explanation or to feel acceptance. I already felt a lot of the things Undrai was saying, but I hadn't fully given myself permission to say, develop or live them. No one ever said anything; I could feel judgments from the voices of my upbringing, Christian beliefs and societal conditionings. My self-discovery, seeing God, my purpose in me was exploding thc walls and boxes religion, race, gender and societal expectations spent years to construct. Undrai became a mirror and living proof that revealed not only was I not alone, but he was evidence that the wisdom of my truth was worthy to be thought, lived, shared and it was craved by others, necessary and attractive. Undrai remembers saying, "TracyMac, you remind me of the silent promises I made to myself."

I realized that there were some relationships I could not be myself in, though I was scared, I left some of them and many of them left me, too. One of the first things I remember Undrai saying was, "Mac, sometimes you have relationships and when you let them go your purpose will always allow you to attract different relationships, only upgraded." I wondered how he knew... He didn't know at the time that he was becoming proof of that to me. I had no reluctance or fear of jumping into a depth of relationship with him because I wasn't afraid of me, the fullness of my truth, especially with him. We are thought partners, friends, fellow coaches, speakers and authors offering who we are to the world, on purpose! I wanted to share our relationship with you.

WHO IS UNDRAI FIZER?

Undrai Fizer is a man on a mission, constantly evolving into his ever progressive thoughts. He is a lover of himself and learning, and ever evolving to love himself and his life. He is also a gifted musician and recording artist; using the sounds he creates to speak the language of wisdom, consciousness and enlightenment. But it hasn't always been this way for Undrai. What if you didn't love yourself or thought you should or could be loved by anyone outside of your family? What if the only relationships you had with greatness was built with in the expanse of your own mind, but never feeling the permission to live it? Well, that *was* Undrai. Growing up in Lake Charles, Louisiana, there was a little boy who once felt the only way he could accept himself was to feel as though he was one with God. He was a child who knew that, he felt it, but couldn't share it. Maybe because he didn't know how to share it, what to share or with whom to share it.

The closest way he could feel that permission was going to church and having a spiritual experience within the confines of the walls of religion. It was a boxed freedom. He knew God was with him, but when it came to most of his relationships, he felt he wasn't good enough to be kept. It wasn't something he made up; it was based on how some of his relationships taught him to behave. It had nothing to do with being a Christian or not being saved, but when it came to human relationships, he felt that there was always something better or someone better than he was. Within human relationships, can you imagine feeling and wanting to connect with someone else, and not being able to get to them because you felt like you were being in their way? That's how Undrai felt. As he grew older, most of his relationships were temporary and he had the experiential evidence that people were only with him until something better came along. It was learned behavior as a little boy and even a young man.

TracyMac: I can identify with that so much because I felt that growing up in church. When you're the PK or the bishop's daughter, you feel like every relationship is there to get through you to them.

Undrai: Yeah, oh yeah.

TracyMac: And that can make you feel kind of used by people. And some people do come into our lives that way if you let them.

Undrai: If you let them.

TracyMac: What was the changing factor, what changed for you, when you begin to see differently?

THE SHIFT

Undrai: When I really embraced the vision that came from my own thoughts, it was back in 1991. I had a question. I had a ministerial friend/associate, and I explained something to him. I always had these outlandish or adventurous visionary thoughts. I just felt that I didn't have the permission to be the one to execute them. And I finally took a chance on myself, which was a form of loving myself, which was a form of learning to love me. In '91 when I finally spoke of this particular path or vision, and I accepted the fact that I would be the one to introduce it and I kept it. I think that vision was the Divine's way of getting me to love myself. I think it's God's way of helping us how to learn to love us by loving what's coming through us. I started to accept the excitement that I was significant. And when I began to accept the adventure beyond what I had in the bank or what clothes I had or what lack of style I had, it gave me an excitement. It sort of gave me this new alter ego or this thing; it gave me this shift of this new person that I got used to, who I started loving my mind. I started loving the fact that I was smart, that I was intelligent, that I did have something to offer. When in years past, I didn't see that in myself at all. I had friends, but they didn't know how much I needed them around me. They didn't know I used to live temporary because I knew eventually this relationships isn't going to last. It made me hold tight to people. And it probably was a form of co-dependence too. When I studied about it later, I saw myself in so many ways as the enabler. I saw myself as the victim. There were just so many problems, man, I had so many of them. Everything else was just better than me. Until my shift in '91.

TracyMac: So with this shift, you felt brand new, you had an awakening; I am smart. I do have something relevant to say, these visions are credible. And you know how now they use the terminology when you say "I felt brand new", did you have relationships that said you were "acting brand new"? How did this new consciousness in its initial stages, affect your other relationships?

Undrai: I lost some. I lost some. I was talked about. And I actually saw how my relationships actually felt about me. Some felt I was full of arrogance. It made me wonder, now who was I before? Some things you see and some things you're blind to. I was blind. Some things you want to be blind to. I saw what I actually felt about people, or saw from people, I saw it from the past. So I lost the majority of the relationships or was treated like I had a disease. Who is he? And a lot of my relationships were in church. So a lot of my church relationships suffered. I heard them talk about me in third person. I heard different things, and it made me wonder, what I was actually giving them or what was I really chasing them for. So I had a rude awakening. My self-awakening was beautiful, but my relational awakening was rude. My relational awakening, it turned to be rude. It was rude to me. Some friends I still have now, but it made people wonder, what's up with you. I didn't know the awakening had shifted my persona or my inner vibe. I didn't know that it would reach that far. It was beyond just having something new to say. It actually shifted my way, my psyche, the vibe that's in my body. People embraced the former me, the person who was afraid. When I began to think of myself and say, you know, I don't care, if you understand and ask. And they made me pay for it; they made me pay for my discovery by their silence and they turned away.

TracyMac: How so? Through them breaking off relationships with you? Was that like one of the major ways that they made you pay, per se?

Undrai: Yes, by not accepting me in public or by not allowing me to feel the camaraderie. By making me feel I was on the outside. We're going to make you suffer like—You can think what you want, but we won't be there. They had grown accustomed to me constantly seeking their advice or their acceptance or their camaraderie. They never sought mine. They allowed themselves to be the magnet that attracted me. Once I changed the rhythm of the relationship I saw how they really felt about it.

TracyMac: So Undrai, what do you say to someone who may feel different in their current surroundings, whether it be spiritually, mentally, economically, emotionally or business? It may not be an awakening like yours or rude, but everybody goes through these different transitions in life when it's time for change. So what would you say or how would you encourage that person who's in a group of people that knows there's something different that has to take place, so they can be comforted by the difference?

Undrai: I could say believe in yourself. I could say, God has you here for a purpose. I can say a lot of positive things. I can say there's no one else like you in the world, and this is why this is happening and it'll feel good. It'll feel good temporarily. You'll feel the peace in somebody finally acknowledging you and saying that you matter. You'll feel the peace when someone else is saying it. The challenge is hearing your own self say it and embracing what you say to yourself. I can say a lot of things and it will make you feel good and it'll confirm how you feel. You'll say, thank you, Fizer. You know, Undrai, you've confirmed what I've always felt. But you need to affirm your own confirmations. You need to confirm your own affirmations. What I will say is, when you hear your own soul tell you, "You know you're different," take a chance on yourself. You need to believe it. You need to believe what you hear your soul tell you and you'll stay. YOU'LL STAY, if you believe yourself. Now, you'll smile if you believe me, but you will remain and be consistent if you believe yourself.

TracyMac: Wooo! That's like, whoa, because that is the beginning of trusting and loving yourself, if you say so.

SELF-DISCOVERY

TracyMac: Undrai, we hear people say it's not about you or self-discovery is selfish because you turn all the eyes and lights on you. Give us a differentiation between self-discovery and listening to your own soul and being one to consistently evolve yourself versus being selfish.

Undrai: Self-discovery is when you finally discover your significance and your weakness and your truth and your lies. It's you discovering why you think the way you do and why you were afraid to think the way you did. You're discovering your truths, the truths that hold you accountable to being greater than you've been allowing yourself. You will also discover your weakness and why you've despised yourself. But you will discover it without hating yourself. You will discover all of your good, bad, questionable, unfamiliar, dangerous, you will finally be confident to see yourself without damaging yourself. That's the power of self-discovery. I'm able to look at myself, beautiful, ugly, crazy, broken—

TracyMac: You said "crazy"...we all can identify with that one.

Undrai: Oh yeah, because we're all a bit crazy. You have to accept that; all of us are a bit crazy, not dysfunctional. We all are odd. Divinely unique, but we're odd. A lot of us have some backwards ways of looking at some things that create issues and problems. All of us are not beautiful to work with, but yet we're beautiful to have in life. All of us have an oddity about us. You will be able to discover it without damaging yourself. Before when you saw your oddity you hid it. You hid it in the ground because you try to create a perfect image in order for people to like you or want you. And now when you really have the power of self-discovery, you discover the power to be hated and still love yourself. I can allow you to misjudge me and I won't hate myself if you do. I will let you hate me and I won't hate myself because you hate me. You've discovered your unique oddity in allowing people to reject you or hate you or misunderstand you, and you will still be in love with you even more.

TracyMac: Anyhow, eh?

Undrai: Anyhow. That was the greatest thing I found about myself. Before, I couldn't stand it if you didn't like me. I went out of my way to make sure you knew this is who I am, not knowing I was creating an image that I thought that person would want. So I would study people to see who they talked to and how they handled people, who are the people that they have in their lives. And I studied it enough to be a chameleon. I'm going to become what they would like. And that's really probably what selfishness really is, destroying and annihilating yourself to create a self that everybody else would want.

TracyMac: Oh my goodness.

Undrai: Maybe that's selfishness. Maybe selfishness is not always me, me, but maybe - I will kill me to be the "me" that you like. I'm going to kill me so I can create a self that you like. I started destroying myself to be what others would want, whether it happens on my career, job, or what have you, people want you to stop being you. Now I know how to be me and give you what you need, but when I have to annihilate me to be what you like, then you need to let me go. And that's what your gifts, your talents, and your vision will do. Your gifts and your talents will provide for you when other people let you go because they wanted you to commit spiritual suicide. Your own power will pay you. That's what our visions are for, because everybody can't take us.

TracyMac: Wow, wow, wow. Did you just say, your own power will pay you?

Undrai: Yes! It will. Yes, it will. Your own power will pay you, because it won't allow you to be outsourced by people who no longer want you to be a source. It'll never do that. It won't do that. I know that. You are always hired by your power. You are always employed by your power. Always! Because some money will force you to stop being you for the money. That's selfish.

TracyMac: You speak with such authority, and I think that's what attracted me to hear you, because it's like it raises the authority up in me, in my own life. Some shifts have just happened in my mind, because I never heard up until today, this moment, the different perception and perspective that you just brought on what selfishness could really be. The mindset of just about going crazy, trying to please other people is way more selfish than just being mySELF. And so we see life and all that you obviously have gone through successfully to be able to have this type of powerful thought and implementation, because I know you don't simply think these things powerfully, you live them powerfully. How have they helped or transformed your purpose and mission in life, and how has this relationship with you been affected within purpose and mission and passion?

Undrai: Oh, wow. It causes me to constantly seek people out or attract people or friendships or associations that constantly remind me of the promise I made to myself. It allowed me to have accountable relationships that don't have to tell me what I said to myself, me being around them silently reminds me, remember what you told yourself. That's what it's done to me. I constantly live out my thoughts. I constantly seek adventurous ways, even if I have to create the adventure myself. I seek out ways to live dangerously, even if I have to create the danger myself. I became bored with the familiar and the routine and the status quo. People say it, but it bored me. Sometimes my wife, Bridget, will tell me, "You're bored aren't you?" I'll say, "No, I'm alright." Bridget will say, "Man of God." That's what she calls me, MandaGod. M-A-N-D-A G-O-D. "MandaGod, looks like you looking to get into something." I'd say, "I'm okay. I'm alright. I'm good. Life is good. But it's alright." But I like to be with relationships that hold me accountable. See, that's what I like. That's why when we connected a few years ago, I was like—we didn't even know one another. Our first conversation we talked for, I think for some hours, like we'd been knowing one another. You knew all of my antics. You said all the sassy stuff. I thought, *Yeah, we know one another.* You just knew, you just knew! It's like, yeah, you just kind of knew. And I thought, *This chick is like a female Fizer.* You know, I remember that. I thought, *Girl, where'd you come from?*

TracyMac: I saw something you wrote on Facebook, and at the time, it was about four years ago...

Undrai: Yeah, it was about four years ago.

TracyMac: Something you wrote literally quickened something. And I thought, *Who is this sounding like me?* But then I had to back up, and I thought, *No, who is this sounding like I want to sound?* Because I felt certain things, but I didn't give myself the permission. And I saw that not only was I connected, but I needed—and I told you this before—to see others who gave themselves permission.

Undrai: Oh yeah, I remember that.

TracyMac: And that's what I recall. So when we talk, and the language, the vibe, the understanding without words and even the laughing and kickin' it, I wondered, *Where you been? Where have you been?*

Undrai: And I don't ever remember thinking, *Okay, now what are you about?* It was like we always knew. I never did, we always knew. And then we met in person and it was like oh, wow. You know, that was cool and it allowed me to attract a relationship that silently remind me of the promise I made to myself to continue.

TracyMac: And, you know, Undrai, I quote you all the time. You live in Texas and I live in North Carolina, but anyone who knows me knows Undrai Fizer. Early on, you said something major that allowed me to get the permission from me when I told you that many people had left me because they felt a change in my beliefs, but all I did was expose myself, my truth. And, you said something that manifested: "Sometimes, you will get new relationships upgraded." Sometimes, people bring us our needs fragmented—this one has this and that one has a little bit of that—but what I needed from five or six people, I got from you. You became about four or five people who had left me. You became them rolled up into one.

Undrai: Oh, yeah! Oh, wow.

TracyMac: And it was just a beautiful thing, and there was no second guessing, and still isn't. You know, okay, this is somebody that I'm partnering with for the rest of my life. This is a thought partner with me. This is somebody I cannot only go there with spiritually, but I can go there with laughter, in depth and brilliant conversations. We've had some wonderful times together and I'm so grateful, which is why I wanted to celebrate who you are to me, who we are together, and who you are to the world. Because I know a lot of people know you. I know a lot of people respect you. And the depth that you offer when it comes to relationships and spirituality, I just wanted people to see that amplified the best way I could. You are the husband to the beautiful Mrs. B. (Bridget Driver Fizer) and a father of three handsome young men, Benjamin, Loren and Zion. You are a wonderful musician and a coach, speaker and a mentor. With all of those missions and knowing that people recognize you and the owner of The Kairos Institute of Personal Discovery, which I'm glad you connected me to that great group of people.

TAKE A CHANCE

TracyMac: Tell us what you want someone to know. I know it's going to be good. How does all this mesh? Everything we've talked about in this conversation, let's close it out with some Undrai.

Undrai: Take a chance on yourself. Take a chance on yourself. Fall, experience pain, and get up. Take a chance on yourself. Love yourself enough to take a chance on yourself. Explore your options. Put meat on your feelings, put skin on them. You have ideas and ways that are in you that are asking to come out. All of your thoughts that you get, that's God's way of telling you to mentor them and make them grow up to be something. Now I could sound deep or extravagant, put the words together that will make me sound good. It'll make me sound like, I'm cool. But the things I speak I'm speaking to myself. This is how I feed myself. But you, take a chance on yourself. Take a chance on change. Take a chance on watching your relationships and your finances and your personal zones shift. Take a chance on yourself. There's nothing ugly about you. There's nothing insignificant about you. Take a chance. I mean, you're hurting yourself if you don't. And you're hearing it in your sleep. You hear it when you drive. You hear it every time you're frustrated. You know, life can be good if you're not agitated. But you know your purpose is revealed every time you're agitated? Every time that something happens that you don't like, you always say, man I ought to—get my—or man, you ain't gonna mess with me no more. Or I need to— Your purpose is always talking through you when you're mad and when you're agitated, and when it's not going your way. You feel like you're in a cocoon trying to get out, trying to figure out something. That's your purpose trying to get out of your skin. It's not you trying to find an answer. It's your purpose trying to find light. When you're frustrated and twisted and rubbing your hands and drumming your fingers and patting the seat and the desk, it's not you trying to figure it out, it's your purpose, it's who you are trying to find its way out. Take a chance on yourself.

TracyMac: And even if you have felt like you have taken a chance, it's probably been a minute; you need to take another one.

Undrai: Just take another one. I mean that's what it is. That's a key word. Take another one. Be a person that gives yourself every opportunity. One isn't enough. Because we give people chances to screw up in our life. We give everybody else more chances than we give ourselves. So give yourself what you give everybody else. Well do the same for yourself. Come back from your lies. If you'll take a chance with your lies, take another one. If you can let them lie to you and come back, you come back.

TracyMac: Well, you know I love you and I am so glad you took a chance on you back in 1991, because I don't think your life could have stood you if you hadn't. I'm so glad that you took that chance at the risk of having relationships that treated you rudely, at the risk of being misunderstood, at the risk of being dejected, at the risk of not having the people that you may have thought you needed, but growing to a place that it's okay to be you. It's okay to be odd. It's okay to be different. Because as we've shared before, that's your edge. Self-discovery's the new sexy, you know? It's what makes keeps you sweet. "Remember, God never sent us here just to believe, but BE! Everything else is to follow…" *The 365: A Personal Compass to Self-Discovery and Enlightenment* by Undrai Fizer – Read that book!

Implementation Guides: Who can help coach your life? How do you handle rejection? What makes you odd? How can you upgrade relationships? What type of relationships remind you of the promises you've made to yourself? How do you define self-discovery? How have you been selfish? How can you take a chance on you?

Chapter Six

Parents are People, Too

"We can improve our relationships with others by leaps and bounds if we become encouragers instead of critics."
—Joyce Meyer

I couldn't blame anyone. I couldn't even blame myself for thinking I was adopted. I made it a point to see my family members as my family and I could rest with being me. I observed my parents and remembered things about them for the first time as *my* parents. My dad was two seconds from being OCD when it came to cleanliness. He and my mom must have believed the saying "cleanliness is next to godliness" as our home was always clean because that's all they seemed to do. Washing the dishes wasn't simply washing the dishes, but washing the dishes, drying the dishes, putting them away, cleaning the counter tops, wiping down the stove and oven, sweeping and mopping the floor and taking out the trash. Cleaning the bathroom involved cleaning baseboards with toothbrushes, making the beds consisted of hospital corners and a tight fit, even if there were no fitted sheets. Cutting the grass included pulling weeds, trimming hedges and watering. And don't forget the car. A clean car in the Jones's house was taking the mats out of the car, scrubbing them with a scrub brush, vacuuming the front and back of their Chevrolet Impala, wood grain down the side, burnt orange/brown station wagon. The point is, Walter Earl Jones Sr. kept clean, clean and Thomasine, my siblings and I, in that order, helped him carry out that mission.

HISTORY/HERSTORY

Being neat and clean was part of my parent's upbringing; it makes sense and is the right thing to do. It was also a way to prove being just as good or worthy. The approval seeking cleanliness is like the scene in the movie *The Color Purple* when Miss Millie tells Sophia, "Your children are so clean. Would you like to be my maid?" That "Hell no." response got Sophia knocked out and locked up. But that pressure for approval flowed throughout late '60s and '70s, and spilled over into every area in the lives of Black folks, especially Black women. In some cases, having to be squeaky clean, study and work twice as hard for half the pay. I was born in that era and that mindset still rears its ugly head today. But it was a different kind of difficult time for Black folks in America back then. They were distancing themselves from being called Colored and Negro, and embracing being Black and proud in America. But that time seemed to be more oppressing for Black men, at least the Black men with whom I was familiar. When Black men were together, they'd joke and laugh loud, eat well, play spades, bid whist or dominoes, and drink good liquor (or act like it was good), but their 9-to-5 jobs seemingly forced them to behave like "yessa boys" and be neat and clean. It wasn't much different for my dad, but he never seemed to have that James from *Good Times*, ghetto-angry-heat seething. The oppression over the men was evident, and the oppression over Black women seemed to be compared to an abuse of the invisible. My parents, Thomasine and Walter, endured this era, and survived valiant involvement with countless others within the civil rights movement at I. C. Norcom High School in Portsmouth, Virginia. Not only on the days of sit-ins and demonstrations, but being denied was a way of life. They suffered racial inequalities, family dysfunction, discrimination and income prejudices and their own unanswered childhood ills and colorism within the Black community.

My parents did their best to attempt to combine and blend two very different religious backgrounds, and had to do deal with and overcome all the other surmounting crap that was happening with the majority of non-Blacks. Sometimes we don't take our parents' lives before they were parents into consideration. We assume they were born as parents the same day we were born as children. They had lives before they had children and it should be realized that parents are people, too.

THEIR STORY

I didn't realize my parents were people, too, until I started deliberately watching their lives, seeing their humanity and vulnerability. They temporarily lost their hero and SHero status when I saw their relationship weakening and they began to talk about separation in 2006. To me, they had been married forever, you know? They had been married all my life and as far as I was concerned, they got married back when God was a boy. I thought they were born married, so how in the world, especially as mature adults and Christians, ever think they had a right to not be married? Who did they think they were? After all, people expected them to always be married. So what made them think they had a choice in their relationship? After an honorable discharge as an E-7 after twelve years of service, owned a cleaning company, served twenty-eight years of ministry, founding pastor, bishop, counselor, and chaplain, and mom's nine years in banking, thirty years as a non-profit comptroller and corporate administrator, founding co-pastor and school teacher, Mr. and Mrs. Jones were legally divorced after forty-three years of marriage. I never thought divorce would show up in my parents only to be used as a tool for genuine reconciliation. What? Who does that? How does that happen? Well, since you want know…

It was 1961 at a baseball game in Portsmouth, Virginia; Walter Jones, better known as Earl back then, was mesmerized by her big doe-shaped eyes. He knew immediately he *had* to meet her, talk to her…so much so that he purposely passed her as she walked with her friend, and took her wallet. Now, he wasn't a thug or thief, he was determined.

"Give me back my wallet!" Thomasine reached, as he toyed and raised it in the air out of her reach.

"I'll give it back if you tell me something."

"I don't have to tell you nothing!" She stood on her tiptoes and slightly jumped.

"I just want to know how you enjoyed that trip."

"What trip? Give me back my wallet!"

"How did you enjoy your trip? Because I know you just came from heaven."

"Oh boy, please!"

Frustrated and her wallet still being out of reach, Thomasine hauled off and slugged him in the arm.

"Stop. Don't hit me, or I'm going to tell my daddy!"

Though she thought it was quite strange that he didn't say "I'm going to tell my momma," which is more common, she didn't ask at the moment because she was more concerned about getting her wallet and not having any trouble. Truth told, she wasn't supposed to be at that game anyway. Thomasine, or Teeny as she was affectionately called, and her friend had schemed up that common high school trick: I'll tell my mom I'm going to your house, and you tell your mom you're going to my house.

He didn't know about the scheme and, at that moment, it didn't even matter because he was hypnotized by her big, beautiful doe-shaped eyes. She didn't want to admit it as quickly as he did, but she was truly impressed by his mature conversation. After he kindly returned her wallet, she could see he was much more mature than the schoolboys she knew. She also assumed he was much older. He was dressed in impeccable '60s style, had a small waist, neat frame and was well groomed. Impressive. His dark skin and nice smile made him attractive, too. Her eyes, her eyes, her eyes, her smile, even her clothes had charm and her overall petite cuteness took them from meeting to courting to love to marriage.

On November 16, 1963, they were married in her parents' home. But after they said "I do" the pace of their relationship accelerated by the speed of tasks, duties and responsibilities. They had one child within the first six months, then another child eleven months later. Four years later, they had another one. They lived with Thomasine's parents for a little while. Walter had always worked, but then Thomasine got a job, they moved out, he went into the job corps, then the Marine Corps, she got a job at a bank, they got saved, they went to church, they moved, they started Melton & Jones Cleaning Service together while she still worked at the bank, they moved. He went back into the Marine Corps as a drug and alcohol abuse counselor, he got out, they moved, he became a pastor, they moved, he became a bishop, she became a pastor and they moved. Between military and ministry, they began to support young military families, they began to shepherd and lead people, they began to teach about marriage, they raised their three children, and influenced and helped other children in every neighborhood they lived in. Their home was the neighborhood hangout. They helped raise their two oldest grandchildren, from infants to school age.

Before they knew it, they were caught up in function, duty, title, ministry and service, and never really caught up in a relationship with one another. There was no fake or façade, just the imbalance of marriage and family life and the busyness of ministry, inundated with serving and being what they believed God called them to do. Throughout the thirty years of ministry and forty-three years of what marriage was supposed to look like, they were experts in working together and knowing one another based on titles they knew: husband, wife, Dad, Mom, Marine, bank teller, ministers, deacon, choir director, praise and worship leader, pastor, teacher, preacher, administrator and bishop. They had an admirable partnership for ministry and people (their spiritual children) and it far outweighed the ministering to themselves as individuals and to one another as friends. The service of people, and duty and function, their marriage lasted forty-three years. It wasn't mundane and robotic, they had great times and celebrated the love of God, church and family (in that order).

Implementation Guides: When is the last time you checked in on your relationship and partner? What do know about your parent's or guardian's history? How were they people, too? What do you want your children to know about you being a person, too?

Chapter Seven

Divorce & Reconciliation

"When there's a divorce or break up, the person may have left you but always know, they didn't take you."
—TracyMac

THE TRUTH OF WALTER E. JONES AND THOMASINE RAWLS JONES

So what happened? How does two mature, Christian people, who taught, met in 1961, get married in 1963, minister and cater to young military families for thirty years, mentor hundreds, maybe even thousands, shepherd their congregation and oversee other pastors and churches, teach marriage and family seminars across this country and others, sharing their core values of being a "ministry of hope and reconciliation within the body of Christ" (Ambassadors for Christ statement of purpose incorporated 1982) decide to legally separate in 2009 and divorce in 2012? Who does that? What in the world happened? It's easier than you may think.

TracyMac: Mom, what do you think happened as to why you and Dad aren't married anymore?

Ms. Jones: Well, Tracy, our separation and divorce didn't just happen overnight. It was years of getting used to things I didn't realize were making me lose my identity and making me feel bound by duty. I loved your dad and our marriage was good, we just didn't spend time on us, our relationship because we were was always doing something or had someone else to take care of. Even in the name of submission. I didn't realize until after we divorced what those things were.

I never took time for myself. Yes, I spent some time alone by myself sometimes and I was okay with that. I knew how to have a manicure, pedicure and a spa day, but that wasn't taking time for myself, that was spending time ON myself not with myself. I did more work for God rather than living the will of God that included getting to know me and your dad. I wore his military rank and his ministry titles and functioned as a bishop's wife and a Gunnery Sergeant's wife and became what the titles required of me. I already had my own career titles in the banking system, teaching school and a pastor, too. I never liked the title "first lady" because I didn't want to perceive anyone else as "second." I didn't like it, but it didn't stop people from introducing me as, "This is Gunny Jones' wife" or "Bishop Jones' wife" when I really wanted them to say my name. I would have preferred, "This is Thomasine Jones, Gunny Jones' wife" or "This is Pastor Thomasine Jones, Bishop Jones' wife." I had a name. I was a person, more than a borrowed title. I read, shared and taught thousands of women the Word of God, how to be a good wife and mother, but I didn't know how to teach them how to be themselves. I didn't know. I also didn't know how to be my own friend, so I really didn't have a clue of how to be your dad's friend. Most of our conversations centered on the needs of our children, other people, the congregation and finances.

TracyMac: *Dad, same question. What do you think happened as to why you and Mom aren't married anymore?*

Mr. Jones: Tracy, first of all, I'd like to say, anything you go through teaches and I have no regrets. I love your mom. Thomasine was my wife. She is a very good and godly woman and the mother of my children. Looking back I realize me and your mom literally laid down our lives for a purpose. I believe our marriage served its purpose in fulfilling the will of God for our lives. We didn't really get to know one another as people or take time to gel as a couple, to experience what we shared and taught. Doing so could have allowed us to serve one another better. We didn't have a pattern, no one to go to. We had peers in ministry and I did have other pastors and bishops who fathered and mentored me, and they taught me how to have a relationship with God and do the work of the ministry. So we did the best we knew to follow a ministry pattern to show people a family pattern. In the name of being a good example for the lives we influenced, we took more time to make our genuine performance excellent, rather than pausing to implement. I didn't know how not to be "there" for people. All times of day or night and any place—counseling, teaching, preaching the Word of God, disciplining and helping others have a relationship with God and their families. We brought our work home with us, carried in our hearts, minds and on our backs, too. Some of this is because at the beginning stages of starting Ambassadors for Christ, I could see there were so many young families and I knew they needed someone and I knew that was me and your mom—our family. I knew what it was like not to have a mother because my mom died when I was nine years old. I knew what it was like to have a father who worked all the time and who was hard on us. With six brothers and a sister, my dad was a single father in the '50s, and we had to grow up quick. I knew they needed discipleship and a relationship with God. I knew I was the one to teach them and your mom knew she was the one who would help me. God knew I needed her to be my help mate and I wanted to be hers. So, early on in pastoring, I asked God, "How am I supposed to take of these people and my family, too?" and I heard God say, "If you take care of these families, I will take care of yours."

My dad, along with my mom right by his side, took care of people via ministry and God kept His promise. Yes indeed. My siblings and I may have gone through some things in life, we could do a much better job of communicating with one another and used less excuses for not getting together and we are far from perfect, but God! God kept His promise to my dad. All three of us are alive and well, living our lives as we choose and we were and are well taken care of because we were taught how to take care of ourselves. I did not have my parents like people thought I did. The church was how I stayed connected to my parents. It was a sacrifice I don't regret because they gave a sense of family to thousands and it taught me to establish, cultivate and cherish a greater sense of universal family and value sisterhood and brotherhood with so many amazing people. I'm grateful! During their interview, my mom and dad talked about how grateful they were to have produced three beautiful children. They talked about how they share a bond that no one else will ever have and they are now friends and becoming best friends.

Yes, you read it right. Currently divorced, but now becoming best friends. They shared how a few months ago they talked on the phone for four hours, the longest they have ever talked on the phone, not only in length but the depth of content. They reminisced about the people they loved and the mighty things God used them to do as a team that they never could have done alone. They were better together, for a time, their children, a people and a purpose. God used him to be the brand and used her to be all about the business, literally.

They didn't know what friendship looked like in marriage or how to explore the depth of relationship. Had they known, they may have anchored instead of starting off by hitting the ground running. They paced, but never left the race. They weren't really together as a couple, but together as a dutiful and functioning unit for the sake of natural and spiritual children. Without regret, it made them who they have become, as well as helped thousands of other people become who they are, too. Ambassadors for Christ, in name and in action. It was a ministry of hope and reconciliation and if the story of their lives continues, if friendship after divorce isn't hope and reconciliation for sixty-nine and seventy-year-old friends, I don't know what is.

Their separation and divorce was a bit scandalous and unraveled in a church and little town, so you can imagine how painful it was to hear rumors, especially coming from the mouths of those they served so diligently. It hurt, and made forgiveness stand up and heal me. I will say some of the rumors were quite entertaining and funny, so much so I told an inquiring mind to believe every rumor she could about my parents because they were more juicy and easier to swallow than the truth. Speaking of swallowing, things may have been different if they had. You know how it is when you're feeding a hungry child who doesn't have the teeth to chew well, so you do it for them. My parents lost themselves in titles, functions, duties, entitlements and expectations. They grocery shopped, brought the food home/church, cooked, set the table, tasted, chewed and spat for their children, congregation and mentees. You see, they tasted but didn't digest it well or consistently enough for their own marital nourishment. That doesn't make them hypocrites, especially when their relationships with God has kept them and when those they served have become grown folk with evidence of being well-fed.

DIVORCE LEADS TO RECONCILIATION

Who are my parents an example for? You. If you are in the military, a pastor, father, teacher, counselor, mentor, mother, working mom, military spouse, woman pastor, and bishop's wife, my parents' relationship is still a powerful example. It is definitely encouraging for those who may be divorced. Divorce doesn't have to end the relationship, On the other hand, some people won't ever befriend their ex. Maybe my parents' marriage was their gift to people. Maybe they unconsciously decided to lay down their lives for purpose, to become a living sacrifice unto God for other people. Even if it meant taking a chance at it being at the expense of their own marriage and their children. Soldiers die for their countries every day, so is it too far-fetched to think the death of a marriage is a result for saving many. Maybe that's a kind of love many have received, but may not understand it enough to give. Walter Jones and Thomasine Jones believe the fruit of their labor has and is coming back in their later years. No doubt my parents are an example of marriage and divorce, however it speaks to you. People don't usually allow themselves to be an example of what the church, religion and society see as something very negative: divorce. I am not encouraging or promoting divorce as a heroic move or an answer. It was simply their resolution and solution to live. *If you are divorced or a long-term relationship ended, that person left you, but they did not take you!* It may hurt; both of my parents were hurt, but relationships and mentorship can help you understand that you still have you!

TracyMac: Mom, how has coaching or mentorship helped your life?

Ms. Jones: I am able to express myself freely, with myself as a woman, in my relationships, including the one with your dad. Your coaching me through the rough times, when your dad and I first separated was a great help! You said something one day that I never forgot and think about it all the time as a way to live. You said, "My spirit proves my beauty, therefore shattering any negative competition or jealousy with another." That helped me so much as a woman to be freer, knowing who I am here to be and what I am here to do. I don't have to toss things all about in my mind repeatedly, because coaching allows me to bring it out, make sense of it and have it read back to me. It holds me accountable to do something about it. It's like writing myself a letter that includes dreams, visions, goals and instructions. I write myself a letter because I know me and I know what to say. I know me now and I want other people to know me and get to know who they are, too. I teach them who I am and I learn who they are. I enjoy that. I can't lie to me and that's what coaching feels like to me. Divorce can simply be a witness for seasonal changes and shifts within relationships.

TracyMac: Dad, you mentioned how you had other pastors and bishops who mentored you. How do you see that level of discipleship and mentorship different from coaching, if at all?

Mr. Jones: God, will You ever use me again? When I left your mom, Ambassadors and Havelock, I wondered if God would ever use me again. I knew I had more purpose in me, but I didn't know if I had passion for that type of ministry. Because if you are not willing to live your purpose with a passion then it's not your purpose. I had friends, peers and mentors who helped me value relationships and unconditional love for people—for ministry, with the evidence of making sacrifices. Not to sound brutal, but

I know that when you sacrifice, you can't do it without leaving some dead bodies in the path. Somctimes even the things that have to die in you. That level of mentorship taught me to take shepherding the lives of people very seriously because being looked up to as an example is not a joke. Preaching tells you one perspective of who you ought to be. Coaching helped me deal with me, showing me who I am, my reality and drawing out a greater sense of purpose. It helped me not to base my purpose on what I do. Your book The Book of Purpose: The YOU Testament helped me see that my purpose is who I am and that God would never stop using me. Yes, I've gone through a lot of things since then and my mission changed. Now I go boldly where I hadn't gone before, on purpose!

Statistically speaking, my parents have more years behind them than they have ahead. They talked energetically about what is and what's next for them as individuals and as friends. They both spoke about living freely, experiencing those things they always wanted to do at their leisure, like traveling more often and enjoying other facets of other people's lives. Teaching and learning more about people in ways they may have missed. They are getting to know one another in different ways and are enjoying discovering other relationships. They even over-talked one another about the peace of living in the moment and be fully present. They realize living in the past is full of depression, living in the future is full of anxiety, so living in the now is best. My parents said they are learning from me. If that isn't an honor, I don't know what is. What is also an honor is I wouldn't be all of who I am and know a lot that I know if it weren't for them teaching me first. The seeds they sowed, the youthfulness they sacrificed—I pray my life is good fruit.

Implementation Guide: What do you know about divorce? What do you know about reconciliation? What relationships can you reconcile, if any? What would you sacrifice a relationship for?

Chapter Eight

Relationships to Ponder—Communication

"When the trust account is high, communication is easy, instant, and effective."
—Stephen R. Covey

Dear Communication:

I'll make this brief. It would seem that we would all seek to be experts when it comes to you, seeing that relationships start, are maintained or end based on how well we use you, or not. You show up in speaking and listening, and behavior and thought. You allow us to exchange messages and signals. You tend to be most effective when we use words to share and impart information. You are why we use radios, letters, music, phones, television and social media; it's all for and about you. Do you get conceited knowing this? Don't because you are simply a balanced component of listening and speaking, no matter the form, you aren't much without them. We all know that you are a key, but how many of us allow you to unlock us within our relationships? Things always go awry when people are closed to you. We blame you by saying, "There is a mix up in," and we all say your name. We also associate you with disagreements and misunderstandings. Do you accept? We say you are also the key for any healthy relationship, especially marriage, and I most certainly agree with that! But, you can be a little tricky when people are opposites, or come from backgrounds where you were misunderstood. What then? What do people do when they are opposites and have to depend on you? They say all good marriages depend on you, great sex and healthy finances, is that true?

Chapter Nine

When Opposites Attract

"Love recognizes no barriers. It jumps hurdles, leaps fences, penetrates walls to arrive at its destination full of hope."
—Maya Angelou

THE TRUTH ACCORDING TO DUANE & SHARON REYNOLDS

How could anyone write a book about relationships and not include one that has all the ingredients of a classic love story? For one of them, it was love at first sight, well…

Once upon a time in Grand Rapids, Michigan, there was a strapping young lad and a beautiful damsel…

Hold up, talk about communication, I'm setting the wrong tone already! Let me start over.

SO FINE

Back in the day he said she was, "FINE!" It was 1981, and Duane Reynolds and Sharon Brooks went to two different high schools. But, as fate would have it, a program similar to what we now know as the magnet program (Educational Park) allowed them to meet. It was a pretty normal morning for Duane, an energetic and outgoing student and athlete. Duane was comical and friendly, which made it easy for him to have friends and be liked. Being a people person wasn't something he was learning in high school, it was something he was born with. He probably felt it was a subject he could teach. He was sitting in class, talking with his friends, and never one to be one at a loss for words, his lively speech was suddenly interrupted with a delayed "Umm,

umm, umm…" His friend's conversation slowed to silence, looking at Duane and then looking to see what captured his attention. She was beautiful. No, she was FINE! The songs, "So Fine" by Howard Johnson and "She's A Bad Mama Jama" by Carl Carlton had created a mix tape in his head, to the beat of his accelerating heart, yet slowing, purring, "Umm, umm, umm." That's the language of youthful lust or love used when a young man's eyes have been smitten and his vocabulary was rendered useless. When Duane saw her…when-he-saw-her! She was beautiful, no, FINE! Was it her skin? Yes. Was it her eyes? Yes! Was it her hair? Yes! Was it her body? Yes!! He didn't even have a clue of the maturity and brains that were all wrapped up in this beauty. It was a day he would never forget, umm, umm, umm!

On the other hand, her hand that is, she couldn't not quite recall the very first time she saw him. To her, he was a guy in the class. This beauty was studious, sharp and one who sat at the front of the class. Though her intelligence was innate, learning was a skill she chose to craft. Not being a social person, she went to school to learn and that she did! Duane was there to learn, too. He learned in school, but he wanted to learn more about her now. Her name was Sharon Brooks. Using his competitive edge, with laser focus combined with a little swag and charm, oh it wasn't swag back then, it was "cool points," he went bankrupt using his cool points on Sharon. She authenticated them, counted them and made him work to use them. But, being the competitor that he is, it worked and she bought in. He wooed her and she didn't mind it at all. They started by having those awkward exchanges of information to talking all the time. Though opposites, communication was a commonality they enjoyed. They talked one another right into being sweethearts and started dating October 1981.

Everything was going pretty well until one day during their Black History class, there was an open discussion about interracial adoption. During the discussion, Sharon unashamedly voiced her opinion that interracial adoptions didn't really matter to her because she wasn't going to have any children anyway. Duane took it personal. After all, his plans were in jeopardy, and being readily outspoken, he said to her and in the hearing of the entire class, "Sharon, if you're going to be with me *you* are going to have some babies." The class erupted with laughter. Sharon was not going to have that *and* have Duane assume she was going to allow him to be a committee of one for Planned Parenthood, or allow him to think he could control her like some teenage husband! Opposites strike back! She immediately engaged him a in a lively discussion and an exchange of ideas and also stated, "No you didn't! You aren't my first boyfriend and you won't be my last!" Did she really say that to the senior class president? Oh yes she did. That was a rift, but they forged ahead into the world of boyfriend and girlfriend. It was also an early sign of how different they were. What would come of this?!

In February 1982, Duane's high school was hosting a Valentine's Day dance. And, since Sharon was his umm, umm, umm girlfriend, of course he invited her to come. But, Sharon was not hardly the social butterfly, plus she didn't attend his high school, so she was not going to subject herself to be put under the microscope by being the topic of whispered conversations like: Who is she? What is *she* doing here? So she chose not to attend. That was her final answer, Alex (Jeopardy)! But, that didn't stop Duane, Mr. Opposite, from going. He was outgoing, an athlete, senior class president and he could dance. That night, he may as well have been dancing to "All Night Long" by Lionel Richie because that is what he did! Duane danced with several different young ladies and he was such the dance man, he also danced with teachers. While he was at the dance getting his dance fever on, little did he know that a rumor would surface that he had kissed a girl at the dance and that it would travel all the way to Sharon. "Rumors" by Timex Social Club hadn't come out yet, but that didn't keep Duane from being a victim. He didn't do it. Sharon didn't know whether to believe him or not, so they broke up.

After graduation, Duane left Grand Rapids and enlisted in the United States Marine Corps. Although they broke it off as boyfriend and girlfriend, they decided to remain friends and would exchange letters. In the letters, they were able to keep up with how each other was doing and what each other was doing. Duane had traveled to a few duty stations and ended up in Yuma, Arizona in 1985. Sharon was planning on going into the Army and it wasn't because she was gung ho about being a soldier, it was the benefit of having the Army pay for college. She wanted her Military Occupational Specialty (MOS) to be in journalism. She wanted to become a broadcast journalist and do the Oprah thing, way before Oprah came along. Sharon's mom threw her a party with the works. A DJ, an Uncle Sam cake, family, friends and neighbors were invited to say bon voyage. The next day, she packed up, went to the Military Entrance Processing Station (MEPS) and was ready to go. She had sworn in, and just before boarding the bus to head to basic training, they couldn't find Sharon's name and information in the computer. There was no evidence that she had been processed. Feeling that was an obvious sign that she wasn't supposed to join the Army, Sharon went back home. Her plans to go to Central Michigan for college, with an internship and a scholarship, fell through as well. At eighteen, she left home and moved to California with relatives.

During that time, Sharon had received Jesus Christ into her life, as her Lord and Savior, and committed to living a Christian lifestyle. Although they both attended church in their youth, they couldn't say they had a real relationship with God. They'd talked about Duane coming to see her and because he wasn't saved, she wasn't sure if this relationship would be a wonderful romance or if it was of the DEVIL! Sharon started praying for Duane to accept Jesus Christ in his life, too. Maybe she inspired Helen Baylor's "Can You Reach My Friend?" Though she stayed in contact with Duane, she was not in a hurry to get married to anyone, including him. On occasion, she would talk to her grandmother about not wanting to ever get married, but if she did it would be to someone like Duane. He was her exception. As you know, God answers prayers and they show up through people. In this case, Duane showed up on her doorstep. He had given his life to the Lord, too, because of the evangelism of two Marines who would not give up on witnessing to him. Their last names were Thomas and Shepherd. So, now, Sharon and Duane were now good n' saved, in love, married and they were getting their communication skills down to a science, but still opposites.

Opposites do attract. Here's more proof. See, Sharon is a self-proclaimed pack rat. She's analytical, observant, she can be critical, and she's a conscientious, no nonsense type of person. She's comical and likes to laugh, but it still should be correct. Why not? And then we have Duane, who's very energetic, wide open, full steam ahead; if he thinks it, he will do it right then, and if doing it like that doesn't work, he will do it in another way next time. He doesn't do a whole lot of pondering. While someone is still talking about it, he has completed it and is off to the next thing. He has a sense of humor and enjoys laughter, be it at or with. Did I tell you they were opposites and still are?!

After twenty-nine years of marriage, they are still opposites, but champions at communicating and are still going strong. They are so opposite, she's right handed and he's left handed. Yin and Yang, Venus and Mars—rocking it, Grand Rapids, Michigan and Havelock, North Carolina style. Boy, you should see them on a road trip. He may strike out not exactly knowing how to get to wherever they're going and she would be more likely to break out a map, map out the trip, and check the accuracy of the legends and proofread it, too. And, together, they WILL get there! Talk about proofreading…

You see, Sharon is a natural born proofreader and she has no respect of person. She loves to read and her children get that from her. When they were younger she would have them read the newspaper and give them a quarter for every error they could find. Who does that?! Sharon Reynolds, that's who! No one is safe, not even Duane. Remember I mentioned how they exchanged letters? They exchanged letters from the time they were in high school until they got married almost five years later. They love to communicate, so that meant there were lots of letters between them. Being a pack rat…no, a caretaker of all sentimental memorabilia, Sharon kept all Duane's letters. Duane, being her opposite, did manage and keep up with several of the letters Sharon had written to him. One day, years later in their marriage, Sharon had come across all Duane's letters. He liked that and wanted her to know he had kept hers, too. It was a sweet moment because neither of them realized the other had done so. Sharon started to read the letters he'd written to her and it went something like this:

> *Dear Sharon,*
>
> *How are you? I'm doing good. I know you enjoying living in California and I am come see you soon and I hope you are looking forward to seeing me to.*

Duane read a letter she'd written him and it went something like this:

> *Dear Duane,*
>
> *How are you? I hope you are well. It was great hearing from you and to answer your question, I am well. Please let me know when you are planning to come see me. I'd be happy to see you, but I do not like surprises.*

They laughed and reminisced, reading letter after letter, the more recent the letters, the more evident their love and heart-felt intentions. But suddenly, someone gets the great idea to switch letters. He would read the letters he had written to her and she would read the letter she had written to him. As Duane began to read, he noticed his letters had been met with a red pen he didn't use. A proofing, red pen. Sharon had performed grammatical surgery on his letters without anesthesia. She loved reading what he'd written to her, yet she couldn't resist wielding her red pen of correction. Yep, she would take out her red pen and correct his love letters.

Sharon said, "His run-on sentences were the worst and correcting his use of to, too and two…I would have a field day."

Duane said, laughingly, "How dare she correct my love and the feelings of my heart?"

Sharon responded with a smile and without pause, "Your feelings were fine, but your grammar was terrible!"

How does being opposites work for them in this relationship, without living a life riddled with dysfunction and unhappiness, forcing one to get along without losing yourself in an argument? Sharon and Duane believe that it is their relationship with the Lord first, then seeing their being opposites as a gift of balance. While Duane stays on "ready" mode, Sharon pauses and questions everything. She will ask questions, do research and now she has the convenience of Internet reviews. So, whenever he wants to experience the next endeavor, she finds out all the what, when, where, who, why and how. And, how! But, she realizes her need for his energy, his sense of adventure and wanting to explore options that serve their lives in every way. She knows that if it weren't for him she would be debilitated by analysis paralysis. Balance!

Duane: You don't realize you're the opposite of someone until you are already attracted to them. That's where the trick is. Because if you knew that someone you were attracted to was so diabolically opposed to a lot of the things that you do or like, you would just avoid that person most of the time. Because you just want to flow in rhythm with others who are enjoying and liking the same things that you like. But, that could be a very dangerous road. We have known each other thirty-two years now, and I value the fact that we are opposite. It requires us to communicate. I also value the fact that we had children at a young age because our focus on our children and our family did not allow us to get stuck in our uniqueness. That required us to communicate. Our children needed both of us, the balance of who we are, and our relationship as a couple and for the family. Our children are so much like both of us. They are a lot like me in some ways, they are a lot like Sharon in other ways. The children are not pigeonholed into one thought process.

Sharon: The balance that we are has helped both of us because we've rubbed off on each other. He has definitely brought me into some extroverted experiences. Now I won't say that I have totally converted. I am comfortable being who and what I am and even though we are opposites, Duane has helped me grow tremendously. We have influenced each other because we aren't afraid to communicate! It allows us to consider a perspective we may have never considered before because we listen to and challenge each other.

They may be a wonderful example of balance and healthy communication, but it doesn't mean that everything has been perfect. They have had their share of ups and downs and trials and triumphs. Their story is one of resilience and overcoming relationship, health and financial challenges and it is also one of foundation and security, because their relationship has withstood their challenging differences. They're not afraid to challenge one another lovingly and have those lively exchanges and expose very different opinions. That's communication at its finest! There are a lot of cases people fear knowing what their spouse thinks because maybe they wouldn't love them as much, maybe they will put their marriage at risk by not being able to say what they really feel or think. They don't have those kinds of inhibitions, so their relationship is stable enough to withstand it.

There is a place to say what's on your mind and there's a place to honestly filter truth. There is also a time where you pray with and for your spouse. Their story is also about accepting and loving one another, as is, and being able to fall in love with one another despite the huge amount of baggage and differences that couples tend to bring into relationships. Duane and Sharon came from extremely tumultuous environments. Balanced communication wasn't talked about or carried out properly in most situations. And, what kept them from bringing that chaos into the relationship they attribute to their individual and collective communion with God. Their relationship with God, through Jesus Christ, was encouraged and fortified by being mentored and developed, and having loving relationships within the local church.

FAMILY, CHILDREN AND CHURCH

The local church was another area that Duane and Sharon had to learn to balance and communicate. At church?! Yes, darling, at church. Duane and I worked at Ambassadors for Christ together. Sometimes I wondered if there was a contest or a healthy competition for who could get to work the earliest or stay the latest. A progressive church, whose members were made up of mostly active duty military families, between the ages of twenty-one and thirty-five, required a lot of work, especially before there were computers and smartphones. So, both of us were there during the day, we had service two nights a week, leadership meetings one night a week and choir rehearsal one night a week. So, sometimes it was just easier to stay at work, go get something to eat, bring it back and be on time for the next service meeting or rehearsal. Let's not even talk about outreach, conferences, symposiums, supporting the other churches my parents (Bishop and Pastor Jones) oversaw. That way of life was all I knew. I wasn't married at first and didn't have a child. But, Duane was married and he had one, two and then three children. And, that's where their relationships with communication and balance had to be strengthened. Sharon was involved in the church as well, but not nearly as much as Duane. She knew that having a relationship with God meant everything, and it didn't require church attendance for everything all the time. I'm sure opinions were voiced, she may have even gotten the side eye from some of the saints and some may have assumed that she felt her children were better than others. But, it wasn't about that at all. She wanted her children to, first and foremost, have a relationship with God, be involved in the church, do well in school, be active in extracurricular activities, and be involved in vocational and educational opportunities that would offer a plethora of experiences.

During that time, they also ran a business together—Sharon's Cookies Supreme. Sharon is an excellent baker and had created cookie recipes that people may not die for, but they are so good, people definitely loved and paid for them. What started out as giving cookies as gifts to friends and family that were baked in their home oven, grew into having a store in the then Twin Rivers Mall, in New Bern, North Carolina. It started out with just Sharon and Duane and they ended up having accounts, subcontracting with other stores, providing delivery services and hiring employees. Business boomed! Those cookies were some of the best I ever tasted and if I play my cards right, whenever they come to visit, they make me say umm, umm, umm, too!

Sharon and Duane have always been innovative and progressive thinkers because Sharon is aggressive in thought and Duane's nickname should be Action Jackson! You can't stop this duo from leveling on their own terms. Now Sharon works with the city of Havelock and Duane is the Executive Director for the Boys & Girls Club of Coastal Carolina. They attribute the success of their relationship and marriage to each of them having a personal relationship with God, and sharing in that with one another. They also give props to communication and do that openly, honestly and often. They allow their differences to be what binds them together. They also credit the foundational relationships within the local church they had from 1986 to 2012. It wasn't passing "Hello" or "Praise the Lord" or "How are you doing?" but real relationships where covenant, deliberate coaching and mentorship were taught and implemented.

According to the truth of Duane and Sharon, there was more show than tell, more encouragement than criticism and more sisterhood and brotherhood rather than ordinary back-of-the-head religious membership. There were systematic classes about discipleship, marriage, family, children, sex, finances, leadership, homeownership, entrepreneurship that were paired with and just as important as Bible study. You see that common in churches now, but this was happening in the '80s, '90s and beyond. We still have and choose to maintain a very viable relationship with one another and many others because of the holistic relationships cultivated back then. They experienced being taught more about the Kingdom of God rather than preached at about it. Duane and Sharon Reynolds have successfully raised three children.

Their daughter-in-law, is the other half of the reason they have two beautiful grandchildren.

When I asked Sharon and Duane what they look forward to doing in the future, I wasn't surprised to hear them say spend time together in their empty nest and being with family and friends. They passionately spoke about being grateful for their children being taught the Word of God from the time they could hear, and wanting their children and grandchildren to have a relationship with God, too. They want to spend more time doing all they possibly can to make sure those foundational principles and way of life are instilled in their grandchildren and their grandchildren's children.

This is what can happen when opposites attract and choose to communicate: two people can come from damaged backgrounds, fall in love, have a relationship with God, get married, be zealous about ministry involvement, raise God-fearing and socially-conscientious children, become entrepreneurs, unite their polarizing leadership skills, serve through community and government, enjoy healthy relationships with friends and family and still enjoy a lively discussion and exchange of ideas. When opposites attract they communicate. You are truly the balance of listening and speaking, and Duane and Sharon are handling you quite well.

Implementation Guide: How well do you communicate? How can being opposites work for your relationships and parenting? How can you not perpetuate generational dysfunction? How do you balance work, marriage, family and ministry? How can mentorship and coaching play a part in your relationships? What do you feel the role of a local church should be, in relationship to balancing family roles and responsibilities? How do you reinvest into your marriage and intimate relationship?

Chapter Ten

Relationships to Ponder—Changes: Church, Coaching and Clients

"I like to see myself as a bridge builder. That is me, building bridges between people, between races, between cultures, between politics, trying to find common ground."
—T.D. Jakes

Dear Church:

As I address you in this missive, I want to thank you for being my gateway to my relationship with God, spirituality and community. I am so grateful for all the times I didn't "forsake the assembling" and the people or the "two or three gathered" who have touched my life. I would not have connected with them had it not been for you. You were the foundation of my relationships with music, my family and many of my friends. No matter if I was a member or attended for a short time, congregations like Emmanuel in Portsmouth, Virginia, Pilgrim's Rest Christian Church in Harlowe, North Carolina, Holy Light Church of Deliverance Portsmouth, Virginia, Marshall Chapel Baptist Church in Jacksonville, North Carolina, Deliverance Evangelistic Temple of Jacksonville, North Carolina, God's City of Refuge, Newport North Carolina, Ambassadors for Christ Fellowship Center, Havelock, North Carolina, and Harlowe Community Chapel, Agape Fellowship, Family Worship Center, Kingdom Outreach Center, were all in Okinawa Japan. All of those bodies of people help touch, change and transform my life. No, I wasn't hopping around on you, military moves and going to college were the reasons I got to know so many different denominations and interpretations of you.

I went to the altar at least three times for salvation, countless times for other reasons, was baptized three times—baptistery and a river and, yes, the water was cold, ice actually. I was filled with the Holy Spirit, with the evidence of speaking in tongues in my teens. I heard some of the most profound, thought-provoking and inspirational messages. I prayed, read, fasted, sang, taught and cried. The denominations ranged from African Methodist Episcopal to "non." No matter whom, when or where, those places and experiences helped me develop my relationship with God and people. I thank God for them, their pastors and leaders.

My parents' church, or should I say our church, was Ambassadors for Christ Fellowship Center (1981-2008) and my dad used to say, "The church is meant to be a living organism, not just a religious organization." (Remember that.) I love how you bring people together and even how aspects of religion, from a positive perspective, have been the infrastructure that kept Black folks hopeful during slavery and allowed us to "Lift Every Voice And Sing." Oh my goodness, your music is ALL that! You, a Hammond B-3 organist, a bassist, drummer, keyboardist and a handful of powerful singers are a match made in "We're-About-To-Have-A-Good-Time-Now" City! Now some of your lyrics and song book theology, I could never really get with, so much so, I used to hum on those parts.

Your fellowship is a conduit to extend families, support and benevolence. Your presence can also bridge communities, nations and governments together. You have a way of serving inspiration and encouragement that's second to none! And though your services still seem to be the most segregated hours of the day on a Sunday morning, you have crossed racial, gender and even denominational lines to magnify God. Now, I will tell you, denominationalism is perceived by some as riddled with hypocrisy and confusion and that it may be. Yet it is also a way for everyone to choose from a buffet of how they choose to publically connect with others of like faith. Various forms of religion and other spiritual practices can do that, too.

MY SHIFT

Church, I had a shift from you back in 2001. I was still attending, but my pregnancy kept me out a lot and being on bed rest gave me a lot of time to pray, meditate and hope. After all, every day I was in jeopardy of losing my baby. To keep a positive mind, I also used that time to reflect, think and read. I'd have my various translations of the Bible, lexicons, commentaries and concordances, and self-help books spread out over the bed, trying to answer questions about me and my life that I could not find. I had those same questions—Who am I? Why am I here?—that played Wimbledon tennis matches, like Serena and Venus, in my mind ever since I was a little girl. They got louder because I wanted to be able to tell my child who I was so she would know who she was and could be, and I had nothing to offer that satisfied the responsibility I felt.

Chapter and verse were a start for me to find my answers, but even as sacred as they were, I didn't want her life, possibilities and descriptions tongue-tied to one book. Something in me always felt God was greater, more creative, could evolve and had more to say beyond sixty-six books. Church told me who God was and all about Jesus and everyone else in the Bible. But, maybe because the services were monologue, I didn't hear much about me, other than what I wasn't supposed to do. When I would even think about asking about me, I'd hear people say, "It's not about you. It's about God!" I'd keep quiet, but think real loud, *Isn't God in me? How else do we see God other than in and as us? How do we make "it" about God if we aren't doing and being whatever "it" is?*

TWO QUESTIONS

When I was eighteen, I wrote two questions in my journal and no answers followed: Who am I? Why am I here? And nothing. When I was twenty-one years old, I'd go to the beach almost every night to feel free, be alone and hear a "Peace Place" of my own voice that had been drowned out by sermons, society and service. (That's why I named my LLC.) I could speak to me there and I would listen. One night those same two questions visited me, but this time it was so strong, I felt like the crisp night air, the sound of the waves and the seagulls were asking me, too. The wet sand under my feet, as I walked along the shore, randomly picking up shells began to soothe my mind. The peace, wisdom, acceptance, success and wealth I experienced in those moments felt like me. They felt like home. They felt like I AM. They filled me up, but I didn't know how to make them fit into the framework of my life. I didn't know I could be them much less how to let them be me. So, I held them hostage to my beach experiences.

I still had those two questions wearing a bald pattern in my mind, and still, no practical and relevant answers stood behind the question marks. Being on bed rest forced me to take time; I was determined to find out and all I had to use were the resources I had been equipped with. Now I did read other books, but they always had scriptures to point me back to the Bible. Nothing is wrong with that, if that works for someone else, but I wanted more than to exegete a text and re-read, rehearse and regurgitate things like:

> *You are the head and not the tail.* Okay, well if I'm the head, who is the tail? Do they know? How can all of us be the head? Isn't Jesus the head?
>
> *You are the righteousness of God in Christ.* Well, who's isn't "in Christ" if He died for all? What does it mean to be righteous and what does that look like other than preaching the do's and don'ts that include Sunday morning's "what NOT to wear," but yet "come as you are?"

Then I began to study verses like: I am accepted in the beloved, I am one with God, a friend of Jesus, justified, redeemed, a recipient of grace and forgiveness. I knew them, but this time I saw them differently and posed more questions: Okay, if I know this, how does it look in my life other than at one of your services, church? If I'm one with God how does that feel? How does that live everywhere and behave practically with evidence? If I am one with God and Jesus is my friend and He died for my sins, once and for all, why would "they" still keep me sin conscious and God keep hell as an option? Is that how you treat children and friends? Why were we so segregated, saints, sinners and ain'ts, if we were all God's children and friends and you were God's house? Why do I have a relationship with God and the only way it was validated by others was attending your locations or organizations? What if I had a relationship with God and didn't go to church? Would God still love me? Would God still know me? Know me?! Do I know me a part from titles, duties, functions and labels? Who am I anyway? Why am I here? Whoever I am, there has got to be more to God, me and life than what I was currently experiencing within myself, as there was no shortage of activity and things to do.

Now don't get me wrong, I was taught well (thanks Dad and Mom) and I knew about vision, destiny and some elements of purpose, but my involvement with you, church, groomed me to be a part of a beautiful organization, but I was ignorant, self-ignorant about my own organism. Who am I? Why am I here? Those books spread out over my bed were giving me one perspective of information, but I was determined that the answers to those questions were going to come with implementation. I stopped reading those filled pages and began to write, filling the blank pages of my journal and they filled my life. My words were sacred. Why couldn't my "text" be just as sacred as the authors of those books, including Genesis through Revelations? Huh, why not? Weren't they men (human), too? Why no women? I mean, it is believed that Samuel wrote the book of Ruth and Mordecai wrote the book of Esther. Women didn't write? I wasn't trying to be defiant, I simply realized I was the only one qualified to answer those two questions for me and my answers would be just as sacred. Why not?

SELF-DISCOVERY

I realized my bed rest was my greatest wake-up call. It awakened me to a different perspective of spirituality and consciousness and at that time, I didn't even know what to call it. I began to feel the same peace, wisdom, acceptance, success and wisdom I'd feel during my beach experiences, only this time I wrote to them as them, personified, as if they were a part of me. I was losing the feeling of being self-ignorant. This was the start, but…my, my, my…it was a conscious beginning of self-discovery. I began to realize who I am here to be and what I am here to do. Church, you weren't anywhere around and I became less and less afraid to ask and answer questions. And, God wasn't afraid of me, my questions or my discovery. Was I afraid not to be with you? Yes.

I knew that I had to take a break from you to hear my answers and write my text. Of course you would be a significant part of my foundation, but I couldn't let you or anyone else override my experience and call to purpose. I couldn't multitask you and me. You couldn't get mad at that because I will tell anybody if I never set foot in one of you again, I have been with you and faithful, enough for five lifetimes. I loved you so, and from my experiences I could no longer allow our relationship to continue as it was. I know a lot about you and we spent most of my life together. After all, my dad even started one of you in our house back in 1981. I don't regret a day, a service, Bible study, meeting or rehearsal. As much as I have mentioned you thus far and may even say your name again, you know as well as I do, we hardly ever see one another.

ENOUGH ALREADY

When Owen got orders to Okinawa in 2003, I decided that was my chance for you and me to really take a break. But, as habit would have it, I couldn't. I didn't. I felt guilty. The churches I connected with in Okinawa were very nice churches and family-oriented like Ambassadors, yet I couldn't plug in 100% because it was my intention to take a break from you before I ever got the island. I wasn't mad with God or church folks. I was frustrated with my own rut and outright tired of you, and just about sick from not knowing me. You hadn't changed, I did. And, in a lot of ways, you still haven't changed. My attendance wasn't allowing me to show up in my own life. I had served, taught, sang, worked, cooked, cleaned, traveled, showed up early and stayed late for years…too many times to count. Say amen, church!

It wasn't until late 2004 that I had to stop completely. My not wanting a relationship with you was causing me to have a negative relationship with God, all because of years of association—as if you and God were one and the same. I was being hypocritical and judgmental because I was in my own funk of habit, not relationship. I didn't want to be there. I didn't like me that way. I quit. I knew God was where you were, but I knew God was everywhere else, too. I wasn't even sure if God went to church as much as I did. Some of my Japanese friends showed me other places God was, too. So, I took a chance on being rejected, talked about, being called a back slider, and I don't know if they did or not, or if they even noticed. I did hear about folks praying for me and Lord knows some felt sorry for Owen, thinking he had "lost control of his wife" (HA!) not realizing he was feeling the same way.

I had to fan the flames of the sparks I kept believing, knowing, feeling and experiencing. The answers to my questions came in the form of discovering my purpose, mission and passion. Some people see those words as interchangeable, but I had to break them down differently in order to live them. I wrote about that extensively in my first book and I'll share a little about that later. But, I knew I wanted to help people, especially leaders, business owners and organizations, with relationships, self-discovery and self-development. Maybe some of them felt tired and tangled up like I did or some organizations could stand to rekindle some "organism characteristics," due to them being comprised of individuals.

LIFE COACHING

I read an article about life coaching while sitting in a doctor's office in 1998. It talked about life coaching from the perspective of executive and business coaching. I thought, *What if people had something like that in their everyday lives—a listening ear, the right questions able to set and achieve goals and have accountability without control?* I didn't look into it again until 2002. I wanted to help people that way. Counseling alone was far too heavy for me and I knew the seriousness and responsibility of helping people with their lives, but I didn't want to just talk. I wanted to listen to what they wanted to be and do and help them with the solutions and get results to do the damn thing! I wanted them to have a life-changing experience, and not clone the way I did, but assist them with the way of their unique journey, grid of life and purpose.

I was discovering who I was here to be and what I was here to do and enjoying life much more abundantly! Now church, some people, a lot of people, can experience self-discovery while having a relationship with you, and that's good for them. I've coached them well, too. I couldn't. The walls were too thick and confining for what I knew I had to do. I'd hear people say, "We've got to get out of the four walls," but when we/they did, we just built a better box with new walls out there that looked just like the walls surrounding us. The way I was getting to know the God in me, and how purpose and mission were answering my life's questions, God didn't need the walls or the boxes to use me.

MY FIRST CLIENTS

I started coaching and my first client was in the Air Force. I was coaching him, but couldn't tell him what it was because it wasn't "church related." He wouldn't have that. I couldn't present it to him as if he needed help, mine or anyone else's. He wouldn't have that either. Plus, I was still working some things out for me as I was coaching him. I just called them "inspirational talks" and being unrefined as a coach, we'd "talk" for hours. Then coaching allowed me to help people transition, be it off the island or back to the United States or within some of life's transitions—welcomed and unwelcomed. When those in the military are getting out or retiring, the government has a TAP (Transition Assistance Program). But, what I found out, through our own transitions, is that though that program deals with geographical, financial and some career transitions, at that time it didn't deal with the dynamics of relationship transitions. Not dealing with the nuances of self-ignorance, relationships can be abused and destroyed. A military mind is conditioned to give and receive orders and instructions, without questions, and once those parameters are non-existent, they, too, begin to ask: Who am I? Why am I here? Much like church folks—orders, instructions and commandments beyond the ten. I knew my method of coaching was Godly and spiritually based, but didn't require church walls, especially when those I wanted to serve didn't need them, have them and in many cases didn't choose that experience.

WHERE ARE WE NOW

I became what I needed. I became what my parents needed. I got certified, Owen got certified and he and I became what we needed. My natural gifts, chosen mission and experience qualified me, and the education and certifications I chose to earn simply give lift and illumination to what I do. Business owners, leaders, organizations and fellow coaches are who I serve well. Though I can speak and am a public speaker, I love to hold a safe space for those in the limelight for when they leave their stage and postures of performance. Who hears them? Who is there for them? I am. I serve as an unbiased listening ear, a relationship strategist and a confidant to help them mastermind personal decisions. I love it!

So church, I spent so much time with you from the inside looking out, I had to see you from the outside looking in. I am not regretful or angry with you, and recent evidence will show that I do visit you from time to time, more often than I have in years. My *framily* (friends who have become family), the Campbell's (we'll talk about them later) are members of Riley Hill Baptist, in Wendell NC and that church has embraced my daughter through their youth activities and affiliated teen program, so you know other than youth activities, Owen and I won't let her show up there without us. We were asked to volunteer at their annual community day event and of course our answer was yes. They are a down-to-earth congregation of close-knit families who are worshiping God and have an outstanding youth ministry. Those ladies work hard and serve well. I honor them! Several of Jayda's fellow Top Teens of America and the Top Ladies of Distinction who serve as their mentors are members and also serve at Riley Hill. They do an impeccable job of serving their community. I'm grateful for those two groups, who make a difference, they matter and they work well with and through you.

Church, I do believe in your viability as an organism to facilitate relationships to maintain a sense of Godliness, collective inspiration and encouragement, benevolence and a sense of community. There are so many other locations that offer great hope about you. Now, I don't want to hurt your feelings or get into more trouble with people than I already may be in (oh well). But, as I close, there are some parts of you that if you don't change, you will die as an organism because, overall, the organization seems to be killing you. People won't even know you died because their organizational habits will assume you are still alive. You have to change. Maybe over time, like most of us, maybe aspects of you have become self-ignorant. You may want to discover or re-discover your purpose, shift your life's mission and rekindle your passion, too. I don't know, I could be wrong because for the most part, I am now on the outside looking in. But, I will tell you in my second closing: I hear you. I see you. You matter. I am here to help. Will you let me? If not, love me, anyway.

Implementation Guides: What is your relationship with church? What do you believe about religion, church and God? What relationships have you formed through fellowship? Does church differ from religion or denominationalism? How can the Bible be your example of writing your own sacred text? How does God speak beyond scriptures and religious books? Is it possible to have a healthy relationship with God apart from going to church or religious gatherings? How can you appreciate or become consistently involved with positive activities that help or assist your community? What questions do people have that church and religion are not answering?

Chapter Eleven

Unique on Purpose

"The more you like yourself, the less you are like anyone else, which makes you unique."
—Walt Disney

THE TRUTH ACCORDING TO KISHA LEE

I met Kisha Lee about three years ago when my thought partner and friend, Undrai Fizer, had a speaking engagement in Salisbury, North Carolina. Because he lived in Houston, Texas and had come so close, Owen, Jayda and I took a little Sunday drive to Salisbury. When we arrived, the event had ended and he introduced me to the pastor and his wife, a very inviting and kind couple. I met several people in passing and then he introduced me to Kisha Lee. There was something about her that was fun, exciting and different. There was a familiarity about her I couldn't quite put my finger on. We knew we'd never met before, yet we had a mutual feeling that we had. We had a lively conversation that lasted no more than about five minutes. We exchanged information and realized we both were living in Raleigh, about five to ten minutes from one another. You know how you meet someone and you intend to follow up, but you don't? Well we didn't do that! After realizing how much we both were committed to living lives of purpose, it was exciting to know there was someone who was not only ready to have the conversation about purpose, consciousness, spirituality and many things perceived weird and different, but who lived it. She's got some serious dibs on the Law of Attraction.

ON PURPOSE

She is a small business owner of Purpose Productions and Photography and if you ever see her work, it's obvious she is on a mission and is extremely passionate about what she does. When I learned her website was http://www.purposeproductionsandphotography.com—my coaching niche being self-discovery and relationships as it relates to purpose, mission and passion—I knew that this connection would be purpose filled. We had so many things in common, from growing up in the church to being PKs (preacher's kids) to getting saved and having real relationships with God at a young age to always having questions about religion, denominationalism, spirituality and the role of the church in our lives. But, on the other hand, our lives and so many of our experiences were completely different. Not only were our experiences different, but one of the things that makes Kisha Lee attractive is that she is different and she loves it. Kisha Lee, and yes I always call her by her first and last names, is a thirty-eight-year-old, Black and Native American, and her grandfather was from India. She has a ten-year-old daughter named Naija, whose name is tattooed over Kisha Lee's heart.

Kisha Lee: Naija is my only child and I am currently in one of the longest relationships I've ever been in in my life. I love my life. I have had a really long journey and I come from a very strict Christian background. I was very okay with that because there was nothing else I really wanted to do growing up. I actually really, really enjoyed going to church as a child. But, there was always something more I wanted to know about God. My journey is all about my relationship with God. When I was ten years old, I could hear God—I would talk to God and God would talk to me. One of the defining moments as a child was me and my mom would always go to church together, we were like church buddies. I remember always telling her I heard God say this, I heard God say that. One day she was in the kitchen stirring a pot and I walked in and said, "I heard God say…" and she turned around and said, "You hear God more than anyone else I have ever heard in my life!" That moment I began to question myself. I wondered if I was weird because I took her statement very negatively. Until then, I thought everybody heard God like that. I thought it was normal. And, I didn't know that everybody else didn't hear God the way I did. She may not have meant it negatively, but that's the way I received it. And, that was the first time I ever felt like I wasn't normal. I also felt different because not only could I hear things from God, I could also see things prophetically. I could visualize things before they would occur. But, before all of that, when I was around seven years old, you know how you think thoughts and you can hear your own voice in your head? This is going to sound strange, but ever since I was a little girl my thoughts spoke with an accent.

Now I already told you Kisha Lee was different and now I know you're thinking that this has crossed over from different to weird. C'mon, how does a seven-year-old little Black girl, who lives in a little town like Sanford, North Carolina hear her own head-voice in an accent that sounds a little British, or Australian and sometimes a little Caribbean? And guess what? She had never been to those places.

Kisha Lee: I don't know why I heard my own voice with an accent and I didn't know where it had come from. You have to realize that everyone in my home, all of my relatives and everyone in the town that I lived in spoke with very strong southern accents. My outer voice was like theirs, southern and country. But, my voice I heard in my mind spoke with an accent and even at that young age I knew that was way too different. I knew it was something I would have to hide. It was easier for me to adapt to what I heard from my family. But, every time I was alone I had to speak to myself in that accent out loud. I had to. In order for me to have some type of balance, I incorporated my inner and outer voices and people began to say I talked "white". So, I suppressed it because I didn't want to be that different. I felt like I would just have to live and die with it.

No one can understand this; how could I explain it to anyone if I couldn't explain it to myself? There was no one I could talk to about it because I knew everyone would think I was crazy. So, then when I felt the negativity about hearing the voice of God, I knew that with my inner voice having this accent, there was no doubt that this would have to go with me to my grave. I began to suppress and shut out my ability to see things prophetically as well.

MARRIAGES AND CHANGES

Having to hide this was having to hide who she was and that caused Kisha Lee to experience things on her journey that would have made most of us give up and die. She would have short-lived relationships with different men. She has been married and divorced three times before she was thirty years old. She was eighteen years old when she first got married. She was still in high school and that marriage lasted a year and a half. Her second marriage lasted nine months. Her third marriage lasted five months. Now imagine having these experiences growing up in a small town, being heavily involved in the church and living in the "Bible Belt."

Kisha Lee: It was so painful for me. Because people will not let you live things down if you allow them. People didn't have a clue of what I had gone through. On top of being married several times, I had been raped three times and I had gotten pregnant with my daughter when I wasn't married. Now you have to take responsibility for the things you have done, the things you haven't done and failures. But, people didn't realize that in those several marriages it wasn't even my fault. I do take responsibility for my end of things, but I refused to live with abuse. The first thing people say is, "Hey, you have been married and divorced three times. What is wrong with you? Why can't you keep a man? Why can't you just be a good wife?" They always ask what's wrong with you, they never ask what happened. I had people that would not even talk to me because I have been married and divorced three times. And, understandably, whenever I did have a new relationship, the man would be distant because he didn't want to be number four.

I understood how it looked. I knew it didn't look good. I didn't care how it looked. What I knew was that I had to make a decision for me and my daughter. My daughter was born into the third marriage and I had to leave it in order to survive. Why would I stay with a man who put his hands on me and almost threw me over a second-story balcony? So you make a decision and you have to stick with it even if it carries negative weight. Those experiences have taught me to take my time, really get to know someone, and not just dive in or fall in love with being in love. But, I learned I had to own all my decisions and mistakes and not blame someone else for what I repeatedly attracted into my life. I strongly believe in the Law of Attraction. I had to take responsibility even if the decisions I made had warning signs. I chose to marry every man I married. I've always been spontaneous and I still am, but maturity and purpose has taught me to make sure my relationships are purposeful. I'm currently in the longest relationship I have ever been in. I have been with him for three years and we are not married. But, what got me through the pain, the rejection, the broken relationships, including the one with myself, was my relationship with God. God is Source. God is Spirit. God is Energy.

Hold up! Where does all this God is source, God's energy come from? She grew up in the church, she knows the Bible. And, at twenty-seven years old, she was an ordained minister, preaching and teaching the Word of God and even training other ministers. But, when she got pregnant with her daughter she hadn't yet gotten married for the third time. She chose to refrain from ministering because of her convictions and not wanting to be hypocritical or a bad example. That didn't even go over well because the church that she was a part of practiced a level of forgiveness that is rare in most churches and didn't hold it against her enough for her to cease ministering. But, she stopped anyway. That was different. She was different. She also realized that she did not want to ever preach or teach and know the truth of God. Her relationship with God, the same God she kept hearing from even as a child, grew beyond just hearing or getting a word for people, but she was at a place where she craved getting to know God beyond her religious experience and outside the four walls of her church. Her journey would consist of enjoying her relationship with the church, but not being controlled by it.

When I met Kisha Lee I had no knowledge of her story, nor the pain and rejection she was able to overcome because she was so energetic and genuinely excited and still very spontaneous. But, she wasn't wild and out of control; it was attractive and fun with a little edge. Her personality was one that would encourage gentle risks and explore God-given what if's that were purposeful and powerful! I didn't know her past, I didn't know her triumphs and I didn't know about the accent. Kisha Lee eventually became a part of one of my coaching groups. And, she and I had a very blended relationship because we were able to discuss God, Jesus, the Bible, spirituality, business, family, relationships, and ourselves. We could talk about faith, hope, love, purpose and things like the Law of Attraction, consciousness and share our visions, but yet we would hold a comfortable space for her to be coached. We would meet for breakfast once a week to have our catch-up and coaching moments. One day at breakfast Kisha Lee said, "There's something I've been wanting to tell you, but I don't know if you will see me differently."

Our conversations had gifted me with the knowledge of some of her experiences and because I knew how colorful some of them were, I was like bring it on! Now you have to know Kisha Lee is always bubbly and energetic, but on that day it was different; she seemed nervous. And, I felt the need to assure her.

"No matter what it is, I will still accept you for who you are, as is. If it is something I can help you with I will, and if it's something I can't help you with, we can find someone who can. And, if it's criminal activity, I will be sure to visit you in jail." She smiled so big, as usual, her eyes tightened and shut and chuckled, and put both hands over her face.

With her hands still covering her face, she said, "I didn't know I'd ever meet anyone who would ever understand or accept this. I don't even know if I accept it myself." She went on to tell me about a man she had met who speaks with an accent simply because he chose to. She told me how she felt from the time she was seven years old about having this accent in her mind, that she was ashamed to speak with her mouth. Just because she didn't speak it with her mouth did not mean the accent changed. She lived all those years hearing one accent and speaking another. But, when she met this man, his freedom, vulnerability and daring to be different was not only a sign of sanity, he was proof that he could do it and not be carted off somewhere wrapped straight jacket, she could, too! I listened to the compassion in her story. I could hear the fear of the assumed rejection she'd grown accustomed to living with, and I could see the excitement and the desire she had of wanting to hear herself, be herself.

"What kind of accent isn't it?" I asked her.

She smiled so big, as usual, her eyes tightened and shut and chuckled and put both hands over her face. She even tried to hide her face behind her napkin.

I said, "Is it that funny? Is the accent a comedian?"

She smiled so big, as usual, her eyes tightened and shut and chuckled and put both hands over her face again, and this time she tried to hide her face under the table.

When she sat upright, she was still laughing and there were tears rolling down her cheeks, and that's when I knew that she wasn't just nervous she was scared. She was scared as hell. She heard her mind's accent when she was alone and there had been times when she entertained family and friends by toying with her accent. And, even when she was inspired and in the presence of the man she had met she didn't want to use it in front of him, fearing he would think she was mocking him. So, this was the first time she would tell someone, be serious about the risk of having them think she was crazy, too. This let me know that even though we had become acquaintances and friends and had collaborated on business ventures, Kisha Lee didn't realize just how accepting I am. So, I coached it out of her. I asked her the right questions, allowed her to answer her own life without judgment and I created a space for her innate accent to emerge with audible voice, seriously. It took a little bit, but as she began to speak with this accent it seemed so natural coming from her. Her entire persona gently shifted. She became "rather posh," actually. I listened to how she heard her own voice ever since she was seven years old, thirty-one years suppressed.

I was so grateful to be there to hear her sound. It wasn't a joke this time. That's when I realized it was because it was so natural to her, the confidence in which she spoke her voice wasn't afraid of being heard, seriously and out loud. She was afraid of how other people would hear it and perceive her. She was a mom, she was in the longest relationship she had ever been in, she was a business owner, she has family, she has friends, and clients and none of them had ever heard her speak seriously this way.

She was scared of rejection. She'd already experienced that in her life and had overcome it and was afraid it would plague her again. I will tell you now, she overcame it and now speaks with an accent that can fit in so many different places in the world. It's so natural for her that when I hear her speak now, I honestly can't remember what she used to sound like. Every great coach, teacher or mentor learns from their clients, students or mentees. This experience with Kisha Lee taught me to dare to be different. And, just because you won't listen to the truth of who you are and how you are to express the voice of your being unique, it doesn't mean it ever stops speaking.

Be YOU

Because of Kisha Lee, I see how we put so much emphasis on the fact that because a person hasn't visited or lived or is from a certain place they don't have permission to speak with an accent or vernacular. You should see some of the looks I've gotten when I tell people about my friend Kisha Lee. We easily accept someone who speaks an entirely different language, but give people like her the side-eye when they put a twist on their own. Weird. Can a person choose to speak differently, even if they haven't had a geographical move? Who says the language and dialect is controlled by where we are from or where we live? Whether you have a country accent from North Carolina or a twang from the hills of West Virginia. Or whether you have a northern accent from New York or a different accent from New Jersey. We have to realize that accents are only a way we use our mouths to form the sounds of consonants and vowels.

There are people that choose to change their accents if they grew up in the country and now live in the city. You have people that choose to hold on to that accent and not be moved just because they have moved. My husband is originally from Charleston, South Carolina, and those who live in certain areas have a very distinct accent I love, but he only chooses to use it on occasion. Not to allow someone to speak in the authentic way, or have them assumed strange may lean more toward being small-minded and weak. Some people choose to enunciate differently because of an experience they've had, others may choose that being themselves comes out in a different dialect, whether they heard it since seven years old or not. What if being yourself comes out having to be married three times? Is it worth it to be yourself?

Kisha Lee was fearing being ridiculed and rejected. But, once she began to share this with her partner, family and friends, colleagues and clients there was no rejection. Don't get it twisted, no one cheered. But, there was no rejection. No one left her. Kisha Lee wasn't rejected because she stopped rejecting herself. And, what she did not have the tools, experiences or maturity to do at seven years old, she could do as a woman of purpose.

Kisha Lee: I appreciate people when they allow you to be you. I want people to be free and happy. I want people to experience joy and peace. I want people to experience their purpose in life. If people can discover their purpose, they are more likely to live their purpose. And, what is beautiful about my life is not only did I discover my purpose, I live my purpose and I get paid to do my purpose. My past, my pain, my purpose and my accent have paved so many opportunities for me. Purpose uses them ALL! I have always consistently evolved and overcome, so when the coaching came along and the opportunity for me to become completely free, met me where I was, I was ready. But, coaching helped me further understand who I am and why I am here. I have always been different. But, who isn't? Who says what normal is?

Because I love God and God loves me, I have authority to minister love everywhere I go. I have authority to be in a relationship or not. I have authority to take care of my daughter. I have the authority to work for myself or with someone else. Knowing my purpose has given me the ability to accept who I am, to love who I am and be okay with who I am. I will tell anybody not to be so hard on yourself, accept yourself, love yourself and don't be afraid to be yourself and open up to yourself. You may need to get help with that and if you do, it can help you be complete. I feel so full and I am complete because I know my purpose and I am accomplishing my life's mission. My relationship with God is heightened because I have a greater spiritual awareness and I don't have to hide who I really am from God, from me or from anyone else. I know what I am and even if that is different, then different I dare to be.

Implementation Guides: What if you felt different all of your life? Have you? How? What have you said about someone who has been married multiple times? Who sets the standard for "normal" or the status quo? How can you own the decisions you've made, without blame?

Chapter Twelve

Relationships to Ponder—Listening

Dear Listening:

Let me start out by saying when I found out how life-changing important you are, I was motivated to become your most improved student. You helped me realize that when I put you first, you put me first.

You have a wealth of wisdom to teach and share, and thus far, I have learned your first lesson was to use you with me first. I found out it helps me immensely when it comes to using you when I'm with other people, especially my clients. I could do so much better when it comes to Owen and Jayda. Keep that straight for us, will ya?! You aren't as busy as you could be. In some cases, you are underemployed and unemployed. So, while you're chilling, can you fix that amongst some other things? I would like for you to help me make sure I use you well, too, because I love to teach and coach—the quality of my work depends on you.

You're actually pretty easy to be with, but a lack of relationship with you allows many to presume you're difficult and self-serving. So many of us learn about your counterpart—speaking—but where do we take a class about you? Where's a "How To Listen Class" and who will attend? Remember if there is one, you may have to offer it for free and even then, don't expect to pull a crowd. Make sure you dress up, because nowadays, marketing and promotion says people want to see something and their attention spans are in a hurry! Talking about you can make people feel they are being restrained or controlled not to speak.

I mean, calling myself a "motivational listener" gets me the eyebrow raise and I've even had a few people say to me, "How boring," It may be that some assume you to be boring because of the outward stillness, but if they would only take time to get to know you, they would see that you are so freakin' active that one can't only use their ears. Most have asked me what it means to use you motivationally and with our experience, when I explain, I can tell when they stop using you. Sometimes I show them better than I tell them, and as purpose and mission would have it, they are motivated because you are beautiful and attractive.

As a motivational member of your tribe, I hear people's lives, what they say and what they don't say. You are actually very insightful, entertaining and far from boring. You accept communication in any language and translate. You even have a very intriguing way of animating, which is how I've come to know you, motivationally. You have the ability to enlist every sense and vital organ to get your point across I don't know how to explain it but sometimes you can be so demandingly loud you have to be broken down in layers. Since lives and souls have sounds that vibrate through experiences and stories, how can we appreciate the melodies, harmonies, lyrics and tones if we don't use you as the appropriate hearing aid? Understanding the art of you aids in our hearing. I understand there is a difference between you and hearing, though some feel its minor, it majors in the art of communication. Hearing is being aware or capable of hearing sound, but listening is to pay attention and tune (with) into it.

Everyone wants you so desperately when it comes to them being heard, but not so much when it's someone else's turn. There are so many assumptions, since the unspoken can be misinterpreted; especially when the spoken is un- or underappreciated. I so agree with sound consultant, Julian Treasure, who did a *TED Talk* entitled: "5 Ways To Listen Better" (Treasure, TED Global, 2011). When I watched his presentation, all my bells and whistles I didn't know I had about you went off! In seven minutes and thirty-six seconds, he spoke to my life in a way that confirmed what I felt, needed and wanted others to experience with me.

You, Listening, are an art that is being lost. But, not so fast; I can hear and see you and I am not alone by far! The value of you was reiterated when I was completing one of my life coach certifications at Coach Training Alliance. I am grateful for my coach and coach mates. Professionally trained life coaches are effective because we don't make others hear our own brilliance because they could take it or leave it. But, as we listen to them, ask them effective, thought-provoking questions, encourage them to set and achieve big goals as they discover their purpose, and develop their mission with great passion, they hear their own brilliance and wisdom and can experience you, their way for life!

With our ears, we hear the voices of others, as well as our own and some of us are most uncomfortable with the sound our own voice makes, we don't like it, yet want others to…we are so quirky! I love to hear unintelligible conversation when I'm at an event because I know people are conversing, communicating and exchanging sound and lives. I love the sound of music, laughter and waves, and I am grateful you used my ears to hear it. But, the most intriguing thing about you is when ears are not needed. You show up when we think, read, feel and see. We are among the deaf and hard of hearing, which helps me understand a relationship with you requires access to our entire being. If their hearts, minds, bodies and souls can speak in order to fairly communicate, they use you, too. In fact, you go everywhere because that's where sound is; even sounds our ears aren't privy to, like our thoughts, minds or hearts. People have been known to say these things speak. I agree, and would go farther to say they speak first. You know we know their sounds, yet they are the first voices we ignore, especially our own. Certain moments, facial and emotional expressions have a visible sound and a relationship, and sometimes the ears aren't invited to every conversation.

So, look here, though I'm good at presenting, I know I will learn a great deal with my speaking course because I want to level up on being transformational. As balance would have it, I want to level up with you, too, so I'll continue to teach people about you. So before I go, will you agree with me in prayer about you? Don't worry, it's short. God, help us not to neglect or ignore the power of Listening. Help us to remember my friend is a vital part for the yin and yang in communication and our auditory medicine. This mighty friend of mine can effortlessly render dysfunction powerless, not because Listening is that forceful, but when we use this sweet and invisible power to connect with ourselves, it opens our eyes to see and better understand the language of someone else. God, help us not to forget or lose my dear friend, for without Listening, we may be in jeopardy of forgetting and losing communication with you.

Chapter Thirteen

Relationships to Ponder—Unmarried, Sexuality

To The Unmarried:

I will tell you first hand, it's better to have peace by yourself than chaos in a relationship! I hear people say there are no good men or women left. I don't believe that for one second. I do believe there are plenty good men and good women who are being overlooked. I dated different men before I was married, and long before self-discovery, someone shared the acronym with me to be U.G.L.Y. Be UGLY!? U Gotta Love Yourself! I took that to heart and date or no date man or no man, I loved me. It wasn't about manicures, pedicures or clothes and shoes. Loving me meant loving my mind, even if I wasn't the smartest. Loving my soul, even if it wasn't the purest. Loving my body, even if it wasn't the finest. I paid deliberate attention to how I felt about myself and talked to myself in my own mind. I had some jacked up mental tapes just like everyone else, but I did my best to create and play positive tapes in my mind about myself, that way, if a man did or said something derogatory, it was foreign and unacceptable. I loved me first. Yeah, I may have been perceived as "too good" and those who felt that were right. But I was very accepting of men and to a fault, I saw them as brothers and friends, when they saw different. So communication became key. But I had to have the communication down with me first. I had to love me first! Love you first then, set the stage and issue the invitations.

Who can make you happy? You! Become who you are looking for. If you make a list, list what you want from you, what you like about you and that will attract someone else's expressions of those desires. Do you really want to be married or be in a long-term relationship? Be honest. Now your answer has to be authentic, consistent and in the open. But no need to be loud about it because everyone is not meant to hear you. Don't pray two-faced prayers or send God mixed signals. Know what, how, when, where and how you want – starting with YOU! Be okay with you, just the way you are. You will attract people who are okay with themselves their way, and because of that, they will be okay with you too. You don't have to go-a-looking if you just show up, show up whole not in percentages. If you don't think you can, you won't.

I haven't dated romantically in over two decades, but I have and do have time alone and out with men, personally and professionally. That's a date, just not sexually charged. All of us are single but many are not socially or legally coupled off, either way, we're all connected. Yet, we are all individuals and sometimes people lose their individuality when they marry or are in long-term partnerships with a significant other. They tend to forget and are smothered by relationships that forget there is a "me" in team and there are two "I's" in relationship. Balance requires those times when we choose to give up the "I's" sometimes for the sake of us and we! It's even sweeter when we can go beyond saying "you are mine" to "you are me".

Because it's been so long since I was unmarried, one may seem to feel that I may not know a lot about that status, or that what I may know could be very outdated. I will agree with them that the dating scene has change drastically since I was in it. But what I am hip to and savvy about is how to build relationships with men, and as a woman isn't that what dating is all about, getting to know a human being not hooking a husband or wife. It's not something I've read about in a self-help book or something someone told me. My relationships with men and women is how I live. Maybe the relationship I have with my brother and other childhood male friends made connecting with men easier. Owen is my primary and best friend. He's my husband, my lover, my child's father, my business partner and confidant. Some of my closest friendships and partnerships are with men.

Thus far, many of my clientele have been men. One reason I believe men hire me is, I listen and let them be themselves within a professional coach to client relationship. Also, they don't feel they have to get approval, permission or consent from their wives or significant others to invest in themselves for coaching, or anything else they feel can assist in the betterment of their lives, most women say they do. The other reason is though they are more likely to be heard, they are rarely listened to when it comes to things they feel most vulnerable about. They don't have all of the answers, they have questions too, they have weaknesses that need to be supported and have strengths that need to be balanced and appreciated and not feared and constantly challenged... everywhere. None of us have all the answers, anyone who thinks they have all the answers hasn't heard all the questions. When it comes to black men, I've heard a lot of people describe the black male as angry, that may be true, but from my experience he is hurting and is in pain. Who cares? Who knows? Who sees? Who's willing to listen? Who's willing to hear his mind? Who's willing to help? I am one of us who does.

Through relationships, purposeful relationships that I build and the sense of community that is established is greatly based on knowing who I am, my purpose and my mission in life. Owen also has relationships and friendships with women, because I can't be every woman to him and he can't be every man to me. The sexuality and our marriage is not open, but the intimacy to share in genuine personal and professional relationships with people of the opposite sex is. He is my only in several ways and though he is a very "good thing" God so graciously shares with me. He is not *MY everything* in all ways, vice versa. That's one of the mistakes I feel some unmarried people make when they go into a relationship and what can destroy a good marriage. It's also what keeps us fresh! With so many things that have changed on the dating scene over the past 20 years, like sexual influences from the media, internet and speed dating, I can't intelligently speak from experience on what it's like for those who are unmarried. What I do know is when there is an energy and a chemistry between a man and a women, it just is and cannot be forced. That hasn't changed since the beginning of time. Keep it as real as you want it.

Implementation Guides: How do you love yourself? What is your perception of those who are unmarried? What do you want from you? How do you feel about dating? How can you maintain the "I" in your relationships? What type of relationships is your life sending invitations to?

SEXUALITY

Dear Sexuality:

You are very good and feel so right, yet at the same time, you seem to mess up everything for many relationships, especially when you go rogue. Let's keep it real, everyone who is having sex ain't married and everyone who's married ain't having sex! You can guilt trip, attempt to control, beat folks with a bible, buy chastity belts, arrange marriages, use scare tactics, educate and religiously condemn folks all you want. People are having sex, lots of it. Well, except for some married folks. I can't count how many married couples I know, have coached who don't have sex at all, haven't had sex in a long time and in some cases, would rather not…ever.

Sexuality, as you know, is a physical exchange of pleasure, hopefully enjoyed by both. But how so, if characters like "The It's All About Me Mandingo Man or "The Academy Award Winning Orgasm Faker" show up in the bedroom? I know the upbringing of my Christian beliefs taught me sex before marriage is a sin. So does that mean no sex or less sex after marriage is one too? When most Christians talk about sex they'll bring up the scripture, "Marriage is honorable and the bed undefiled but whoremongers and adulterers God will judge." (Hebrew 13:4). Forget the whoremongers and adulterers for a second, let God handle that. But let's pull back the sheets on the word undefiled which means, pure, free from stain or blemish, having no faults;

sinless. Some folks believe that means, when it comes to sexual expressions within the confines of marriage, you can do no wrong. Have at it any way you BOTH like it! Two consenting adults who decide to engage in acts of sexuality, to include penetration or not, must realize the significance of the exchange. Whomever you have sex with is a part of you, in some way, forever and that increases your chances to become more like them. So, don't have sex with someone you wouldn't want to be. Create boldly, set strategically and be a choosy lover, like the quality of your life depends on it. It does!

Implementation Guides: How comfortable are you talking about sex and sexuality? What do you believe about sex? Before marriage? During marriage? After marriage? Whether you agree with it or not, what do you know about various forms of sexuality (LGBTQ, polysexuality, etc. not talking about "it" won't make "it" go away)?

Chapter Fourteen

Relationships to Ponder—Weddings, Marriage and Infidelity

"I love you, and because I love you, I would sooner have you hate me for telling you the truth than adore me for telling you lies."

—Pietro Aretino

Did you know the main reasons the marriage license is issued is for proof in the event of death or divorce? Only twice in the twenty years we've been married have we had to present our marriage license. Once was to the church to get married and the second time to the military so I could be put into DEERS (Defense Enrollment Eligibility Reporting System). That was required in order for me to become Owen's military dependent. That gave me an identification card to use at the commissary, military exchange, get discounts at stores on Veterans Day and get health insurance coverage. But, we have had a baby together, financed houses, cars, got in and out of all kinds of debt together, traveled, joined churches, and social groups, partnered in business, etc. And, no one has ever asked us for our license. So, when you hear people say, marriage is just a piece of paper, though the union and commitment is more than that, the paper is basically for "if death do you part": relationship or physical death.

Have you ever asked where the wedding or marriage vows came from? What is the history behind the ring or exchanging rings? Why do we offer a diamond ring for engagement? (You may want to ask the DeBeers Diamond Company the latter. What an ingenious marketing campaign! You also may want to ask them if diamonds are so rare, why are they everywhere?) The wedding and the marriage are completely different commitments. So much emphasis is placed on taking care of the wedding that it is assumed the marriage will take of itself. One is a party and a play for others. It is a day, a moment that includes costumes, scripts and a well-planned, catered meal and choreographed dance. The other, marriage, is a duet of butt naked improvisation, learning the two-step and stepping on toes while enjoying takeout sometimes instead of that lavish catered meal to keep from taking each other out! You are ever evolving, taking a chance that your different evolutions will sync. You have to be able to laugh with and *at* one another, as some days are a joke and others you may have to laugh to keep from crying! So much time, creativity and effort are placed on the wedding day. According to the "Cost of a Wedding" web site, "The average wedding cost in the United States is **$25,200**. Couples can typically spend between **$18,900** and **$31,500**... most couples spend **less than $10,000**." This does not include the cost for a honeymoon. (June 11, 2014, http://www.costofwedding.com/)

Yet, when it comes to *investing* in the marriage, some couples who I have encountered clear their throats and raise an eyebrow over the average cost of couples coaching sessions. The average cost being around 5 to 10% of the low end, and a day long maintenance workshop being 1% of the cost of an average wedding. Most couples invest *no* money on maintenance, outside of a date or a trip. No matter where traditional wedding vows came from, was there a subliminal vow somewhere in there that says, "We will *not* ever do anything to consistently invest in our marriage, unless we are paying our lawyers for the divorce?" I had a potential client tell me he wanted to hire Owen and I for couples coaching, but his wife said that's what their date nights were for. And, if you feel the same way, work the hell out of your date nights, be creative, be deliberate and be consistent. I don't know if it worked for them or not. I never heard back. I know Owen and I needed more to get over and maintain. We didn't have access to a helpful coaching program when we needed it most. Our date nights weren't enough, we weren't comfortable being that vulnerable with any of our friends at that time, we didn't feel church folk would understand without condemnation, and we were supervisors on our jobs. We were leaders in the church and too saved for "secular" counseling. Now that's some ignorant and pompous ass stuff right there!

But those were *the* main reasons we have become what we needed and offer pre-marital coaching and coaching for couples, too. We did our work and endured learning the hard lessons and earned the experience, professional and educational credibility to create a listening space, a judgment-free zone for other couples and leaders, who don't feel they have anyone whom they can trust to help them to either do the work to love it, or do the work to leave it alone. My parents didn't feel they had that safe space either. Having already overcome our ignorance, pride and foolishness, we help keep others from handling it alone, unnecessarily. We reach out for maintenance, too—directly and indirectly—consistently and remain teachable to the married and unmarried. Yes, don't get it twisted, unmarried people can be very wise and hip about relationships.

In marriage, things happen. We happen. Nobody is the same person they were when they said, "I do." I don't care if they just said it yesterday. Those words can cast a mist, no, a fog and you may wonder, who am I now and who in the hell is this?! As I was growing up, I never had a fairy tale image in my mind of what marriage was/is. No knight in shining armor movies played in my head. All I knew is that I didn't want to be married because from what I could see the woman got the crappy end of the deal. It wasn't solely based on my parent's relationship but every woman I knew had to do it all: look pretty, keep the man looking good, keep the house looking good, keep the children looking good, cook, clean, feed, drive egos, cars and attitudes, wipe butts, counter tops and wipe away her dreams, carry children inside and outside of her body, groceries and problems, not get sick, slouch or look stupid, stand in heels, alongside and through hell, have to spank and wear *Spanks*, keep her weight down, bear the weight and wait—She had to wait while the man had the first and last word and got to do whatever, and in some cases whomever, he wanted. I didn't want a thing to do with that mess! As matter of truth and fact, I don't have a thing to do with that mess now. We didn't make a contract, but we share in the construct. But, I didn't want no parts, plus it was hard for a man to impress me, let alone a couple.

I did get married of course. I love my husband and there is absolutely *no* doubt in my mind that he loves me, because I can be a piece of work. There! I said it! We love one another as husband and wife and we don't have to. Some marital relationship behavior embraces the notion, "To know me is to love me." Most times that translates to, "IF you love me, you owe me." Love makes no credit checks and has no desire for indebtedness. Love makes obligation sterile. Love waits without weighting. Where Love (REAL/ly) is, there is no obligation because Love is not controlled by the dysfunction of entitlement, but willingly and consistently submits to the respect and honor of mutual commitment. Twenty-one years of friendship, twenty years of marriage and eleven years of business partnership with Owen McNeil has taught me: Love is not controlled by and cannot thrive within the dysfunction of ownership or entitlement. But, Love willingly and consistently yields to the respect and honor of mutual commitment, and the freedom to enjoy and support individual betterment!

Implementation Guides: How do you see the difference between a marriage and a wedding? How can you invest into your marriage or your relationship? What do you believe about entitlements within marital relationships? Who, what or where is a safe space for you to be vulnerable with your marriage or intimate relationship?

MARRIAGE

"The goal in marriage is not to think alike but to think together."
—Robert Dodd

If you are married, were married, want to be married or know someone who is married, marriage has affected your life. I remember a time I didn't want a thing to do with getting married-at-all-ever. I didn't mind a "friend," a date, kiss, with a little extra sum-sum, but I did not want to get married. I didn't need it. I had my own place, my own car, I was working, and I had a "friend," so why would I need to get married? The last thing I wanted was having to lose my identity and having some man come along to tell me what to do. Now, you have to know this was coming from the mindset that almost every time I heard the word marriage, the word submit followed close behind. And, the definitions and examples I saw of submission was directed toward women and not at all attractive. It wasn't because of a negative relationship with men. I can thankfully say I have never had a negative relationship with a man. I've had my heart broken, but even those times, I never saw the man to be negative. The issue I had with the word submission was the overtone of my experience was that the woman was perceived as incapable of making decisions on her own or needed a man's approval. My experience overrode what I was exposed to, so I was fine all by myself!

Then a man came into my life who I wasn't looking for, didn't pray to get or make a list of criterions he had to meet. We were introduced. We met. We dated. We loved. We married. I met Owen in May 1992, and had I made a list, he wouldn't have been on it. He wasn't in church, he didn't have money in his wallet or in the bank and he wasn't driving the perfect car. As a matter of fact, he had a tricked-out Volkswagen Jetta with a whale tale on the back and a Playboy Bunny on the front license plate. I wouldn't have made his list either. I worked too much, I was sickly and I wore my opinion on my face to keep a man from having to ask me for anything other than friendship. Neither of us were "looking" for one another because we had relationships going with other people. I saw him as my handsome friend who had beautiful dark skin and the most perfect teeth, whom I didn't have to impress. I was open to converse because he was genuinely kind. He had no game, his persona didn't match that Playboy Bunny on his license plate, he was well-spoken and well-mannered, honest, caring and carried himself with excellence. His level of maturity was attractive, he was easy to talk to and he listened. He was open to making new things happen in life, he wasn't stuck on a belief system, and he had a sense of humor that was reserved for those he loved.

I wouldn't have put those things on a list back then. Once we decided to form a committed relationship, I realized I had met myself, only different. He wasn't some fairy tale prince charming, he and I were expressions of one another, only he came wrapped in broke and a Playboy Bunny car and I came wrapped in doing more for anyone who'd ask than I would for myself and carrying everyone else's problems masked as illnesses.

I told him why I didn't ever want to get married and he listened. He understood. Then he said, "Why do you think ours would have to be like that. We can do this however we want." I committed myself to be with him for the rest of my life that day! I didn't need a preacher, priest or paper. The only reason we had a traditional marriage ceremony is because of my relationship with the church, my dad was the bishop and my mom was the pastor. I didn't want to shame them or give the appearance I'd compromised my beliefs. I would have been with the same man, the same day and love him the same way, but I wouldn't have changed my last name, we wouldn't have exchanged rings or repeated the traditional vows in public. It wasn't hypocritical. We believed in the bond, but not the box. You see, a wedding nor the rings can't (ever) determine the value, quality or the status of the relationship, no more than having a watch gives you time. What does determine the value is knowing your self-worth – your individual purpose, mission and passion and the frequent and deliberate decisions to work in tandem. We went on with it because we believed God wanted us to be together. We wanted to our life's purposes to be supported, developed by one another and experience exponential success, you know, "one can chase a thousand, to can chase ten thousand..." There so many powerful things we wanted to do and we knew we couldn't pull them off unless we did them together. The wedding was for people. The marriage is for us. We enjoy our marriage our way. Marrying Owen McNeil was one of the best decisions I have ever made in my life!

Though the years, and counting, I am still so much in love with me, with him and with us! We enjoy a very healthy friendship and marriage. We also enjoy friends who are of the opposite gender. We don't divide duties and functions based on gender. We share in responsibilities and privileges based on gifting, purpose, mission, passion and time. We communicate well and often. It works for us, our way. We don't "let" one another do things. "Let" only lives in our home in Jayda's space. I can't ever remember the word "submit" coming into our conversations unless it was about an application, proposal or paperwork. Don't get me wrong, "submit" is not a dirty word, it means to yield. We yield to one another in a way that even if we aren't on the same page about something we are committed to being in the same book! Our marriage is traditional from the standpoint of how we have agreed to engage in sexual intercourse. That's saaweeet!!! Monogamy works best for us and we found that out after experiencing infidelity.

INFIDELITY

I want to share a perspective about infidelity. Why? Because it can lead to why so many marriages end in divorce! Somebody has got to talk about why so many end. Be it incompatibility, sex, communication or finances, somebody or two somebodies did or didn't become or do something. There are not many marriages and long-term relationships that haven't experienced some form of infidelity. Without defining a word I know you already know the definition of, let me share some synonyms of infidelity which are: unfaithfulness, cheating (informal), adultery, betrayal, duplicity, disloyalty, bad faith, perfidy, falseness, faithlessness, false-heartedness. If you research the etymology you will see "want of faith, unbelief in religion; false belief, paganism, unfaithfulness or disloyalty to a person." When researching most of these words in a thesaurus, you will see the synonyms and statements like, lie, suppressing truth, deserting one's allegiance, two-faced, using deceptive thoughts and actions to support untruths, deliberate disloyalty.

When most of us think of infidelity our minds automatically turn toward sexual or intimacy trespass. But, our perceptions seldom encompass the emotional, financial, mental and within all aspects of communication within a relationship. Infidelity expresses itself when you lie, cover up, manipulate, use deceptive tactics to consistently conceal anything from your partner or spouse that you know good n' well they would vehemently disapprove of or, if they knew it would threaten the architectural definitions of the relationship. Be it a man, woman, conversation, credit card, loan, savings account, professional decisions, thoughts that have turned into active imaginations are (all) forms infidelity.

I hear you thinking, "Some forms are worse than others!" And you may be right. Because if you believe that, then you probably also believe some (perceptions of) sins are worse than others. Like, murder is worse than lying or stealing is worse than cussing or drinking is worse than watching a blockbuster R-rated movie. Your perceptions of sin, level of sin consciousness or your threshold for acceptable sin, may equate with what you believe about infidelity, especially when you rate the areas you don't happen to be guilty of differently than the ones you are or have been guilty of. Infidelity is a creative thief that can also creep in as self-righteousness and render you disloyal to humility and vulnerability. It can steal from the brilliance of your imperfect humanity, all while you're checking smartphones, installing GPS, alarm systems and cameras, waiting to catch it showing up as a burglar in the bedroom. Is that a buzz kill or what?!

Talk about a buzz kill. Owen and I have experienced emotional, financial, several aspects of communication infidelity and yes, even sexual infidelity in our marriage. Yep! I cheated. He cheated. We cheated. We lied. We blamed. We hid. We were ashamed. Don't be shocked at us, maybe you have too. Take your own temperature then ask your significant other to take yours too, if you dare. Be easy now, it's not for the faint of heart. We decided to pull up my big girl panties and his big boy draws and deal with it! We faced the truth. We told the truth. We did the work. We overcame and are no longer ashamed! This book is a tell-nothing-but-the-truth-about-a-lot, not a tell-it-all-right-now saga. So, if you want to hear how to overcome the challenges, to grow your relationship and friendship into a thriving Semper Fi!, you just have to attend one of our "Better Together? Better

Together. Better Together!" couples workshops or experience the intimacy of our extremely successful couples coaching program. (Shameless plug!) We chose to overcome and move forward in our traditional marriage. But, that's not the story everyone can tell; some divorce, some stay in a miserable marriage and some love anyway.

Implementation Guide: How do you define infidelity? How has someone else's infidelity affected your life? How your infidelity affected someone else's life? How can you move beyond it?

Chapter Fifteen

Love Anyway

"I'm not particularly political. I'm not particularly denominational. I'm not worried about any of that."
—T.D. Jakes

THE TRUTH ACCORDING TO MARQUIS HUNT

Have you ever met someone who was so brilliant that whether you agreed with them or not, you could appreciate their mind? My first knowledge of Marquis Hunt was seeing a quote he had written on *Facebook*, shared by a mutual friend. I can't remember what the quote said, but every other quote of his I read ended with "Love Anyway." His quotes and his "signature" caught my attention enough for me to connect with him in 2008 and we've grown from there. We would speak frequently by phone to exchange lives and have conversations about God, life, love, community, and people all the while understanding they were no really different. In 2009 I flew out to Little Rock, Arkansas to meet Marquis face-to-face to discuss having a convergence with a group of people he led called the LifeXchange. The plans to have a convergence with a large group of people didn't happen, but the convergence occurred between us. Marquis is an intelligent conversationalist and who I would like to call a modern-day philosopher. He is an outstanding soprano saxophonist, a writer who uses language with a level of depth and texture that is not only thought-provoking but challenging.

GOD CHEATED?

I remember one day when he and I were talking about Jesus and what his relationships may have been like and we reminisced about our church experiences as children and young adults. We talked about how great of a man Jesus *had* to be and how committed to his purpose and mission he was. And, I said, "There is no reason why we can't be just as committed to our purpose and mission in life as Jesus was, not because he died for it but because he lived, before and after death to prove it. And, when Thomas asked Jesus, in John 14:5-6 to show him the way, Jesus said: *I am the way, the truth and the life.* Jesus didn't say his name, he stated his purpose—way, truth and life." And Marquis stated, "You are right, we are to be the way, the truth and the life, and if God gave Jesus just a hint or a smidgen more power and authority than he gave us, then God cheated. And, God wouldn't do that!" Something shifted in me that moment because of what he said. I realized, God wouldn't do that! I started calling him Dr. Hunt after then. We had other conversations about family and marriage. Let me tell you right now, I am not the same person I was when I got married! But his view on marriage was quite intriguing. I just had to let you in on the mind and the truth according to Marquis Hunt and in the end whether you agree or not you will have experienced a LifeXchange and the ability to use your power to choose to love anyway.

TracyMac: Thank you for letting me interview you Dr. Hunt. Tell those reading or listening a little about you.

Marquis: Hello Dr. Rev. Evangelist TracyMac. And, I say that because normally whenever we speak, I tend to do something of that nature so that I can first hear you laugh, second to hear you call me a name that gives me an invitation to love you, and third because I am just ornery sometimes. And, on a serious note thank you so much Tracy for inviting me into this conversation and into a dialogue that is shared by many people who trust your voice and your insights. I'm grateful be a part of this conversation. I am a lover of life. I am a lover of people. I am a recording artist and professional musician and my stage name is "MarQuis." I'm a thought leader, a writer, and a conversationalist. Most of my life is centered on having conversations that push my conversation partners to think about who they are or rethink who they are. And, as usual each conversation and each relating partner serves as mirror and a reflecting device that allows me to see myself in ways that I hadn't before.

TracyMac: So Dr. Hunt, who are you?

Marquis: I don't quite know how to specifically tell you who I am, other than I am always evolving, redefining and becoming aware of something I didn't know. As of late, years after we met, I probably was better at answering that question five years ago than I am right now.

TracyMac: Wait a minute Marquis, why is that?

Marquis: Because back then I thought I was clear on quite a few things. And, as I continue to live, those things that I was presumed clear about, I find the more I live the more information, and the more details and the more exhaustive my personal awareness becomes. And, I am more convinced that the infinity of information lives more prominently than the absolution of information and insight.

TracyMac: Now Marquis you know how we go. Break it down.

Marquis: Which one?

TracyMac: All of it.

Marquis: Let's break it down. There were certain things about relationships I thought were final. I've learned since then, that each new relationship exposes and offers me an awareness about life I wasn't aware of before and is essentially designed to give me entrance into a space of awareness that I was not yet present with. Every relationship presents itself as a new moment.

TracyMac: Marquis, how did you come into this type of thought process that you have?

Marquis: It has been a gradual process. I am so appreciative of my church experience. I grew up Church of God in Christ (COGIC). We enjoyed ecstatic spirituality that helped give me entrance to trust things that didn't seem intellectually reasonable, like speaking in tongues, shouting, dancing, running around the church, screaming and hollering for no apparent reason other than feeling something on the inside. Growing up as a son of COGIC and the youngest of nine children, with a mother and father who were married until my father died, I grew up in a very traditional idea of family. With the exception that I wasn't really close to my siblings, I was one of two brothers and seven sisters. My brother left when I was nine or ten years old to go to college. It left me with five older sisters who were still at home. I was probably a bratty brother so I didn't really get the experience of being close to my sisters. So, I built a relationship with my childhood best friend I am still friends with him to this day. He is like a brother to me. I built a sibling type of relationship with someone who was not biologically connected to me. That was the start of me becoming comfortable with nontraditional ways of relating and building devotion to someone. But, I still pursued traditional romantic relationships. I was under the impression that one special person, was made for me that was fit for me. And, I tried several young ladies and women to get to that perfect person.

After trial in error in 1988, I settled on that one person who I married. At least I thought that one person I married was the one and only who would answer all of my emotional angst and my forlorn tendencies for romance and for companionship. But, when I went into that relationship, even then, I was young I was married at twenty-one with the traditionally Christian mindset. I left my mother and father in cleave to my wife. And, what I discovered probably eight to ten years into that relationship was that I met my wife, on a journey of what I call self-discovery. When I met her I was in progress and in pursuit and in process of discovering Marquis. What I was taught to believe was that the Marquis I was discovering was this man who was supposed to be a husband. And, that was one dimension of finality that I was going to reach. Except for after I had lived and gone through several life experiences in relationship with her, I realized I was still discovering me. I was not the same Marquis who she met or the same Marquis who met her while living in the same body, technically, sort of. I was still being transformed by new experiences in meeting people and having new ideas. And, after eight years I realized I was still in progress, and still discovering myself, I realized something else quite profound. Every moment in my life is valid and open to a discovery of the Marquis that is equally valued and should be equally profound. When I heard that awareness, I could no longer fit the traditional version of relationships into my head as something acceptable.

THE LAW OF RECIPROCITY

TracyMac: When you heard that and of course it touched you in a way you needed to express it, or chose to express it. What was life like? Would you have situations where you were warring within yourself, within your marriage, within your beliefs?

Marquis: When I came to that awareness it was devastating. And, it was supported by other ancillary relationships and mentoring relationship that I had with my pastor, my father and my siblings. It came to a head in my relationship I have with my wife. The idea was to experience fidelity in my marriage. Which became a non-issue after I became aware of infidelity after three years of being married. Therefore making the sanctity of fidelity not an option. But, love was available. Love was available for me to love and forgive and I continued to live in the relationship and had more experiences like this. I had a question come to me about the whole notion of the law of reciprocity, you know, you reap what you sow? The question came to me, can I ever reap a fidelis relationship? It was peculiar because at that moment, as I had been faithful for ten years. I use the term faithful loosely, in the strict sense of how we see it traditionally, meaning I didn't have a girlfriend, a lover, or partner outside of my wedded union. When I had this question come to me I began to question, not the marriage, but if the law of reciprocity was legitimate. Did God have the capacity to give me a marriage, and give me what I had sown into it, which was fidelity? And I realized it was physically impossible to have that unless I went through a divorce and got a new wife.

TracyMac: Okay, you felt like if you reap what you sow, I've sowed fidelity and faithfulness as it pertains to a Christian marriage. I have been faithful. If I'm going to reap that, I can't reap it from this marriage because it's already been tainted with infidelity. So, the only way I will reap fidelity is that this marriage is over with?

Marquis: Yes, and when I began to reason it that way I began to think it was absolutely absurd. You mean I have to dismiss someone because I am in need of something that can't come to me? And then I asked a new question: Is this what marriage is all about? Does love demand that I put someone away because I can't have something that I want. I couldn't reconcile love doing that. Especially in the Christian context when it was all about forgiveness. It's all about reconciliation. So, I was in conflict with this law of reciprocity. Then, I had a new question, is the law of reciprocity about this necessarily? Because while I may sow a seed, I don't reap a seed I reap a fruit, a plant, flower or a tree. Because what goes into the ground is not what comes out of the ground. I began to expand my mind. Because what God showed me was that love has the capacity to come to me in many dimensions, as does fidelity. The new question was will you allow yourself to receive it even if it doesn't fit the traditional version of fidelity, love, truth, honor, longing? This is where truth began to blow my mind. I did not have the emotional space to hold on to this thought without crying. Everything in these moments was imploding on me. I had to say goodbye to things I had valued my whole life. The version of traditional marriage, traditional family, traditional heaven and traditional hell, it did not fit anymore.

TracyMac: When it didn't fit anymore and something as meaningful as marriage became the catalyst that opens your eyes to other areas, you questioned the interpretation of a relationship with God or the interpretation of scriptures and traditions that you have been reared by, what do you do? Someone may be saying I am traditional, I am in a traditional marriage, I am a Christian, or I have religious beliefs, I'm a member of a traditional denomination and I value those traditions but something you just said caught my attention. I have sown in some areas and didn't reap in those areas, how do I work with that?

Marquis: Number one is important to identify the seeds. It's important to identify the type of ground. This is a common parable Jesus offered: good ground, fallow ground and thorny ground. When we sow honestly and with integrity, we have to open ourselves to the experience of Spirit, which is #1 formless and #2 has the capacity to become any and all things at any given moment. Often times what retards or what we experience is being withheld from our harvest, has a lot to do with our perspective of what we're looking for. Some of us are literally looking for the seed to come back to us in that same version. Take for instance, when we sow money we want money to come back. We don't expect ideas or ingenuity, or education, or a home or food to come. Anything that can translate as seed for resource can be fruit. I was looking for my wife to love me exclusively. By exclusively I mean, she was the only person who could love me this way or should love me this way. What became problematic about that, in the context of being human, is because we know forgiveness, judgment and error. And, as a human, I may choose at any given moment not to love somebody. I may wake up on the wrong side of the bed and as holy or as nice as I am, or was yesterday, I could wake up and decide to be evil and mean or smart ass or jackass. In that moment does the person who loves me, who loved me yesterday, who loves me this morning; do I have the right to withhold love from them and does God have to honor love not getting to them because I held love hostage? So this was blowing my mind. Do I have the right to hold love hostage, and then demand that if love shows up for that person who I am withholding love from, do they have to say no to love because of their commitment to me? How can you say no to love without saying no to God? How can you say no to love without saying no to truth? How can you say no to truth without saying no to freedom? And who in their right mind is going to say no to God, to love, to freedom or against truth? Only the insane do that! So in that moment I realized that none of the presumed sacred unions that we have, have the right to hold love hostage because of some contract we made yesterday or yesteryear. That is absolutely absurd.

NEW VOWS?

TracyMac: In hearing that, not holding love hostage and not withholding love and using entitlements, contracts and vows, I am not the same person that I was. I got married when I was twenty-four and now I'm forty-five and I am definitely not the same person I was then. Owen was twenty-five and now he's forty-six and he is definitely not the same person he was then. We are not the same two people who stood at the altar. We both have evolved. Some of those evolutions have been in rough times. Some were natural. We have had to choose to love one another daily because we can't take for granted that that person will choose to love us the same way every day. So, Marquis how do you feel about the expressions of love? If someone says I love you but the way I express my love to you is different, or the way I choose to look at it is different? What if someone says, okay I see the seed, and I can change my perspective of the fruit coming back different. But, in traditional relationships, how does one say I can't get love or expressions of love from my spouse or partner this way, and so I won't hold love hostage, I'll receive love from another person this way? Where's the limit? Does there need to be a limit? How do we determine the limit, or is there one?

Marquis: I will answer your question with a question. Why does there need to be limits? We believe there needs to be limits because we don't believe we know how to behave without them. So, limits are something we create usually to legislate or to bind certain aspects of our world in order to keep them like we need them, for us to have the experience we think we want. Let's talk about belief and faith. Belief is something we all have its part of the human agency that none of us can get away from. We all believe something. Hardly any of us believe the same thing, although we believe we do sometimes. However, beliefs change and are not to be confused with knowing. This is one of the biggest problems in our humanity. We often confuse what we believe with what we know and we hold ourselves hostage by certain ideals of our past. As it pertains to our vows, it is not even reasonable to think we know what's going to happen five days from now. We really don't know. Our lives tell us this because every day is brand-new, everything is different. Some things are commonly the same, but the nuances of those things are different. For me to marry someone and for me to tell myself I know what I am going to be twenty years from now needless to say ten years from now, and then I'm going to make this promise.

It is a problem that is absolutely unnecessary.

TracyMac: Marquis you just got in trouble with at least 85% of the people reading or listening, say it again and clarify.

Marquis: Those promises are absolutely unnecessary. We don't have to make a promise for a moment that doesn't exist. We don't know what will happen, good bad or indifferent. A train wreck, winning the lottery, a war, a job we have - so at best what we can do is create an idea, or a version of what we want the world to look like and that's okay. As long as we are honest about the fact that it is an idea we have but not something that has to happen. I can say to you, it is my intention to love you forever or it is my intention to love you forever with the awareness that you may become something totally different than what I expect. So, in that moment, my covenant is to love you even if your best version of self does not include me. That's love...

TracyMac: Say that again.

Marquis: I will make a covenant to love you now, even ten years, or twenty years from now, with the awareness that you will change every day, even several times in a day and that your preference will change every day. I will love you without requiring you to maintain the preference you have today. And, I will love you even if that preference does not include me.

TracyMac: Oh, I think you may have stepped in it now Dr. Hunt. I'm going to sit by the hole with you but I think you're about to walk in quicksand.

Marquis: But there is only quicksand if I calculate the plausible potential to lose. But, what I understand about God, at least the God we celebrate is that God does not run out of God and that love does not run out of love. Yet we create relationships on the notion that love is in scarce supply. So, we believe that if someone loves the person we love that we will convince ourselves that, that person will love them better than we love them. So, we create restrictions around the relationship, in a traditional sense that says, you are obligated to be loved least because you have to stay with me. Now that sounds absurd when you hear it that way yet it is how most of our traditional relationships function. We're saying this relationship with you is good enough for me and what I am to you should be enough good for you. What that does is limit me to my own beliefs of being insufficient Even if that person loves you better than me, you are obligated to be loved less.

TracyMac: In traditional relationships we tell someonc, don't even talk to someone else to see IF they can love you better than I can. We don't allow our spouses or significant others room to enjoy relationships because of that fear. We don't want them in the presence, have lunch dinner or phone conversation because we fear that someone else could love them too. Even though that love does not have to take on the sexual connotation, most thoughts are driven that way. I am in a very happy traditional marital relationship. People have to realize that no matter how happy you are your spouse or significant other cannot be everything you need all the time. You cannot be everything your spouse or significant other needs in relation to the opposite sex. If that be the case someone's ego is too big, or someone's life is being lived too small. That's too heavy. So, even if you love someone of the opposite sex it does not have to be a romantic or sexual love. But, you can experience a level of intimacy and the key is allowing yourself and your spouse to be free. Be honest. Be authentic. We are still two vibrant individuals. Two individuals who still have a right to have fun and have friends and be expressive and have relationships and have partnerships, because we cannot meet that person's every human need they have for the opposite sex and the plurality of genuine relationships.

Marquis: And neither were we designed to do that. This is why we have the multiplicity of people. It is physical evidence that the two of us are not enough. If the two of us were enough to two would be all we need. Even in the mythical narrative of Adam and Eve, we have the need to be fruitful and multiply. Multiplication is critical to the process of the evolving as a human and the ever evolving idea of what humanity can be. Can you imagine if it was just Adam and Eve, how limited the version of humanity would be? How much we would not know, how much we would not have discovered or how much God would not have discovered of itself? We are constantly convinced, largely because how we are educated in our schools, our families and our religious institutions. Society and our religious institutions, teach us that we are insufficient, depraved and that we are limited people. So, we move into our relationships with the perspective of limitedness and we say of these relationships that they will give us the ability to expand beyond our limitedness. But, then we try to say this is good enough for what I am and I don't want to know the better me, and there's no need for you to know the better you. Essentially, this becomes a judgment against the self. If I believe that someone can love you better than me, that may be true, for what frightens me is my own beliefs of my own insufficiency. And, I'm not satisfied with insufficiency and I'm not satisfied with not being enough. Because if I believe I am really enough, I don't need to create restrictions for anyone. Because I'm irreplaceable, I am irrevocable, I'm indistinguishable, and I am invincible. But, we babysit and we nurse these false notions. Human relationship is not about the ownership of the other person. So, the idea of marriage is that this person is my property.

THY KINGDOM COME

TracyMac: I am in a traditional marriage and it works for us but we treat one another non-traditionally. No ownership, we treat one another like the individuals we are and are not obligated by an archaic mindset of marriage but we are driven by the love of friendship and evolving relationship. People treat the marriage vows as holy as they treat the Ten Commandments and they're not even in the Bible. Go figure.

Marquis: We pray thy kingdom come, thy will be done on earth as it is in heaven. According to Matthew, in heaven there is no marriage nor given in marriage. I've been married for twenty-four years. If we are really trying to usher in the kingdom of God from the Christian perspective, we should try to usher in what the kingdom of God has in it. Which is no domination of another person. There's no need to dominate another person. We are to be a kingdom person. We don't have to confine ourselves to yesterday's version of who we are. We have managed relationships and it has been an attempt to memorialize who are at the moment of discovery.

TracyMac: But Marquis if we're not bound to be who we said we are and who we committed to be, where it is the stability and how do we all keep from becoming wild asses? And that can bleed into other relationships, I want to be a father today and I don't want to be a father tomorrow or I want the responsibilities and benefits of marriage today but I don't want them tomorrow. Or, today I'm going to go to work today and tomorrow I'm not. Where is the balance in this freedom of being able to evolve and embrace the next version of ourselves?

Marquis: In truth, the next version of ourselves even exist in that moment that were looking for balance. It exists in that moment, when we are negotiating whether we want to be responsible or not. We can ask ourselves the question, am I considering not being responsible? In that moment we get to visit, am I really have this conversation with myself? Am I honest enough with myself to know this is happening? All the while knowing and having the awareness that you are fully qualified with a resource to be irresponsible. In these moments the people in our lives are visited with an invitation to love us or they are visited with the temptation to disregard or discard us. These moments are abiding. There is no better moment or inferior moment to be in the space where love is a choice. Love can always be the choice, even if I am alone. Even the presence of another person, love can be the choice. If I'm contemplating abandoning my children love is a choice. And, I also have to determine that if I am the best person to be that employee or that father at that moment. And, that's where community, life coaching, mentorship and relationship comes in. When I get to the place when I'm trying to determine what love is and what love does, when I can't perform or when I find myself limited or thinking myself limited, love at that moment changes its demonstration. I am not less of a father, husband, employee or friend because I recognize the entrance of another soul who has the capacity to stand in and to intercede for, stand in prayer with, to mediate, or to repair. It becomes incumbent upon me as a human and a spiritual being to recognize the limitations of who I am physiologically and biologically, and also to accept the gift of God in the presence of other people. This becomes a part of my relationship obligations. To step aside and to make room for, just not I, but the Christ that lives in me. That it essentially means the expanded "I." When we become even more aware of who we are we realize we are not just ourselves. I am not just myself. I am in conjunction, in communion and in connectivity of the whole life of God. This is why the multiplicity of relationship exists.

If we could, all of us, walk into a room and do what Jesus said in John, I have come that you might have life and have it more abundantly. If we could all walk into a room with that awareness and also walk into a room with the awareness that others are showing up with the same intention, then it will be only reasonable for us to allow them to experience the allowing of the fullness of God, to manifest itself in the way it did desires and sees. We have been taught to live from a protective vantage point of survival and it has the human condition locked in misery and pain and in war and anxiety. It is what we have believed about ourselves that we are limited. With that said, how can we deny love? How can we deny ourselves and others the opportunity to be expanded by love, through relationships? Why would you love someone and at the same time tell them that I don't want you to be loved more than I can? Our books, our schooling, our churches, our love songs, our magazines and our televisions tend to promote this notion that the way we love is limited. And why would God or Jesus be offended that we exceed a representation of love? It is absurd notion that love is limited. Love anyway.

Implementation Guides: How do you feel about non-traditional relationships? How have your traditions changed? What do you believe about the Law of Reciprocity? How do you feel about traditional wedding vows? What's the difference between what you believe vs. what you know? Does love have limits? Why or why not? What does it mean to love anyway?

Chapter Sixteen

Relationships to Ponder—Speaking and Listening, Again

Dear Speaking:

I would have a bone to pick with you, but God worked it out! We go way back. I didn't use you a lot until I was in my teens. I had a lot of questions and things to say, but my head and heart didn't think you could handle their weight. But we moved on and that's not the bone I had anyway. The bone I would have picked with you was you taking way too long to show up in my child. You don't remember? Let me remind you…

JAYDA

Do you remember when I was in my late teens, and I had severe endometriosis and was told if I could conceive it would be extremely difficult? Well you know I told Owen about that before we got married in 1993. He wasn't fazed about it at all. There was a time in 1995 where I had taken a few rounds of the fertility drug Clomid, but we never had any positive results. We decided that we would enjoy our lives together and when it came to children we had my nephews, his nephews and nieces and all the youth we had come to know at the church. In 2000, I had some complications with fibroids and we scheduled a date for surgery. I was scheduled to have surgery on a Monday and the weekend prior our church had taken a trip to Kings Dominion. We left early that Saturday morning and got back in the wee hours that Sunday morning. When we got back home, the light was flashing on our answering machine that sat on our nightstand in the bedroom, but I was way too tired to listen to it. We had to get up and get ready for church Sunday morning.

No excuses, not even Kings Dominion. I felt funny the day before and thought it was because of the heat, and that Sunday morning I still felt a little strange. Owen said it was because I hadn't eaten much at the park, so he got up early to make me one of his famous omelets. I ate the omelet; it was so good, but a few minutes later I found myself in the bathroom leaning over the toilet.

I still felt strange so I decided to take a pregnancy test. It was more than two years old, but I had an unused pregnancy test under the bathroom sink. I used it. There was a faint +. Owen was ironing and I took it to him. I had no words; I just had the pregnancy test in my hand. He looked at it and I expected to hear something that they would say in a Hallmark or Lifetime movie, but he smiled from ear to ear with those perfectly straight teeth and said, "YES!!!!!!! Aww girl, I told you my soldiers march strong! Now your mama and your daddy are gonna know you been doing the nasty!"

I was in too much of a hurry to think about it; I felt numb anyway. I brushed my teeth again, took a shower, put on my stockings and slip, fixed my hair and rushed out the door to church. Later that evening after we had returned home, I went to the bedroom and there was that light flashing on the answering machine. I had forgotten to retrieve the message.

As I listened to the message, it was the doctor's office saying that they needed to schedule a pre-op appointment before they removed my fibroids. So they were postponing my surgery date until after the pre-op appointment. I called Monday morning and they told me I could come in that Tuesday for a sonogram. So, we went to the doctor and as they squeezed that cold gel on my stomach and then moved the sensor all around my lower abdomen, I saw so many fibroids as the technician pointed them out to me. Then, the pace of the sensor began to slow and she began to rock back and forth. I didn't say a word yet because the pregnancy test was old and the pink + was so faint, maybe I wasn't pregnant. The tech stood up quickly, and said, "Hold on for just a moment, Mrs. McNeil. I'll be right back." She retuned ten minutes later with my doctor, and turned the monitor slightly away from me. For a few seconds, the two of them muttered under their breaths and I couldn't quite tell what they were saying. But, just as I was about to ask if anything was wrong, the doctor interrupted my thought and said, "Mrs. McNeil, that's a heartbeat!" A heartbeat? Do fibroids have heartbeats? I was still in denial. I guess he could see the confusion on my face and he said, "You're pregnant." I didn't know what to think. It was as if I was wearing a Greek comedy and tragedy mask, where one side of my face was happy and the other side was sad. But he said something that if I could have registered any level of excitement it was quickly deflated. "But I'm not sure if it is going to be a viable pregnancy. That baby is in there with a lot of big fibroids." The doctor had great bedside manner, and so did the technician. They see so many women, I know they didn't have a clue of what was going on in my mind. He told the technician to have me set up an appointment and come back when I noticed blood. They sent me home to have a miscarriage.

We went to the doctor the next day and again there was a little heartbeat on the monitor. The doctor explained to us why the pregnancy would probably not be viable, but they would monitor me. And, again they sent me home to miscarry. We didn't tell anyone that I was pregnant because we didn't want to have to tell them that I wasn't. I was about six weeks pregnant at that time, and I continued going to work, going to church, doing activities with our youth group, and singing and writing music with a group called Fresh Oil. We didn't tell a soul. It wasn't until I was almost four months pregnant before Owen and I told my parents and our friends Ebony and Dalton Hill. They are the kind of couple everyone needs to have in their life. We told them without having to say, "Don't tell." By the way, you should hear their "miracle baby story!" My pregnancy was physically and mentally rough. I was on bed rest for most of it. My doctor was doing a great job of making sure I didn't get my hopes up to carry full term or to even be a mom at all. But, God! We had a healthy baby girl named Jayda.

Now, speaking, I hope I didn't bore you with that story because I know you are wondering where you come in. Jayda was such a good baby and an intriguing little toddler. She smiled, danced, laughed and played way more than she cried. But she wouldn't talk. I could ask her what she wanted to eat and she would open the refrigerator, or raise her arms for one of us to pick her up and point to it. But she wouldn't talk. I could tell her to go get the blue brush, the baby lotion, her Sippy cup and she would bring all of them to me. But she wouldn't talk. Often times I tried to teach her to speak, in hopes that she would repeat after me. Hearing herself, knowing that it wasn't as articulate as I would say it, and she wouldn't try. When she did, she jacked up words like nobody's business, she called McDonald's French fries "hi-hi's" and applesauce was "ibba dib bi la!" (Lawd! My po lil baby girl.) But, "daddy," "mama," "tan tu" and "mo peeze" were understood by all.

I knew she was sharp, I knew she was smart, I knew she could hear, but why wouldn't my child talk? Where were you, speaking? She was two years old and her pediatrician recommended I have her tested. As any new parent would do, I took her to get tested because we were about to move to Okinawa, Japan and her pediatric exam was part of the medical screening. The test results were not good at all. They revealed that while Jayda scored off the charts when it came to the cognitive parts of the test, the other scores were so low she qualified for the exceptional family program. The exceptional family program was the program the military had in place for families with children who had some type of disability. They couldn't tell me what it was, so I didn't believe it. I wouldn't believe it. Call it denial? Go 'head. I don't care. I signed the waiver not to allow her to be a part of the program. Jayda, Owen and I decided to create our own program as an exceptional family. This is when I realized that communication was more than simply speaking. My child taught me how to listen.

She taught me how to listen to what was not being said. By not speaking, my child taught me how to listen to the eyes, behaviors, silent sounds and feelings. As I was learning these things from her, her ability to talk became less important and my capacity to listen was heightened. We would have the best verbally silent conversations ever! It wasn't until Jayda was more than three years old when she started talking. She never babbled; she just started saying words; connecting them into phrases and sentences. She talked when she got good and ready, and let me tell you she is still ready. At thirteen years old, Jayda has a lot to say but she's not mouthy with it. I am confident she has made up for the first three-and-half years of her life, plus some. She does have dyslexia, but she is in grade level classes with her peers, makes honor roll every semester, plays the violin and refuses to use it as a crutch. Every day, she shows me what it means to overcome challenges! Go, Jayda! Go! Read, baby, read! Speak, baby, speak! Laugh, baby, laugh, and dance, baby, dance!

So, speaking, I know how people use you, what they use you for, when they use you, the tones, the inflections, the grammar, dialect and numerous languages are very important. I realize that out of the abundance of the heart you control the voice of the mind and lips. I also understand that the lips have gotten a bad rap. The lips on our face aren't the ones we have to contend with, it's the mouth of our mind. That's where you are most influential. Our thoughts are more influential than words uttered, even our prayers.

May I say a prayer for you as I did for listening? Some of us believe that this world would not exist if God hadn't used you to create it. I know that you are powerful. I pray, that we will learn to use your power, and allow wisdom to teach us the balance between words that mean everything and words that mean nothing. May we forever be empowered and craft our ability to use you as a mighty tool to soothe and not set fires. Those times when words mean nothing I pray that God will allow your amplification to fall on deaf ears. I pray that you are not abused, neglected or misunderstood, through words, conditions or silence, as much is it is possible. I pray that when our churches, governments, communities, and businesses use you that they will have compassion for the people they serve, as we are no different or less deserving than they. May you continue to be used as an expression of freedom to communicate within relationships and not be offended when wisdom offers you the right to remain silent.

Chapter Seventeen

She Speaks! She Writes!

"I love you forever, I like you for always as long as I'm living my baby you'll be."
—Robert Munsch

THE TRUTH AND A LITTLE FICTION ACCORDING TO JAYDA MCNEIL

The writing below is part of a project Jayda had to do for her eighth grade Language Arts class. The assignment was to write about a past experience. She was instructed to write about as much as she could remember and she decided to add the fun of fantasy. You may ask: Why would I put my thirteen-year-old's homework assignment in my book, especially knowing her challenges in all core subjects because of dyslexia? First, because I can. Secondly, for someone who wasn't supposed to be here, wouldn't speak and qualified for a check, overcomes the challenges of dyslexia daily, consistently makes the honor roll, refuses to take remedial courses and enjoys classes with her peers, has her black belt in Tae Kwon Do, is a great swimmer, a Girl Scout, choreographs dance, plays the violin, etc. I wanted her to be able to add, "published writer" at thirteen years old to her resume, standing on my shoulders. Stand baby, stand!

THE STORY OF JAPAN

By Jayda McNeil

It all started when my dad went to the Navy. He was supposed to go to Spain 1st, but the Navy stationed him somewhere else. So the tough military said, "You will be stationed at Japan and be sure to bring your family." Before that even happened my dad was deployed to Iraq and other places sometimes, and my mom was pregnant. Before I was born, my dad came home to take care of his sweet loving wife and sweet unborn baby, too. When I was 2 years old my dad told my mom that we were going to Japan and my mom was so surprised and energetic and if I had known what Japan was back then I probably would have been the same. "Jayda, Jayda," a soft voice said. I opened my eyes and it was my mom and she said Jayda over and over and rubbed my head and said, "Were going to Japan this morning." I was confused it was early, I can't remember...maybe 6:00 in the morning and my mom waking me up that early at the age of 2 was ludicrous.

We were driving to the airport. We weren't late, but we wanted to be early so I felt like my car seat was sliding around in the back seat side to side. I feel like I was in NASCAR the way my dad was driving. So we got in the airport and to me back then an airport was like a wonderland because it was so many stores and the smell of the fresh pizza from the oven was even better I hardly had any teeth so I had to eat nasty eggs. And it smelled like eggs but it was green beans and the word is making me sick ewwwwww. All of a sudden I smell these strange smells coming from different places. The smell of BBQ, pizza and Asian foods; it smelled like someone passed gas and not the friendliest smell. "We will board our flight in 5 minutes," the lady from the front said so I'm so glad I finished those green beans in time because if I had to eat them on the plane I would have gone crazy. We are ready to board the plane "All seniors and people with wheelchairs go first," the lady said. We were waiting in line to turn in our tickets and waiting for other people to find and take their seats so we could do the same. So we found our seats and I sat in the middle of my parents. I still do it now when I take flights with them. After all that I slowly closed my eyes to go to sleep and all of a sudden I felt a lightness I have never felt before. The plane was going up in the air and that's what the lightness was so I opened my eyes to see what was going on and my mom lifted me up and said here comes Japan and we both waved good bye. After that long wave I slowly closed my eyes and see if I could go to sleep and I did.

"Jayda, Jayda," two voices said. "We are almost there, we were in L.A." How is that close to Japan? We had to sleep there because there was typhoon there and a typhoon is like a hurricane it is just called something different. My mom and dad gave me a big huge hug and kept singing "I love you Jayda o yes I do I love you Jayda o yes I do I love you Jayda o I love o Jayda mommy loves you and daddy too" and that did it, put me to sleep…I was knocked out.

BAM! I was in a different country. How long was I sleeping? It was hot in the airport and I was so confused on what was going on at the time but I wasn't concerned about that. What I was concerned about was how did I get in a different country? Wow, if I knew what I know now about Japan I would have been all over it but since I was 2 I didn't know what Japan was all about. I thought it was a person. At first it has been 2 months since I was in America and it is so different in Japan. The weather is different the laws are different and my parents had to drive on the other side of the street. But I lived on the base where other military families lived. Every time my mom went to the store I went to the store. I went because we didn't know anyone there in Japan yet. Plus if it is a different country there is different money too so we had to get new money since we were living on base they used American money but yen outside the base.

It has been 11-1/2 years since we moved from Japan and I was in preschool there and I met people my age and my mom has met people too at her job. Sometimes if she couldn't take me to preschool she would take me to her job and that was so cool at the time because going to work with mom was amazing. My dad worked at the base and I don't think he went to war at this time when we were in Japan, but he was still in the Navy working at the office stuff for the people going into war. My first day at a new preschool and it was terrifying but yet so welcoming at the same time. I was 3 years old; didn't like to talk and couldn't talk for some reason, but I could understand what was going on and what people were saying. So when my mom open the doors to the preschool I wasn't scared or anything, but I didn't want to go and plus I left my old friends at the other preschool, but my mom said, "Don't worry. You will go to this preschool sometimes and the other preschool sometimes okay?" So I nodded my head yes. It was 3 weeks since I have been in this new preschool and it is so much fun and I have already met new friend plus I can speak to other kids my age and the teachers and my parents. And this preschool took us on field trips and one of my teachers named Ms. Debbie was a scuba diver and my other teachers was named Ms. Linda and Ms. Amada. I think Ms. Linda spoke Spanish and sometimes she tried to teach us Spanish, but to be honest I didn't pay no mind.

It's my birthday and I'm so happy with the party. I'm turning 4. My birthday cake is amazing and all my friends are here even my new friend Pagie, she is 3 years older than I am, but our parents met and she came to my house. She is 6 and she lives in the states now too. We go see her and her family sometimes and they came to see us. But anyway I had a Barbie cake with a real Barbie and the bottom of the cake was her dress. Ms. Debbie made my cake and put lavender colors on it. It was so pretty and I was so thankful for that birthday party. I had everything I wanted and needed and it was a sunny day on my birthday and the prefect weather too also my birthday is in spring. In Okinawa Japan that's prefect weather. But in the states not all the time like in the spring showers and rain and that's a problem for me.

I can't believe it, but the good news is I'm going to a new preschool that preschool was ok but terrifying because that teacher did not play. As a matter of fact that's what made me start to biting my nails was because of her. I'm not going into details and I didn't get in trouble just to tell you that. If you really want to know what happened ask me later … Sometimes when my dad picked me up he knows I was feeling sad and we would drive down this dirt road after preschool and we both would get grape sodas and Japanese grape soda are so good. I loved those days.

What, we are going back to the states? I can't believe it my dad is retiring from the military and he said when I'm 5 years old we will be planning to go back to the states. I forgot all about that deal. My, how time goes by fast. I asked my parents when we are leaving and they said around August and I said ok. It is just April and is a long time to have fun with my friends. Now it is May and only 4 months till we are going back to the states and I can't wait meaning in a good way and in a way bad too. My mom told my teachers that I was going back to the states in 4 months and they came up with an idea. They make a book with all my artwork and the notes. I wrote them when I went to the doctor's offices for field trips and other places too. And they took lots of pictures of me too. They would give me the book on my last in Japan. It is June and there only 3 months away from us leaving to go back to the states.

The moving people are coming in our house to take the stuff to the states so when we get there we will have our stuff and also the stuff we didn't want any more we gave it away. It was hard for me to give some of my stuff away and it still is at age 13 sometimes. My house was empty my dad has retired my mom had to quit her job it is time to go. Today is my last day to go to preschool and I said good bye to both Ms. Linda and Ms. Debbie. Ms. Debbie let me try on her scuba things and it smelled like fish but I looked good in it even though it was heavy. The teacher gave me the book of all the stuff I did when I was in Japan and I didn't have any true emotion like I do now and so what I did was instead of crying I pouted because I didn't want to leave my friends and my teachers. I wasn't ready it came too soon. So the next day my parents woke me up the same way they woke me up when we were leaving to go to Japan. So we had the house emptied already, left the hotel room, we locked the doors and retuned the key to the front desk and we left to go to the airport. It took 3 days to go back to the states and when we got on our first plane flight me and my mom were listening to music.

Our last flight was the worst because our plane food was TERRIBLE. We had some kind of brown meat and that was nasty and some kind of vegetable and green beans and cake I was so excited. But when I took that single bite I wanted to throw that cake out the window of that plane because a cake is supposed to taste sweet. That cake tasted like everything on that plate got mixed together and had a baby. Thank God my mom had some gold fish and saved my life. Finally we made it back home and waiting at the gate is my aunt, my uncle and my grandparents. I was so excited to be back in America. But one thing I can't live without now and that is fresh Japanese food. You have to try the sweet and sour chicken and the nice sticky rice. The fresh sushi with teriyaki and soy sauce the heat from the teriyaki and the coolness from the cool sushi wrap. Oh you just can't replace such an art of beautiful foods. If you could go to Japan that's the first thing you have got to try.

Chapter Eighteen

Relationships to Ponder—Business Support or Sabotage

"A business that makes nothing but money is a poor business."
—Henry Ford

Dear Business:

My relationship with you is something I'd rather express in this article I wrote about you, rather than talk to you. People have this way of claiming it's not healthy to mix you with personal, well as far as I have experienced, you two can walk hand in hand. But for the sake of the reader/listener, I'm not sure if it's that mix they have to be concerned with or if it's a matter of how they support or sabotage you. I won't judge, so I'll simply talk about you to them and let them decide.

"It's not my business to tell yours, but please tell someone about mine!" That is a statement I often use when some of my clients aren't too thrilled, at first, about anyone knowing they have hired a life coach. Some people are proud to say they have a coach and others not so much. Business and executive coaching carry a sense of pride whereas for some people, getting life help from anybody for anything is taboo. I remember clients literally hiding everything about me, and that worked as I was hiding from me, too. That was okay when I first started, and it isn't my place to abuse confidentiality. But, I no longer coach anyone who is ashamed of the process because a shamed process produces embarrassed results and that's a waste of time and money.

Having sense enough to reach out for help is BOSS! If you can handle your dream all alone, it's way too small. Life coaching is one way to expand and employ your purpose. Coaching, by far, has been my most rewarding profession and I'm good at what I do. That didn't hit me until some time ago when one of my clients called me "The Relationship Broker" and "The Purpose Whisperer." Yep, that's what I do. I get to help people with their lives and that is a responsibility I take seriously. I take my business seriously and sometimes business has more to do with how people see your business more than how you practice, no matter what type of business it is.

I've been a professional life coach for almost eleven years and it took making a five-year plan and seeing it through before I started coaching full time. My previous federal and state jobs kept a nice check coming in very consistently, but I wasn't fulfilled or satisfied. I knew having my own coaching practice and formal business would be outright scary, but I felt like I would suffocate if I didn't do it. So, I used my vision like oxygen to breathe, until I could manifest it. As I continue to inhale and exhale dreams, visions and goals, it is an ever-evolving work in progress!

But I wondered if I would be able to maintain a consistent clientele and grow my business. I found myself having to explain what professional life coaching is more than practicing it. But, it was so exciting! At first, coaching was an inspirational hobby that grew into a side hustle, which grew into legitimate part-time work. Could loving what I do pay the bills and attract financial wealth? Would the Black community that I serve most, but not exclusively, see the value in coaching from me? Would I be able to be a successful owner of a business?

I mean, I'm a woman, no family members or friends who I could count on in the local area, I was also new to the area and this…this *is* North Carolina. Oh my! But, scared and unsure, I *knew* I could be successful. Absolutely! So in 2011, I started my business full time, with all other options off the table. I resigned from what I could to executing my life's missions! This was when I learned that no matter what type of small business you start or own, there are many ways it could possibly be destroyed or supported by the hands, mouths and actions of family, friends and colleagues. I also learned the power of networking can really help with that, but networking is all about relationships. Networking counts, but relationships matter. A lot of times the success of your business may have very little to do with your business practices, systems, core values, mission, vision, networking, systems, sales, promotion, marketing, profit and loss statement or business plan.

Those things are *extremely* important and so are the ways other people, especially those closest to small business owners, handle the business of business. Let's keep it simple and take a look at the two lists below to see where you may fit in. Choose your 10! Are you hurting or sabotaging, or helping and supporting small businesses, maybe even your own? To ruin or sabotage a small business, especially of someone you know:

1. **Always ask for a hookup**—Don't worry, after all, you're a *real* friend and deserve it.
2. **Expect them to provide services or product for discount or free**—There's more where that came from.
3. **Pretend to ignore their efforts**—You are way to cool to act like you notice or care.
4. **Wait for someone else "big time" to appreciate their greatness to get your approval**—Your reputation is too important to be the first.
5. **Support from a distance and throw socially and politically correct shade**—They won't figure it out.
6. **Assume your social media presence is enough**—Like the hell out of their posts, pics and pages and never show up, hoping they never expect you to show up for real, especially in public.
7. **Be nosey and wait for "it" to be over** - They could fail, ya know?!
8. **Compare them to people on TV you don't even know**—Everyone should "blow up" overnight. That is what happened with all the people on TV, right?!
9. **Offer grand suggestions void of help**—After you tell them everything they should do, leave immediately and stay very busy.

10. **See their changes as threats to your "norm"**—Punish them with your absence.

Do all of those things and they could be out of business before you know it. Or, here is another option: if you want to help or support a small business, especially of someone you know:

1. **Be the first one to invest**—Money, time, service or support, there are no genuine offerings too little.
2. **Expect to pay full price**—Discounts are for superstores and overruns, require value instead. Treat them like the businesses you don't expect discounts from now.
3. **Acknowledge what they are doing well**—Let your praises outweigh your criticisms.
4. **Prove how "big time" you are and be their loudest cheerleader**—Confident people pose or fear no threat from another's noble achievements.
5. **Ask how you can help, it's mutually beneficial**—Paying it forward always gives back.
6. **Show up consistently and be authentic with your support in public**—Secret support feeds your ego, but leaves their confidence hungry and the relationship starving.
7. **Join in! Ask them how they are doing instead of what they are doing**—"What are you doing" can be perceived as nosey versus "How are you doing" which fosters a sense of active concern and care.
8. **Encourage them where they are and appreciate the evidence and level of their successes, right now**—Nobody gets everything right the first time or all the time.
9. **Offer suggestions that you can support and only ask questions that you are willing to help answer**—If you see a need, fill it or positively encourage them toward having it filled.
10. **See your progression and theirs and create ways to shift, change and grow together**—Personal and professional

relationships change, structure your life to accommodate and be accommodated.

The help and support list is *not* for the faint of heart or the self-ignorant. Everyone isn't meant to be an entrepreneur, but everyone can think and behave entrepreneurial (take risks and initiatives that help make profit). Business ownership is one thing but having an entrepreneurial mindset is a way of life for movers, shakers, motivators, change agents, visionaries, community builders, posterity providers, legacy-leavers and those who want to see creativity, wealth and overall economic betterment. If that's you, follow thru – not only via position, but with passion!

I've witnessed these behaviors first hand, and among fellow business owners. But, it's not to get bitter, but to have the courage and vulnerability to be better. Business owners can make productive changes and call a thing a thing! It's a reality that can easily be corrected. Small business owners leap into ownership to be free—ask and get paid for what they are worth or, choose to barter, provide pro bono, and have partnerships and collaborations that can be a win-win, creating exponential business growth at their leisure. Offering strategic referral benefits and value incentives are empowering! But, if you want to devalue or bankrupt a small business, destroy credibility and professional relationships and contribute to unnecessary aspects of entrepreneurial "failure," use one word that is bound to make those things happen—hookup.

If you want to be part of something greater than yourself, empower communities, uplift and have a sense of unity in celebrating minorities, have a sense of global pride and experience the unlimited possibilities of positive reciprocity, then deliberately practice the "Support List." It's just that simple! You can even post and repeat it, which could make it even easier to live it. Create a "support movement!" Our individual and collective futures depend on this kind of power action to be better, do better, and expect more—absolutely, and on purpose!

Chapter Nineteen

Invincibility & Determination

"If you seek truth you will not seek victory by dishonorable means, and if you find truth you will become invincible."

—Epictetus

THE TRUTH ACCORDING TO FRANDREA MADDEN

I met Frandrea over twenty years ago. She was nineteen and doesn't look too much older than that now. She is the poster child for the saying "I don't look like what I've been through." Born in California but raised in Toledo, Ohio, she is a sibling to seven, a mother of three, and a grandmother of three. She has earned her bachelor's and is pursuing her master's degree, and is currently working as a behavioral specialist. Frandrea grew up in the inner city of Toledo, and came from a very dysfunctional family. Her mother had an eighth grade education, and her not having employment opportunities added to the hardships that already came with the territory. Forget hardships, life was hell. But she expresses gratitude for living in a home with dysfunction because she was kept from greater dysfunction that existed outside of her household. Frandrea got married at nineteen years old and, as she puts it, it was by the grace of God. She knew her marriage occurred at a time when she needed to be rescued.

Frandrea: I know my marriage was an orchestration to get me out of Toledo, Ohio. I was fragmented and I was in some very unhealthy relationships. My household was riddled with physical and sexual abuse. From the time I was ten to the age of thirteen, I was sexually molested by my stepfather and he had molested my older sister before he molested me and he had a pattern because he began to molest my younger sisters.

There were instances where I had been molested by my brother. Though it was short lived, being molested seemed normal. We were extremely poor and sometimes went without food; we went without utilities and there was physical and psychological abuse as well.

PREGNANT AT THIRTEEN

Frandrea: The sexual abuse from my stepfather resulted in him getting me pregnant. I was pregnant by him at the age of thirteen and had my daughter at the age of fourteen. Believe it or not, my being pregnant was a saving grace because had that not happened he would have continued. I'd even attempted suicide a few times, but by the grace of God, I failed at that! My stepfather ended up going to prison for molesting me and my sisters. His going to prison also left us homeless, and we moved from house to house.

We experienced eviction after eviction and, one time, we lived in a house where half the house had been burned down, and we lived in the half that wasn't. During difficult times, my mom pimped us out to a local drug dealer. She claimed she was sending us to his house to help him clean, but she knew what was going on. We knew what was going on because it was our bodies being sexually abused. He'd help us out financially when we didn't have food. And when we didn't have lights, he'd run an extension cord from his house to ours. That was life as I knew it. I was used to chaotic and abusive relationships. I needed a way out; I knew this wasn't right, but I didn't know what right was. I needed to learn how not to see a dysfunctional relationship and not run right into it. All I knew was this wasn't it. That's why I said my marriage rescued me. It was the first time I could live differently. I didn't know love. I didn't know how to love or how to be loved. I didn't know anything about good relationships, let alone marriage. I was thirsty. I needed love.

HOW IN THE WORLD?

I wondered how Frandrea was able to stand on her story. I wondered how she was able to not pass blame, and not carry the weight, or does she? She says she knows God is sovereign. She talked about the Scripture that says, *"A double minded man is unstable in all his ways."* She said she can't say out of her mouth that she trusts God and believes God and knows that He's an orchestrator of her life, if she blames people for standing in her way or doing something perceptively negative. She believes that *"All things work together for the good of them who love the Lord and are the called according to his purpose"* (Rom. 8:28). She's been through hell, but thank God her life is flame retardant! She is not psychotic; she does not abuse her children. Stereotypically, she could've been a prostitute or on drugs. But she sees God as the beauty in her ashes, and the foundation of her relationship with God is what she stands on, which is greater than the pain of her story. It wasn't easy at all, but she was determined to do the work. How in the world does someone arise out of those ashes and live a life full of purpose, carries out her life's mission and does so with great passion?

Frandrea: I realize that what happened to me nor my titles, the past abuse or even my accomplishments—those events and actions do not define me! They are not the sum total of who I am. The positive events give me the motivation, but I choose to show up as invincibility, freedom and courage because the molestation and abuse did not break me. When I realized my purpose and God allowed me to see myself through the eyes of purpose, I see someone who is strong, whole, and lovable, and someone who is loving. God is teaching me and allows me to look into myself even deeper, I see a psychologist, a counselor and a friend, and I am creating those things. I see can see them, but I'm not just sitting here waiting for God to make them things happen. I'm learning that He has given me the power and the ability to my faith and partnership with him in a collaboration with him to bring those things into existence, and do the work.

When she got married and that relationship became a rescue, from her self-destruction, yet it was another relationship that saved her life. It was her relationship with Jesus Christ. Her marriage provided an opportunity for her to move to North Carolina where she became a part of a local church, and she and her husband gave their lives to the Lord. She still had issues, still suffered from the aftermaths of almost every form of abuse, as well as years of thinking molestation and poverty was a lifestyle. But she became a faithful member of a church that taught the Word of God and offered counseling, twelve-step programs, classes on marriage and a holistic approach to relationships and a sense of community. She was able to get help and as she healed she was able to help others. She and her husband attended Ambassadors for Christ for years and with the help of Bishop Walter Jones, Pastor Thomasine Jones and many other members of that church, they were able to better their lives and the lives of their three children.

Frandrea and I didn't see one another or really communicate from 2002 until she became part of one of my coaching groups in 2012. I had moved to Japan for three years and returned to the States, but we both moved several times in between. During her consultation, it was apparent that she was ready for a journey in self-discovery. I knew I could help her discover her purpose, become even clearer about her life's mission and offer her a sustaining energy in excellence called passion. It wasn't because I knew her; I know a lot of people, some a lot better than I knew her and I don't feel I have to coach them. They may not "feel" me either. Some of them don't feel self-discovery is necessary for their lives. And if they don't believe it is, I don't either. Simple. Plus, no matter if you are coaching or selling water in the desert, you'd be crazy to think people will come to you simply because they know you. But I was glad to speak with her.

It wasn't so much what she said or what she didn't say, I could hear where she was. By listening to her life, it was obvious that she was experiencing transitions and indecision on every level. She was in transition, not crisis. From my experience, you can't coach people who are in crisis. Crisis, no – transition, absolutely! She had recently gotten divorced, she had moved, her boys had been living with her but she and her ex-husband co-parent and felt the boys were at the age that it would be more advantageous for them to live with him. She had changed jobs, had just finished her bachelor's degree and was working on her master's. She didn't say it, but I could hear that her life wanted more than what she was currently experiencing and the best time to discover who you are and why you are here is when you realize you don't have a clue or are at a crossroad. Self-discovery loves to ride in on the wings of transition, and based on all the transitions she was going through, I knew if she did the work she would fly. How could she benefit from these wonderful benefits of leaps and progression? What was the difference between prior counseling, therapy and twelve-step programs and coaching from her perspective?

Frandrea: Coaching has been my key. You know how you can have that door that gets kind of stuck? You have the right key for it, but it just doesn't quite unlock it? So you have to take it back and get it sanded down more and once you get it sanded down, it fits into the lock and clicks. My relationship with God gave me the right key all along, but coaching sanded down that key, unlocked that door and opened me up. All those years I prayed, "God, who am I supposed to be and what am I supposed to do?" Coaching clicked and answered those questions for me. You taught me what purpose was and I was able to discover and experience my purpose myself. My purpose is not what I'm doing, but it is who God has created me to be. I am invincibility, freedom and courage. It goes beyond being a wife, a mom, a student or a psychologist.

Coaching led me to healthy relationships. When I discovered who I was and began to express that in my relationships, they became healthier and they supported who I told them I was here to be and what I am here to do. My life isn't perfect, but I couldn't tell you whose life is any better, because I know who I am and why I'm here! Even with the good, or the seemingly bad, my life is good and God is good to me. Because of my relationship with God, the foundation I was taught with the Word of God and now with coaching, I realize you have to open yourself up to the idea that someone can help you help yourself. Even though our answers lie inside of us, coaching is not about somebody telling you what to do. Coaching is all about helping you discover the answers that are in you. It's Christ in me who is the hope of glory, is greater is He who is in me than he that is in the world. Coaching allowed me to tap into that glory, that greater.

Coaching help me grow beyond the four walls of the church and it has taught me that the best relationship I can have is the relationship I have with myself. Because the relationship I have with myself teaches other people how to treat me, it helps me set appropriate boundaries, it gives me a clear frame of reference and it allows me to be able to look inside me to find and be the answers that God has created me to be. It doesn't matter if it's spiritual, personal or professional. It is an external guide that helps you guide your inward course yourself. Just to have someone listen to you, ask you the right questions, hold you accountable and help you set and achieve your goals is what coaching is all about.

It is okay to reach out to ask someone to help you with your life. It's all about relationships. Frandrea has an amazing story and the facts of what was done don't have to be a burden on the truth of what is (now). Frandrea has discovered her purpose, her spiritual DNA. My friend and fellow coach, Cherri Walston, shared with me that your DNA are your Divine Natural Abilities. In my first book, *The Book of Purpose: The YOU Testament*, I talk about your purpose being your spiritual identity: Who you are. Your mission is why you are here: What you do. Passion is the skill and excellence: How well you do it. Like Frandrea, you are here to allow God to work for you, with you, through you and as you. People get a little taken aback when they get to the "as you" part, but if God can't be you, who can God be? Some people feel because coaching isn't religious or denominationally centered, it would interfere with their beliefs. Coaching can only enhance and amplify what you believe, as long as you really believe your beliefs.

Frandrea didn't have to have a relationship God and then coaching. God is in the coaching. You bring who you are, or aren't. I dare not take the credit for her growth, and no one else should either. She grew before then; she already had the key, but it just needed to be sanded so it could open the lock. She had the nerve to ask for help and got it, but SHE did the work! What is the work? Everyone is different. You find out as you get it done! Frandrea's life is primed for continual success, her way. Her future is much brighter than her dark past. As she completes her master's degree and with her career path, she is becoming what she needed—a help, an advocate and counselor. Her thesis will be about abuse. Who better to shed professional light than someone who has gone beyond survival? She will help them realize the abuse was only a moment in time and doesn't have to negatively affect lives, especially as they experience self-discovery.

Frandrea: After I finished my last class for my master's degree, I will be enrolling into a PhD program in psychology. I live my life with the passion to do well, and do no harm to others. I want to make my life better and impact people who are in my life in a positive way.

I believe her! Because anyone can live a life that says, "Because anyone who says, "Abuse, stand DOWN and die in the presence of invincibility, courage and freedom," and lives a life that proves it, I believe! Frandrea continues to successfully overcome because she is a witness and has life-changing evidence that she is not afraid to do the work. I am excited about her life and the coaching relationship we have, as well as the friendship we have developed. As with many of my clients, her life inspires mine and because of her being invincible, courageous and free, I know her DNA, those spiritual identifiers, so much better, too. Like many others, Frandrea is living proof. Be it during childhood or last night, positive or negative, no matter what happened, it is imperative that you realize: You are not what happened to you or what you've done—good, bad or indifferent—nor are you just the one who lived through it, but you ARE the one who knew you would!! Believe that! Know that!

Implementation Guides: What's been your relationship with any form of abuse? What if your story provides all the excuses you need to fail? How can you live beyond past events? What is your relationship like with God? What do you believe about counseling programs provided by a church? Can anybody get a pass to fail? How can a coaching or mentoring relationship help your life?

Chapter Twenty

Relationships to Ponder—Friendships

"There are only two people who can tell you the truth about yourself—an enemy who has lost his temper and a friend who loves you dearly."

—Antisthenes

Friendship can mean a lot of different things to a lot of different people, be it long-term, platonic and, what some people call frienemies. I've always known a lot of people, but felt I had few friends, which is a common feeling most have about friendships. I've been blessed to have some really great people in my life who I call friend, no matter how long I've known them. Longevity is great, yet friendship does not have to know longevity, as long as it understands love, purpose and connectivity. A friend is someone you love, know, like, trust and support. A friend is someone who knows and sees your imperfections and doesn't overlook them, but looks right at them and continues to love you and your stuff. A friend's love is a friend to freedom and an enemy to bondage. A friend frees you to be you, even if you're kind of strange or weird. Friends range from those you talk to every day, those you catch up with periodically, to those you haven't spoken to or seen in years, and it's all-good. A good friend to me is not necessarily someone I invite over and have to clean up for. But if I need to cleanup for something or someone, my friends would come over and help me do it because they were probably the ones who help make a mess anyway and don't need an invitation.

NO WOMEN

There was a time I didn't make an attempt to befriend women at all. I felt there was too much drama. Gender can play a role in relationship dynamics and my platonic relationships taught me that men have drama, too. Men gossip, too. Men can get emotional and argue, too. No matter the gender, I had to realize it's only drama if you choose to be in the play. I also found out that men can be tender, too. Men can listen, too. Men like to shop, too. Ain't that right, Owen? Most women like to shop, I'd rather not. If I want to buy something, I go get it and come out. There's no adrenalin rush, no high and no need to browse. I used to distance myself from women because somewhere down the line I saw them as weak and needy. I didn't want a relationship with any of that. It wasn't until life, experiences, the strength in vulnerability and maturity allowed me to see how strong women are and can be. Now I embrace my sister-friends, partners, clients and colleagues. I enjoy relationships with SHEroes and powerful women! I admire their strength and virtue, and I have the best relationships with some of the world's most brilliant women!

My platonic relationships are very important to me. The men I connect with, I love and appreciate who they are in my life. I love them and the connection and the ability to relate to them without gender being a hindrance. They are my brother-friends, partners, clients and colleagues. Platonic relationships are necessary, but some extreme forms of religion and archaic societal mentalities make them difficult to form. This is why people sneak, hide, and deny innocent dealings with the opposite sex that can become perceptively tainted. People allow it more professionally but why not personally. Everyone has to know who they are in order to form the types of relationships they need. But if a person cuts a gender off for fear of sexual feelings—usually that's what it is—that's a problem that accountability can deal with and solve.

There are times relationships have challenges and issues, that's understood. But those times of having issues and drama should not be the norm. It's only drama if you chose to be in the play. And, it is obligated to continue and intensify as long as you reward it with the applause of your attention. We have all heard that relationships are for a season, reason or lifetime and once we realize which one we are in, hopefully mutually, the shift does not have to be negative. The other type of friendships people tend to deal with is frienemies or "haters." That's not something I give credence to. First of all, I believe you have to be an enemy to have one. Second, "hating" is less of an action but more of an attitude or energy I choose not to accept (period).

Chapter Twenty-One

Missing the Music

"Perhaps the truth depends on a walk around the lake."
—Wallace Stephens

THE TRUTH ACCORDING TO TIM WATSON

It was late 1988 and I had left Winston Salem State University and moved back home. Between not knowing if my financial aid was going to kick in, getting sick and having to pay hospital bills, it was obvious I wasn't going back to school, at not least for a *long* time. Ask credit and debt about that. Especially in a small town, I knew I was going to have to work hard to make the best of it. I had gone to church that Sunday, and really didn't want to be there. After all, I felt like a failure, and I was missing the freedom of college life, even though I didn't use it, I had it. There, I could choose to go to church, and I did, but being back home put me right back in the saddle of *having* to go to church and I didn't want to, not so much. My relationship with God was proving to be there and everywhere! There were so many things going on in my life: I wasn't well, I had terrible ulcers, as a Preacher's Kid/Bishop's Kid (PK/BK), I was skeptical of every relationship, I was working three jobs, trying to get an apartment and a car on my own and I had a lot of questions about God, life, family, love, money and relationships that no one was answering without sounding like a skipping record or script. Chapter and verse didn't always satisfy my questions and sometimes people started sounding like puppets or talking heads. That's where I was when I met Tim Watson. So he didn't stand a chance to become my friend and I didn't make the cut to become his either. Instant foes.

I DIDN'T KNOW

Tim was a young Marine who had become a member of my dad's church. I don't remember being introduced to him, but I do remember the first time I saw him. He had on some suede-looking black and white shoes. I was not impressed at all. There was no need to see anything else. I wasn't mean to him, but because people had tried for years to hook me up with Marines, I befriended, but I didn't want a thing to do with them because: 1) They were Marines. 2) I didn't want to be bothered with anybody. 3) I refused to date anyone who was a member of my dad's church. Too much mess, too much drama and I didn't need the church congregation to be my picking pool. 4 and 5) They were Marines. At that time, the life of a military spouse was not attractive and even when I eventually became one, I refused to be one. I was Tracy, who just happened to be married to Owen, but that happened much later in 1993.

But I didn't even look at Tim as a potential friend. I didn't see him. I doubt seriously if he saw me either. Then, one day I did see him…well not him, I saw his shoes. This time those jokers were purple. Purple. Purple? Purple! Purple woven shoes and that sealed the deal. I could not be friends with those shoes. There were so many young Marines at our church—men and women—I wasn't hurting to be his friend and he wasn't hurting to be mine. I did end up dating one and he proved I really needed to stick to 1, 2, 3, 4 and 5!

And I don't exactly know how, when or why, but we became foes; foes in the name of Jesus. I didn't know anything about him until much later. What I didn't know was that he was a young man from Chicago who had left the big city to join the Marine Corps. He left a life that if he hadn't, he probably would have become a street statistic. Not because of whom he was, but because the negative gravitational pull of drugs, crime and violence would have been hard to resist. I did not know:

- He had just been in the Marine Corps two years and was about to get out.

- He was about to get out of the Marine Corps in 1991 at twenty years old.
- He was going through a divorce.
- He was deciding to stay in Havelock because his life in Chicago wasn't something he wanted to go back to.
- He would have been homeless there, but for some of the brothers in the church inviting him to sleep on their couch for as long as he needed.
- His car had just been repossessed.

I didn't know that it was difficult for him to get a job because what he had learned and been trained to do in the Marine Corps for those few years had not prepared him for a successful civilian life. Military life, especially the Marine Corps organization, is created to train to govern and to discipline people—young people at that—from all different walks of life so they can operate as one lean, mean peace-keeping or fighting machine. The Marine Corps is a culture that is developed for you. Everything about it is set up for you, and it is designed to tell you how to be, who to be, when to be and what to be. When you come out of that, especially at twenty years old, the first thing he had to learn how to do was how to value relationships as relationships and not commodities. Getting out was exciting, but the scary part was he no longer had the support and the security of a military paycheck, a place to live, a place to eat and a uniform to wear. They told you where to go, how you would travel there, what to do while you were there, how long to stay without ever having to reveal why. So when he got out, his eyes were opened to opportunities he had never had or seen, but he didn't know how to get them. I didn't know:

- He found such value in the relationships he had built at the church; that brothers and sisters were not just titles, but he felt those people had become his family.
- He would relate to my parents as his. I didn't know. I didn't ask. I don't know if he knew about all of the things I was going through at the same time.

FUSS AND FIGHT

But what I did know was that I was working at a place called Tire Town USA. What I did know was that I was working as an office manager at a place called Tire Town USA. I had befriended one of my co-workers named Crystal Davis and she is the one who introduced Owen and me to one another. She even invited us to her home for dinner, and that made our acquaintance a little nicer. Mmm hmm! I thank Crystal Davis for the introduction! Tim had been hired to work there, too. The owners were such a hard-working and benevolent couple. I didn't voice my opinion, but I was angry because they had hired him to work there and I and some of my coworkers couldn't tell what they were paying him to do.

I guess we felt like they needed our permission or approval to hire a new employee. Little did we know, they had contracted with him to do the window tinting. Back then, a lot of Marines were returning from Operation Desert Storm and Tire Town USA was bustling! I was working ten to twelve hours a day, and the days were so busy, it never seemed that long. The Marines were getting their vehicles tricked out with stereo systems, rims, tires, and window tinting. We thought he was an hourly employee like we were, and couldn't understand why he didn't have to keep regular hours. We couldn't understand why he wasn't put in the category with the mechanics or the administrative staff. We didn't know and according to his truth, he didn't realize that, even back then, he was an entrepreneur in the making. Window tinting was the only craft he knew he could fall back on, and used it to earn money. I didn't ask. I didn't know. But I knew he knew exactly how to the piss me off. And I knew how to piss him off, too.

Tim: We argued every day. We argued so much that when we didn't it was awkward silence, like crickets.

TracyMac: Tim, that's because you were aggravating.

Tim: I think looking back at it, your name means oil and my name means water in Swahili.

TracyMac: We had slamming doors arguments, fussing and cussing arguments. Yes, cussing. I think I became an expert at it all because of you.

Tim: Yep. And I know you are not one to hardly ever cry, but I made you cry. So for those who don't think TracyMac cries, she does. I am proof!

TracyMac: Yes. And go ahead tell the rest because if I cry because I'm angry I'm ready to fight.

Tim: That's one of the things that make you so good because you have a very strong and passionate belief system. And I have seen the consequences. We won't even talk about what you did to my camera.

TracyMac: Yeah and I think I tried to fight you.

Tim: Yes, yes you did. And they wrote a play about it.

TracyMac: What are you talking about?

Tim: "Your Arms Are Too Short to Box With God."

(Sigh… See what I'm saying?)

TracyMac: Anyway, It's been too long since we have talked.

Tim: Yeah, too long. More than the word "too" more than the number 2. It's been more like a "prehistoric too." I am talking to you right now from my studio. If we were going to connect on anything, I am so glad that it is about relationships.

TracyMac: Tell us about yourself, Tim.

Tim: I am a forty-three-year-old dad, however I do not look forty-one. I look a very pristine twenty-three-and-a-half. I am a dad, I am a husband and I am a philanthropist, well at least in my mind. And I am giving everything that I have that I do not have yet. I'm a very optimistic person; I really enjoy laughing and I enjoy being the best at what I do. I enjoy people and having a good time. I live outside of reality by creating and writing. Why did we fuss and you fight so much back then?

TracyMac: Because you didn't want to listen.

Tim: I think it was because you loved me a lot.

TracyMac: Nope! I didn't know about you.

(But God! Tim is my buddy and friend from way back and still.)

Tim: But you did care.

TracyMac: Yes, I cared and from my perspective, you didn't want to follow the rules. It was all because of miscommunication because I had no idea you were allowed to set your own hours. And you know how I am about being fair. You didn't get dirty because you weren't a mechanic, you didn't get stressed because you didn't work in the office. I wondered: Why are you here? The bays would be filled with cars, I would have credit apps to run, bills to pay and even the owners were working hard. And you would just stand there and wandered around all clean, calm, smiling and joking. They had given me some liberty to kind of run the office, which was my opportunity to run Tim, too.

Tim: But that goes back to my military regimen. Because when I didn't have any cars to tint I didn't know what to do. I was so used to being told or ordered what to do all the time that when there were no instructions and no orders, I did just kind of stand there or wandered around. You gave me a hard way to go. I didn't know what to do. And then what probably frustrated you was because when you would tell the owners of the company they didn't seem to be bothered by it. And I could tell you were frustrated because you were doing about one hundred different tasks.

LET THE MUSIC PLAY

TracyMac: But, what calmed the storm between us was music. It was Fred Hammond and Commissioned, the Winans, Witness, Hosanna and Integrity Praise and worship music. We came together through music.

Tim: Yep. That was the common denominator and the bridge that closed the GREAT catechism that we created. I think inherently we knew that there was something we both needed or could get from one another and we didn't know what it was, and we found out it was music. Music saved my life. When you come from a place that just about everything you've tried you had not completed; I was a professional starter and I was not a professional finisher. Music was one of the things that I did that allowed me the ability to create, write and finish. It allowed me to do something that I didn't have to get orders or feedback about. It could be the way that I heard it that was different, and that allowed me to take pride in something and see that I was able to do something.

TracyMac: Now, Tim, you know good 'n well it took you a little while to get it right. Because when you first started playing, you know we gave you a hard time. And I was the ringleader. But you were a prize winning jokester, too!

Tim: Yep, you and your right hand, armor bearer chimed in in stereo. But if I were you guys, and had to listen to what I was playing, I would have been the same way. I was trying to play and didn't know what the heck was going on. I was hitting keys and they didn't even make any sound sense. But I could not have developed in a better place because you guys gave me so much latitude and room to get it right.

TracyMac: Let me interpret latitude and room. It was jokes, laughing with and at, because it was horrible. But I must say my mom was so encouraging to you and she would say, "Tim, don't pay them any attention. Just don't stop playing." She kicked me out of the choir stand several times for laughing at you. But gradually we began to hear what you heard. Now at first, keep it real, you couldn't play. But as your gift began to develop, you would play chords that the average ear cannot hear, especially the average church, musical ear. How did you develop that and take a chance on notes and chords that the average ear was not accustomed to?

Tim: I needed a way that would differentiate me and set me apart from what was already there. It wasn't anything that people may have never heard before; it was just a way that I could relate to and add color and things that were a little friendlier for me to play. It was a great process of getting to know who I was, even musically.

TracyMac: How did your relationship with music affect your other relationships, then or over time? We don't have to stay back there, let's grow it forward. Positive or negative.

Tim: One thing you can never do is underestimate your passion. It is a living, breathing, ever evolving organism. Music is that to me. I was single when I first started playing and we connected through music. So I had all the time in the world to play and create. It was all I did, all day, all hours of the night and the wee hours of the morning and in between. That was my relationship with music. Eventually I grew little older, I met someone and we were married. And I will not say that music cost me my relationship with this person. What I will say is that the demand that it placed on me not to prioritize or manage cost me my relationship. Why did it cost me? Because I wasn't willing to give up whom I was musically.

I wasn't willing to conform to what a "normal" lifestyle would bring. Most musicians are happiest when they can create. When that is taken from you, or when you give it up for a chance to see if, in fact, you can exist without music in order to be normal, it doesn't always go well. As a normal husband, could I just go to work, and come home, and save money and pay bills? It didn't work for me. I wasn't a very nice person to be around because I couldn't create. I tried that and it didn't work. I did lose the relationship, but I found music again and it found me. You should never give up who you are or your passion for something or someone who is requiring you to do so that you can fit the mold of what they feel is normal.

TracyMac: I so agree, it's pretty much any level of passion, especially when it comes to creating, whether it's music, poetry, writing, graphic arts, authorship, painting, dancing, etc. Anytime you are blessed with the ability to create, to take something from spirit to existence, when you enter into relationships, you really have to know who you are and be in concert with that passion. And that person or people you are in relationships with have to be able to accept it. And yes, there is room for compromise, but your compromising has to have limits, or you begin to become foreign and ignorant to yourself.

Tim: And a lot of times in relationships people are so busy trying to normalize their lives. Take for instance, that musician who gets pegged as weird because he sleeps in the same shirt for a week, won't sleep, or if she won't eat because she's writing. Or, that person who can't maintain finances or a "normal" relationship or employment because of their creative, uncertain, spontaneous and fluid lifestyle. That's not an excuse to create dysfunction; they/we may function differently.

TracyMac: I am not a musician but I used to write a lot of lyrics for songs and even being an author now and one who helps other people create, all of my relationships have to understand where I have to go to create. It gets easier because I frequent that place often. And that place is not a geographical spot, per se, but it is a place of quiet and peace where I need to create. A lot of times it's about being alone. I am so grateful that my husband and my daughter are extremely understanding. They are creators, too. I have lost a lot of relationships and some relationships have become distant because of not understanding that space. How do you balance being a musician, with your current relationships, being a father, a husband, a friend, an employee and an employer? How were you able to balance all of that now without losing your relationships or getting lost in the passion for what you love to do?

Tim: That is something I had to learn to be. I didn't say I had to learn to do. I had to learn to be balanced. I had the misconception that I could balance everything and everybody. Musically and creatively, I had to learn how to be flexible time wise and understand that it wasn't the fact that my craft couldn't exist or coexist. It was the fact that I thought and I was under the impression that my craft could not coexist within a "normal" lifestyle, and I use normal just as a reference. I understand now that is very much so a part of being a husband, and a father, and I work a 9-to-5. I have learned that if I'm going to create, I need to let the person know and understand that they don't have to understand what I do; they just have to understand who I am. Once I understood that, I now have that in the relationship I have.

TracyMac: So you are saying a relationship has to understand who you are and not just what you do. Tell me, as best as you can, because that's so powerful. Break that down and give me a scenario.

Tim: Today, right now, we are talking and today is my son's, Zion's, eleventh birthday. I work and I have a two-hour commute every day each way. So the time that I have when I come home, whatever valuable is to you, multiply that times one hundred to me. So the hour I have with my children is equivalent to the three or four hours the average person has with their children at the end of their day. So because of who I am creativity does not have a time clock. It has a start and stop button and it comes and goes when it pleases. And if you don't go with it you can lose whatever it is trying to speak to you in that moment. My wife understands who I am. And if she did not, all she would see now is what I'm doing. She would see I'm not with my family, and I'm only doing something else. But she understands that I'm being who I am and it is best that way for me and for our family.

TracyMac: To the degree you feel comfortable, tell us who you are.

Tim: I am a creative genius! I say that because I am always hungry for something that only exists where people can't see it. The average eye can't see where I like to exist and live in.

TracyMac: So your family sees you as a creative genius?

Tim: Yeah! But don't get me wrong; they see me as the back massager, the guy who takes out the trash, the guy who cuts the grass and takes care of the car…

TracyMac: See that's what I wanted to ask! When it comes time to go up to the school or take the kids to the mall or make your two-hour commute every day?

Tim: I am still a creative genius. I am an innovator. I love innovation and I love the fact that we have been given the power to create things, build things or make things better and efficient, even with my family and my relationships. I get the most air to breathe and I can move freely when I am being creative and innovative. It's when I'm in that zone and it doesn't have a time slot. It just is. I am all things creative! Because I don't think music is just created to be heard. I believe it's created to unleash and unlock other things that would only be activated by sound. Not by thought alone.

TracyMac: Uh oh, you going deep and you are ready to take us down the rabbit hole. Now I'm going to be with you, but I just wanted you to know where you were going.

Tim: What happened subconsciously with that is that gift or that passion inadvertently draws itself to people who have a "like." That's why we coexist well. We can laugh and joke and have lots of fun, but we also can talk about things that don't exist yet, things that are primed by another person's gift. Sometimes a sound can be the key to unlock so many things.

TracyMac: Sometimes you have to find people who have your rhythm, and that pun is intended. I don't even want to say find because you just automatically connect with people who have your rhythm when you play yours. You said you were a creative genius, when you own that, people who have like creative genius connect with you and the relationship doesn't have the strain. If we go back to the '80s when we used to argue and fuss. We do realize that your music ability and my writing ability took the strain and the effort out of the relationship and we could be cool. We can be cool on different levels. I love you, man, and I think the world of you when you act right. And when you don't you can still get cussed out every now and then.

Tim: And that's cool because that's a part of who we are. I love you too. Together we can breathe. I can breathe with you. When I can't breathe with people, it requires me to use extra oxygen and I can't live like that. I won't.

TracyMac: How important is it for your purpose, mission and passion to affect your relationships? And how important is it that your relationships connect with your relationships?

Tim: It is vitally important. It is as important to me as saving the world. Because if I don't have those vital relationships, then the world, as I know and exist in, is in trouble. I feel better and more secure when I am with someone who understands who I am because they understand who they are and they're the same way. We may not be doing the same thing, but they are the same way.

TracyMac: How have you come into this knowledge, this experience and maturity level as it pertains to relationships?

Tim: The truth according to Tim Watson: I don't know exactly when, all I know is what it meant. It was you. One of the things that I remember is when you told me, "It's okay for you to be who you are." I had heard that before in a song or I read it in a book. But it sounds totally different coming from someone who knows you. I mean really knows you—the good, the bad and the ugly. That meant the whole world to me. It gave me the go-ahead to grow and to be and to continue to create. And that's what I do.

That's one of the things that stick with me, and it helps me even when I feel like I may be too analytical, or too hard on myself or even with someone else. It's okay for me to be me and it's okay for other people to be who they are. When I realized that, it gave me my own oxygen so that I can breathe.

Breathe! Anyone who knows there's something more to them than what their parents, their colleagues, their relatives or even the people they admire are doing. Breathe! But you know there's something else that nags you; that prompts you. Breathe! What I have been and who I am helps people understand that there's nothing wrong with wanting to be more, to create more, or to create or innovate more. It is a calling you have to answer. Breathe! Anyone who feels like I did, who don't feel they are able to be productive and are frustrated doing what "normal" people do, to those people who have abstract thoughts, for those people who think about things that don't exist, to those people I want to say…be strange. Be weird. You are not going to get there unless you're willing to be laughed at and laugh at yourself. Tracy, take that part right there and put it on the back of your book! That was hot!

TracyMac: That's so true, Tim, because you know what? If you laugh at yourself first, they laugh less. (Tim still makes me cry, but now it's because my laughter gets so full it has to use my tears.)

Implementation Guides: Who could you take time to get to know? How can a man and a woman have a platonic relationship before and after being married to other people? How do you balance your gifts and talents with your normalcy required in relationships? What is your relationships with music? How do you balance creativity with reality? What is your genius? Who has your rhythm? What if you feel like you're strange? What if they laugh at you?

Chapter Twenty-Two

Hospitality & Servitude

"People don't care how much you know until they know how much you care."

—Lisa Nichols

THE TRUTH ACCORDING TO LATONIA F. TALLEY

Where does a social butterfly get her wings? She didn't realize she had them then, but this social butterfly, who I call my dear friend, got her wings from Swainsboro, Georgia and boy is she fluttering! I met Latonia Talley in 2003 while my husband was stationed in Okinawa, Japan. Latonia and her husband were stationed there, too. The Talleys are our friends. Not only are she and I friends, but as rare as it is, our husbands are friends, too. That's a miracle in and of itself because neither Owen nor her husband, Henry Talley, want to be bothered with a lot of people, and when they do, they tolerate it while Tonia and I meet people, network and socialize. But I didn't lay eyes on Tonia or Henry first. I saw their daughter Paige.

FIRST IMPRESSIONS

I sat near the door the Sunday they walked in church. Paige was about five or six years old then (she recently turned sweet sixteen—oh my goodness!) and she wore the cutest red dress with the right amount of crinoline or tulle underneath, making it Disney Princess poufy. She had on the matching red laced socks and beautiful red bows in her hair, black patent leather shoes with a cute purse to match. Paige looked like one of the little girls you see in a pageant or on the front of a new church fan. Well of course Paige wasn't alone on my imaginary church fan because in walked her dad, Henry Talley, tall, well-dressed from shoes to tie and haircut, and he wore a no-nonsense look on his face. He didn't look mean, but he had this "What?! I know you see me, now show me something" look, as if he was the secret service. Then, I saw Tonia; she, too, was dressed in red—red suit, red shoes and a Coach bag.

They could have taken the perfect family portrait that Sunday suitable for that church fan. I didn't know at the time that Tonia was an active-duty Marine and her husband had retired from the Marine Corps and was a civilian working for the federal government. She had a feminine quality about her that some hardcore, Oooh Rah women Devil Dogs can lose. I almost didn't get to know Tonia and she almost didn't get to know me either because we'd both heard things about each other that caused a great divide. But thankfully, we were mature and women enough to seek one another out to find out the truth. We hit it off instantly!

I found out was that we had so much in common, but yet we were different, too. We both had one child; our daughters who weren't "supposed" to be alive—Paige was a preemie. We both grew up in small towns, we were the youngest girls among our siblings and both of us had parents who were preachers and pastors. We both had battled with illnesses that had us hospitalized around the same time and almost took us out, and that was before we met one another. Our husbands were not openly ready to pursue being overly social or pursue relationships, we both liked to sing and could sing, and we both had a distaste for mess and messy women. Both of us were ordained as ministers—she as a preacher and I as an elder/ teacher. In so many ways we were alike, but there were other ways we were very different. I found out early on that though Tonia was an active-duty Marine and she wasn't a silly girly-girl, she enjoyed being a woman and enjoyed feminine things. She liked shopping, she liked getting manicures and pedicures, and she would have spa days and get massages. I, on the other hand, consistently enjoyed a good pedicure (still do), but I could do without a manicure because I kept my nails cut very short to maintain my typing and adding machine speed for my job and as a writer, and that would only make for a short-lived manicure. She enjoyed the stress relief of a good, deep tissue massage, and I felt it was aggravating and stressful to have someone rubbing on me. As Ms. Millie from *The Color Purple* would say, "I don't know them either!"

Tonia joined the Marine Corps when she was eighteen and I was days away from joining the Air Force when I was nineteen. Now, if that isn't a stark difference, I don't know what is. Tonia loved to go shopping and she looked the part, and still does. And the only part I wanted to look (at) was not going shopping. I still do not like to shop or try on clothes, but I'll tolerate an hour or so to buy shoes, jewelry and purses. I'd much rather read, people watch and have ice cream in the food court. Owen is the shopper in our home. But Tonia and I grooved so well and found one another's rhythms. Back in 2003, we had a day of shopping I'll never forget it.

COACH BAGS AND SHOPPING

She was so hyped about a sale on Coach Bags that she got me up at the crack of dawn to go shopping. Ugh! But as we all do with our new friends, I was nice and went with her to the exchange on Kadena AFB. I was smiling, but my teeth were clinched. I'm sure she endured plenty of situations where she had to grin and bear it with me, too. (Keep smiling, honey!) But she was so excited that morning, and when I saw that the bags she was looking at ranged from $250 and up, I said, "Girl, I ain't paying that much for no bag, unless I consistently have that much cash in my wallet." That was my line and it worked all the other times people brought up designer anything. She said, "First of all, they are on sale *and* we have an extra 30% off coupon. Second, you probably spend that much for purses you buy that you say keep tearing up. And third, you must not think you're worth it. I am." I thought, *Damn, who does she think she is?* She already ruffled my feathers with #1 and #2, but she 'bout pissed me off with #3. I had to think before a cussing erupted because she was a minister and around that time, I was too, but I was getting flat out tired of church, so as far as I was concerned, I was free to cuss! Plus, it was Africa hot in Okinawa.

But #3 made me think. She made me think. I was tearing up

purses because I liked big bags for all of my and Jayda's stuff and I always had problems with the thread on the handles fraying or the zipper popping and would spend $45 to $50 on a purse three to four times a year. It added up to the same thing. And was I worth it? I worked long, hard and I worked well. That instant, I bought Owen gifts, my dad a brief case and my mom a diamond and sapphire bracelet, loaning and giving people money, each costing way more than that. Was I worth it? Hell yeah, I was worth it! She was a good saleswoman that day because I bought TWO! I still have them and I won't say how many of those and other designer brands I ventured into, but it's all Tonia's fault! After I bought my two, she bought two and put two on layaway, we went to the food court outside, talked, people watched, had lunch at Chili's and later had ice cream at Baskin & Robbins. We shopped my way, too—chillin' snackin' and talkin'. Then, we carried our sorry selves to our individual homes and took a nap. United by Coach Bags and ice cream in Japan, who knew?

We were also different because she likes and still loves to travel and happily invites other people to visit places she's never been before. I travel sometimes, but my preferred travel is taking people places to visit internal places where they may have never visited before and gladly welcoming them to themselves. I see my coaching, writing and speaking as a way to travel within foreign nations to see what I can help them discover. Her method of traveling helps people, too! Same thing, but a little different, right? One of the other things we have in common, then and now, that caused me to connect with Tonia was our innate desire and effortless drive to help and serve people. I was just delving into the life coach profession when we met and I knew helping people, through coaching, was one of my missions. Tonia was spreading her wings, preparing to retire and connecting with organizations.

From conversations and great times spent together, it was evident that she wasn't simply a social butterfly. She was a social butterfly on a mission to make the world a better place by helping women. Before ever being a member of any sorority, before being involved with formal social and charitable groups, she had a deliberate and consistent determination to help, serve, motivate and connect with women. As I witnessed this drive and the natural gift she had, I wondered where hers came from. I knew the Marine Corps' slogan was Semper Fi, but I also knew that being black, woman and an officer, was being a minority times three, and it took more than being "always faithful." I knew that it took something that was fundamentally amazing, something of spiritual depth, something of great purpose and strength and that something started in Swainsboro, Georgia.

SERVICE IN SWAINSBORO

On her way to church, with a station wagon filled with her six children, Mrs. Gladys Whicker would pick up other women and their children. Mrs. Gladys' generosity and hospitality always made room for one more, not just in her car, but in her heart, home and church. And though it was the consistent expression of her heart to provide transportation, the police department didn't feel that way because Ms. Gladys got a ticket for having too many people in her station wagon on their way to church. Can you imagine that?

Ya know my dad did that, too. He would pick up Marines for church, but he didn't get a ticket. But he should have, not only for there being too many people in our rust-colored 1976 Chevrolet Impala station wagon, but for having us ride in the back knowing good and well, the exhaust fumes were backing up into the car. Cough! Cough! Can I tell you the fumes were so bad, my dad had a bottle of Brute in the glove compartment and my mom had a bottle of Impulse body spray that they would splash or spray on us and themselves so we wouldn't smell like "Muffler de Parfum" when we walked into church? The summertime wasn't bad because we'd manually roll down the back-back window, as we called it, and hang out the window, but the wintertime, with all the windows up—it's a wonder me and my siblings aren't glowing in the dark right now because of inhaling toxic fumes and chasing the mosquito truck. But wait, the mosquito truck is another story... I wonder if Tonia and they had a mosquito truck back in the day in Swainsboro, too.

Tonia remembers her mom getting the ticket with much humor. We laughed so hard about it. But she will never forget seeing how her mom helped and served women in and outside of the church, and her dad, Mr. Roy Whicker, was a hard worker, too. And though she did not sit down to take notes, she had a bird's eye view of her mom's God-fearing lifestyle of helping and serving and Tonia carried that with her down Interstate 95 to swear in to become a United States Marine.

SEMPER FI WOMAN

That trip to boot camp was Tonia's first trip down Interstate 95. Honestly speaking, she didn't join the Marine Corps with a number one goal to lay her life down for Uncle Sam, or an overflowing degree of patriotism, and it definitely wasn't because of the uniform. Her number one reason for joining the Marine Corps, at that time, was because of the opportunity to earn a college degree, a degree she promised her mom she would get. Not only would the uniform she would soon be wearing be green, she was green. Fresh out of Jaw-juh, and not knowing quite what to expect, her heart raced as she got off the bus to step on those infamous yellow footprints. How would this young, black female from the South, not only become a fine warrant officer in the United States Marine Corps, but attribute her success in a male-dominated world to the relationships she chose to establish with women? She made it a point to remain teachable and coachable and not to just retain it, but everything she learned she digested and taught someone else. She even talks about how a fellow Marine took her under her wing as a young Marine and helped her with her career and with the simple things in life, including teaching her how to make potato salad.

The Marine Corps was a proving ground for Tonia for so many reasons and a test of endurance of being a minority in so many ways. It became the cocoon that she was able to wrap around her life, accept, grow and develop the beauty of her social wings. It was not easy. She met challenges where she felt discouraged at times, but she could see that with consistent hard work she would overcome, which was also consistently rewarding. Not only the hard work of being an upstanding Marine, but the work she had to do on herself, admitting what she didn't know and learning to ask for help. Mrs. Gladys & Mr. Roy were not at every duty station, so Tonia made it a point to learn how to get help by serving. Although serving was what she saw her mother do and that was admirable, she knew she wanted to serve differently.

Early on in her career, one of the ways her hard work paid off was when she was working in Parris Island, South Carolina as a Drill Instructor. She was offered the chance to have her picture taken to be a on a poster to represent the USMC. She accepted, not realizing that picture would be posted all over the world. If you go to just about any Marine Corps base or ROTC program and see a poster of a black, female Marine wearing a drill instructor's cover (hat), with the name tag: Talley, and the caption below reads "Don't be late for my class" that is this Latonia Talley. The picture was taken over twenty years ago, but for whatever reason the Marine Corps still finds her image and its message to be attractive. Tonia still finds that message to be effective not in the form of a clock (Nope! That's another story.). But in the form of the intention of not being late or slothful to serve, help, appreciate and motivate.

The Marine Corps is where she grew her relationship and the desire to help women. Doesn't that seem odd? Deciding to deliberately have friendships, be a mentee, becoming a mentor, in an environment where not only most men badmouth women, but some of the women heavily criticize their own gender. In an already competitive field, Tonia got the great idea to go to the drill field to become a drill instructor. Because Tonia's hard work kept paying off, she set her achievements high and consistently met them and she is known to exceed them. She knew the drill field would break some women down; after all, it breaks some men. She knew the drill field was competitive, and that not only being a successful drill instructor was a feat, but to earn a meritorious promotion was rare because they only gave out a select few per year during that time.

She established relationships with women, and she zoned in

on those who were perceived as being difficult to get along with. Because she was able to see something in them that needed a friend, she began to understand that some of that perception had to do with the competition, some of it had to do with low self-esteem, a lot of it had to do with being misunderstood and she was not going to allow them to be late for her class in friendship or relationship, not on her watch. She was able to admit her weaknesses by asking for help to learn military requirements and skill she didn't have or know to successfully complete her tour on the drill field. She was able to use her strengths to build their weaknesses and use their strengths to build hers. Though it was the extreme discipline drill field, it provided her the opportunity to meet a need and build genuine relationships with women, some of whom she is still friends with today.

Latonia was able to establish relationships with her male comrades in the military as well, but she found that no matter how she established a relationship with a male, it inadvertently always helped to serve and befriend a female—his mother, sister, friend or wife. Proof: While we were in Okinawa together, one of her fellow Marines was away from his wife and CWO3 Latonia Talley would help him pick out gifts for her. Remember, Tonia likes to shop and his wife preferred that he go shopping with Tonia because she knew her gift would be something she'd love to receive and not something like a blender or a thigh master. *I knew one Devil Dog who gave his wife a vacuum cleaner. Poor fella. Poor lady.* But I will tell you, Tonia's relationship with her fellow Marine and friend was so meaningful, he and his wife flew from California to Virginia to attend Tonia's retirement ceremony and I was able to meet them. His wife was so cool and she had the most gorgeous wine-colored Coach bag I had seen. I wondered if Tonia had sold him at the Kadena exchange, too, with that "Is she worth it?" line. But she connected with them in a way that when I met them, I could be friends with them, too. We connected on social media and still communicate! (Here's a toast to DJ Kool and "*Let Me Clear My Throat!*")

SOCIAL BUTTERFLY ON A MISSION

So being one to help, to serve, to be an expression of Semper Fi and building people up by building relationships with them didn't stop when she retired. Her spirit of servitude, hospitality, gift of inclusion, unbridled camaraderie, and genuine desire to see other people do well has blossomed like wildflowers on Miracle Gro. Because she was able to retire before the age of forty, Tonia decided to continue her service to the federal government and to the Marine Corps as a civilian. She is an analyst for the Marine Corps at Quantico, Virginia. One would think federal service would be enough, but I am convinced that she only works to earn an income to finance her gift of service… oh yeah, and to shop and travel sometimes. Why not! Not only is she echoing the servitude that she saw her mother express, she is also a bridge, teaching her daughter to serve by doing as she does and as she says!

Tonia: I have to leave a legacy and a road map so my daughter can see a clear path of what it means to give back. God has blessed us and we have been given a good life, and my husband, Henry, and my daughter, Paige, are my biggest supporters. I was serving before I became a part of social organizations in a sorority, but I must admit that those organizations allow my service and desire to be of help to increase exponentially. I not only build relationships with those I serve with, but I intentionally build relationships with those I serve. I am a proud member of Delta Sigma Theta Incorporated. I am a member and now serve as second vice president of Top Ladies of Distinction (TLOD), and my daughter serves within that organization as a Top Teen of America (TTA). I am also proud to be a member of The Links, Incorporated. I am an active member of all three organizations because they serve differently and I want to cover all my bases. Each organization meets different needs, be it hosting a charity event, participating and fund raiser, charity walks, giving of my own finances, helping the elderly, participating with literacy programs, caring for the homeless, providing resources for women who have been abused, providing food, clothing and even school supplies for children whose parents don't have the means, and simply being a light for someone who can't see their way to betterment or greatness.

This is who I serve and serve with, but my child is why I serve. People often ask me how do I keep it all together, how do I pull a full-time 9-to-5, serve within three major organizations, still have time for my family, still have time for personal relationships and, most of all, still have time for myself. I've had many people refer to me as a social butterfly and I gladly accept that I fit that description. But one of the ways I keep my wings intact is not forgetting about the relationship I have with me! I am a soldier for self-care. I will tell you I am a priority when it comes to feeding my mind, soul and spirit with good things, serving my body with manicures and pedicures done consistently, getting my hair done, getting a massage, going shopping or taking a trip because I cannot be to other women what I am not first to myself and for my family.

I pray a lot. I know God, and God knows me—that's first—and I know me. Also, being organized keeps my responsibilities balanced. Knowing who I am keeps my life balanced and knowing that my husband and my daughter are supporting me keeps my life balanced. I serve myself not to be self-serving as some may think, but I serve myself so that I can pour into people from my saucer not my cup. Serving and building relationships and friendships is not only what I do, but it's who I am, which makes me not forget myself. Not only myself, as in just "me," but also parts of myself that I have seen in other women. I also have to balance knowing what I need, and what I need from other people. You see, I have relationships in my life that give to me and serve me, too. My husband is my lover and best friend, and my daughter is my heart. My mom was my example and I knew I wanted to be more than that, not more than her, but I wanted to serve even greater and make her and my dad proud. It wasn't only about getting the bachelor's degree I promised her or earning my master's degree, but balance comes from letting relationships educate me so that I could help teach others.

My friendships serve me, too, because they allow me to be

myself, they allow me to let my hair down and relax, they allow me to share my weaknesses and don't treat me any different or judge me, and they allow me to grow without them feeling intimidated. I attribute that not so much because of what I've done, but because of the relationships, including my relationship with God and all the others I have had and do have. I attribute it to being mentored and showing my gratitude by being a mentor, even to my own child by leaving her a legacy of knowing how to express her gratitude through serving and giving.

Now do you see what I mean by social butterfly? I think about Denise Williams singing "Black Butterfly." Not just someone who's breathing air, sashaying into an elitist-filled room to take up space to go to the next party or dress-up in the trendiest gown, although Tonia can do that, too. But she uses her social gifts and qualities in areas that matter to let people know they matter and they are worthy. I'm glad to call Tonia my friend and she calls me hers. Knowing that we're still so much alike and still in some ways a very different, I appreciate who she is because she shows me what's possible for many. Her life is proof to my life that women have do and will get along.

Implementation Guides: What if your friendship starts out rocky? What if you outrank men? How well do you get along with women? Men have issues with one another too, why do you think that is seen differently? How can you connect, professionally, without competing? Who taught you to serve? What legacy are you leaving? Because you serve, how are you being served? How does mentorship benefit relationships with women? Who can benefit from coaching and mentoring? What can't a woman do? How do I not lose myself?

Chapter Twenty-Three

Relationships to Ponder—Social Media

Dear Social Media:

You are indeed a force to be reckoned with and now that I have acknowledged you as such, I believe it's time for me to "reckon." Let me start by reminiscing how you and I became acquainted. According to your records, it all started on October 11, 2008. I got an email from a beautiful friend named Camille Ferguson who wanted me to see recent pictures of her children. I had moved to Japan in 2002 and hadn't seen her since. She didn't have the pictures stored on her PC, so she asked me had I ever heard of you. I had, but I was only familiar with chat rooms and I was skeptical and didn't really know what you were all about. But I wanted to catch up with her. I missed her and her children; I trusted her and took a chance on you. I am grateful and I thank her and you too.

It's been years since you and I were introduced and during that time, our relationship has allowed me to connect with relatives, classmates, reconnect with old friends and be introduced to new ones. I could see their pictures, be aware of things they wanted to share and you helped me not to forget their birthdays. Through your existence, I have come in contact with some amazing people! A few of my closest connections I have now is because of you. I have been able to share some of my best thoughts, pictures and events with them as well. I am grateful and I thank you. You were so cool to me because you were later introduced to me as a conduit to promote my businesses. I could let my relatives, my friends; old and new, network colleagues, potential clientele and the "public" know about the services I offer and how I would love to assist them in every way my purpose and missions will allow. Incredible! I am grateful and I thank you. I recently wrote my second book and, you guessed it, you were one of the main outlets I used to get the word out about it and sell it! I am grateful and I thank you.

I've been thinking about all of those wonderful benefits I have received because of you, and I was wondering: Why in the world would you do all of that for me…for free? Well, like I said, I've been thinking… Maybe I'm alone in this, but I don't think you are free anymore. Let me tell you why, and please correct me if I'm wrong, but here's my "reckoning." I know it's hard for you to keep up with the millions of people who have signed up to use your services, especially when so many of us have so many *friends, followers, grams and links*. But my friend who introduced me to you, and I don't know how or when it happened, but I don't get to see her anymore. For some reason, her information is no longer automatically available to me. I understand that you can't let me see everybody, but I think it's costing me for you to decide who my friends should be. Yeah, yeah…I know. You're going to say that you let me see who I communicate with most, and that may have been true at some point in time, but that's not the case anymore. You're making us seem antisocial and accept being non-relational!

Also, when it comes to my business page, I really feel like you are suppressing the relationships with my contacts because you now want me to pay dearly for advertising to *boost* what I had been saying for free. Don't get me wrong, I know you have to eat and feed your family, too…or do you? When did you get greedy and controlling? You assume who wanted to see and who didn't and it's gotten murky and people started to have face-to-face social relationship issues because they thought their *fans, grams, links* and *friends* weren't communicating. All the while it was you. Those are just a few of the things I wanted to reckon with you about. I know you have way more friends, support and money than I do, so I know you wouldn't miss me if I left. Truth be told, most of my *fans, grams, links* and *friends* may not either. But the most important thing I want to do is apologize to you.

I want to apologize for four years ago when I was playing your games too much, too long, making you work via my laptop, PC, tablets, phones and being mad with you when you moved slow and didn't act right. I want to say I'm sorry for using you as a substitute for authentic relationships, even with my friend who introduced me to you. She and I could have spent so much face-to-face time together rather than staring at monitors and screens. I want to apologize to you for helping people only share edited pictures of their edited lives. I am so sorry for being with you when I could have been with real people, forming real relationships in real time. For becoming addicted to aspects of whom you are and hiding behind you to avoid the work, responsibility and privilege it takes for real relationships, I apologize.

For every time I didn't make eye contact with someone who was talking to me because I was using my phone to check on you, my texts and emails, I apologize. I stopped that three years ago, but I'm still sorry. I hope they will forgive me. The people I used to see at the gym who can't work out without you, families, lovers and friends I see in restaurants that aren't holding conversations or even enjoying a meal because they can't talk or eat without being all up in your business...my apologies. But you know what I just thought about? You have managed to accomplish some pretty incredible things! You do help raise money and awareness, connect people from all over the world, spread just as much news and questionable hearsay as you do gossip; and while you're at it, would you work on stopping cyber predators, bullies and hackers? Don't knock yourself out, that's just a thought. I know you have to crush candy, dash diamonds, farms to sell, cafes to create, poker to play and targets to hit.

Since we met, there are probably some other things I took for granted and it didn't dawn on me that we are going to have to break up unless I am in control of you. By my being in control there are some things I have to do that won't involve you at all. As a matter of fact, it may give you some much needed space. I'll start with taking down some of the things I put on the wall. I thought it was *my* wall, but since we're reckoning, I see now that it's been yours all the while. I'll have to remove people who befriended me just to increase their count and I'll remove myself from people who I can't really count on. Boy, I think that'll take me down around to... (sigh) I'm almost scared to say. So now, I've reckoned and apologized, I won't wait for you to do the same. I'll just give you more space and give my relationships more face.

Implementation Guides: You know your social media, cell phone and other technological gadget habits (or not). What are your relationships with them like? This time create your own questions.

Chapter Twenty-Four

Freedom Reigns

"Relationships based on obligation lack dignity."

—Wayne Dyer

THE TRUTH ACCORDING TO NICOLE WINSTEAD

Many people who know Nicole Winstead call her NiCo, and so do I. When I met her almost seven years ago, and began to listen to her truth, it caused me to listen to another life. I listened to a life in another language, a language I could barely translate and was initially intimidated and, honestly speaking, offended by. Yet, I was intrigued enough to listen to the whole matter, the entire story of her life. That's when I realized the language she was speaking was freedom. Some of it was foreign, yet some of it was akin to my fears, whether I liked it or not. Her truth shows up in the form of an articulate, beautiful, bold, and bald by choice, black woman. Now that's what she sounds and looks like, but this is who she is…

NiCo: If I had a clue as to all I was, I would be a millionaire or not on this earth. I will be forty-eight years old this year. I discover more about who I am daily and I am a work in progress, always. I discover things about who I am within every moment with anything that I do. But for the purpose of this book, I am a black woman who has two children, which makes me a mother, who has never been a wife, who is always a friend and a lover at some point in time. I have many talents. I'm an artist, and I'm a graphic designer by trade. These are the things that I do. I am very creative and I love to write. I grew up in a household with two parents. My father was a physician and my mother was an executive. I was born on the East Coast, but I've traveled throughout the United States. I've always been a free soul and a free spirit. I am a wrong word in the mind. I like to roam a lot and I like to read. And I am polyamorist. I lived in California for about twenty years, until around ten years ago. There, I was in an abusive relationship with my children's father, verbal and physical. I was also in an emotionally abusive relationship with my mother. One day things came to a head with me; my mother, my children's father and I decided to leave California. My mother and father had gotten into an argument and I remember my mother blurted out something about my father that should have never been said in front of me, my children or my father. That statement erupted into an argument. We were just fussing at each other and I remember my oldest child, Chase, getting scared. He got scared and picked up the phone and said if we did not stop arguing he was going to call 911. My mother was trying to get the phone away from him and he ended up getting knocked down. I remember my mother and my oldest child tussling with each other over the phone. Something clicked; I had had enough and didn't want to be there anymore. I didn't want to be in California, I didn't want to be with them anymore and I didn't want to feel suffocated anymore.

That was in April 2004 and I did not return back to California until March 2011 to visit. Now, I have seen my mother since because she would come to visit me and we talked in between. I let things go. When I first moved away with my sons, Chase and Ransom, it was a breath of fresh air. I could sit on my carport, drink a cup of coffee in peace, watch the squirrels go by, watch the birds and enjoy looking at the rain. It was home to me. And I think everybody is trying to escape from something and that's how we all can relate to some degree. And once we escape we have to decide what makes us click. I had to decide my core desires, and what I really wanted to feel. And that's not something we are really taught. We are taught to go along with the flow and we're not taught to think about and articulate how we really feel, that day or that moment.

We have to figure out how we want to feel in every moment. Do you want to feel safe? Then you have to examine that moment. It requires honesty. It requires you to get someone to help you walk through the process and break down what that means and what it looks like. Sometimes it may take pen and paper to write down things, and you work from what didn't work to what does. That is self-discovery and I tried to walk myself through it, but that wasn't working. And I ran across a young lady named Danielle LaPorte who wrote a book called The Fire Starter Sessions. I tried to read that book over and over and over again, and it didn't really work at that time. But she wrote another book called The Desire Map, and that is what began to help me. Her workbook helped me walk through all the desires I had, all of the words, and allows you to delve into having an honest relationship with yourself. This desire map affected my relationships and based on a normal perception it was not in a good way.

SECOND SELF VESSEL

NiCo: It's been extremely difficult for me. There are people and relationships that I walked away from. I even walked away from someone I was in love with because it wasn't healthy. It helped me see that at the end of the day, I am the most important thing. When it comes to relationships, I truly believe that if you don't have an honest relationship with yourself, any other relationship you experience will be a lie. When you walk into lies, a lot of unraveling happens. There is a lot of energy that's not correct, a lot of energy that's false. And as that relationship begins to unravel, the real you begins to show up and the other person stands there and says, 'Who are you and where did you come from? Are we friends?' I remember looking up the word friendship and dissecting the two words. And the word "friend" means second self. The word "ship" means vessel. So I see friendship as having a second-self vessel. But you can't have that authentically if you don't have an honest relationship with yourself, which is the most important relationship.

TracyMac: Nicole I have never heard the word friendship broken down that way. Thank you for sharing that. So when you see that relationship with self is the most important you decide to connect with a second self. You mentioned a word that some may have never heard of or others have only heard of from one perspective. You mention the word polyamorist. Tell us what being a polyamorous is about.

NiCo: I try to stay away from the rote definitions of things but explore. Polyamory to me means loving more than one person. And with some people, the first thing that comes to mind means that you're having sex with everybody. That's not the case. That is polysexual. There is a difference. Polyamory is when you love more than one person and everybody in this world is polyamorous. We all love more than one person and we love many people many different ways. But when it comes to being polyamorous, love is lateral. When you start getting into the marks of possession or saying, 'This is mine,' you start to water down what love is. We give degrees and levels so we can give it its importance and that's where the problem is. I don't see the difference of loving you, or loving my mate any differently. But if we're talking sex then that is a whole different level because TracyMac is not bisexual or polysexual, so we're not going to sleep together, but we can still love one another. And if I called you, you would be there for me, and that to me is love. Now I am also polysexual. And again, that means more than one, and I will have sex with more than one person.

POLY WHAT?

TracyMac: Now wait a minute, NiCo, you are an unmarried woman. And on behalf of some readers or listeners, you are supposed to be married and you're not supposed to be having sex outside of wedlock and definitely not with more than one person. Do you?

NiCo: Hell yeah!

TracyMac: At a time?

NiCo: I have. I have had sex with more than one person at one time. And I have had sex with more than one person at a time.

TracyMac: But do you feel this is every way of wrong in the eyes of society? How do you justify this lifestyle?

NiCo: I don't. I don't justify it because if I were to justify it that would mean that somewhere I believe the rules that have been placed out there and I don't, and that would mean I have some type of judgment and I don't.

TracyMac: I am sure you have gotten ridiculed or the side eye from people who realize this is a lifestyle you embrace. What is your response?

NiCo: I usually don't have one. People will ask me questions, but they're usually not direct questions. The question I usually get is about marriage and monogamy. And my usual response is that I don't, just like I don't believe in heterosexuality. I believe that people should follow their bliss and be happy with whatever they're doing without there being a definition or a label.

TracyMac: Knowing that most of the world, especially the culture we live in—whether it's religious, American, and African-American—usually does not embrace that lifestyle at all. In some cases, it is not heard of within our community this way. When you hear that someone is having sex with multiple partners, people are going to say they are a freak or a whore, especially a woman. So you're saying you don't limit love or who you have its sexual expression with?

NiCo: Correct.

TracyMac: So what is your ideal relationship? Do you ever see yourself in a monogamous relationship?

NiCo: I have been in a monogamous relationship. For the most part, I usually start my relationships off being monogamous and that's by choice because I need to get to know the person who I am with. So I do not open myself up to another person coming into the relationship until I have found a comfortable niche and really get to know who they are and who I am with them.

TracyMac: So are you up front with people when you enter into a relationship?

NiCo: Yes I am.

TracyMac: And what is their usual response? Especially as a woman?

NiCo: I usually get a very happy and elated response. I wonder why? They get wide-eyed and they say they want to be on board. And they say I'm good with it. And then something changes. There is a particular juvenile meltdown that happens with some men that I've noticed and experienced. While they say they are good with it, then experimental portion kicks in and they usually say, 'Why don't we try introducing someone else?' And I'm usually the agreeable one to say, 'Absolutely, that works for me.' We do it; we get together and have a sexual encounter. It's usually pretty good. But then something clicks within the gentleman and it turns into almost greed. And it seems he wants to include another and another and another. But then, when I usually open myself up, I open myself up to more than just a sexual encounter with the next partner we have. There is love involved. We are building a healthy relationship together. Then there becomes a problem with the first gentleman that I was seeing. And it turns into jealousy and possessiveness.

TracyMac: So in a nutshell, you're saying some men, from your experience, can handle it when they are polysexual, but it becomes difficult when they realize you are polyamorous and love is involved. So the ideal relationship with you is...

NiCo: To have another me. To have that second-self vessel. Someone who can walk into the relationship with honesty because I'm not asking for someone who will accept everything that I want or do. I want someone who's going to be adult and human enough to say, 'This bothers me. Let's talk about it.' I'm not saying that my emotions and feelings are all correct, but I am saying this is where I am, can we talk about it? I like communication. And I am a good communicator. I like to talk and express myself. So I am looking for that second-self vessel.

TracyMac: Got you. So, looking for the ideal relationship or partnership, whether it is professional or personal, how does this lifestyle affect your purpose in life? And how does it affect your relationships, past or present? Or how does it affect having your ideal relationship?

NiCo: Who I am, what I believe my truth is in this moment, I think it has affected my relationships and not such a great way. Because I am a bit esoteric. I've heard more than once—which sometimes gnaws me to the bone—that I'm not from here. People have said I'm not from this planet. So it gives me the idea that I'm a bit too much for the relationship that I'm in, that I'm not really understood. I think eventually at some point in time,

I'll end up meeting people or someone who will understand that I am from this planet and I am of this planet. I have something to offer if they can just sit long enough to try to understand. So I think that at some point in time, I will affect someone in the most positive way. But in past relationships, not so good. Now I will say that some of the gentlemen I have been in relationships with, that a lot of the things that I shared with them throughout my life, has helped them. And they say they wish they had listened or did things differently.

TracyMac: Sometimes when people talk about being homosexual, bisexual and even polysexual, that it consumes every part of their lives. People sometimes dismiss that they have families, work and other very acceptable and common aspects of their lives. So even though this may be only a part of your lifestyle, what are you passionate about, what is your life's mission?

NiCo: I am very passionate about the arts. I am passionate about children. And I'm passionate about truth. I am really interested in helping people find their own truth. Not the way I want them to find it, but I want them to just find it. Whatever road they need to travel, I want to help them do that. I'm interested in being helpful toward them finding it. I have always been a free spirit and I am grateful. And even though my parents tried to squash some of that free spirit, they gave me some very beautiful lessons. I know this is going to get me in trouble, but I am so grateful that they never raised me in the church or with religion.

WHAT ABOUT JESUS?

TracyMac: Uh oh! Someone is saying, 'That's why she's polysexual. She's a freak, she doesn't know God, she doesn't know Jesus and she's never been in the church. We need to get her saved.' What would you say to that voice?

NiCo: I would have to ask: What is working for them? What is working for the church? What is working for their community? Is religion really working? Can they walk into a place without judging someone based upon religion? Because I can walk into a room and do that. I can walk into a room and not judge and not base it on religion.

TracyMac: So even though you weren't raised in the church or with religion, how do you feel about it? Whether people are Christian, Muslim, Hindu, believe in Shintoism, Buddhism and the different denominations within Christianity and there are many, how do you feel about those areas?

NiCo: I think the message from these writings and teachings are so beautiful. But I think the structure of religion is what has affected this world and the interpretation of those religions. Because religion has affected me, though I did not grow up in the church because of who I am, I am judged constantly. Religion permeates everything. It permeates our government, our children, it is everywhere. It has infiltrated everything. So it has affected me. Though I am spiritual, I am not religious. I think spirituality lies within a person, it is a layer of who you are where you can go deep into who you are and pull love, faith and hope from that layer without any question, without having to reference a book for it. I think it is something you come into this world with. And I don't know that there are necessarily words that can define it. I know that may be very difficult for people, but I think one of the problems that we have in society is that we are so entangled in language that we are left without emotion and feeling. And I'm that type of person that goes by feeling more than I go by a rote word. Maybe that is the only way I can explain spirituality versus religion. Religion at this point is a written is a word and spirituality is more about feeling in trust.

TracyMac: There is a level of truth in every form of religion no matter the religion or a person's beliefs. The core commonality is that there is a greater power than that which is in us. In Christianity, we have Jesus, the Muslim faith has Mohammed and Eastern religions have Gandhi or Buddha. These are spiritual leaders that people all over the world embrace and worship. If you go back and read any of the sacred texts, the messages are the same. I'm reminded of India.Arie's song "One." The Christian in me, and maybe those who are reading or listening may be saying, 'But it's Jesus only, and everyone else is sacrilegious and you're going to hell.' Tell me, as someone who has not experienced being indoctrinated and religion, what does that sound like to you? What do you hear when you hear people say that?

NiCo: I hear regurgitation more than I hear anything. I don't find the emotion behind it. I don't find the truth behind that when it's said. There are too many questions that come up in my head. If there is only Jesus, then a baby in the womb does not know Jesus until you teach them about Jesus. Just like the Aborigines, they don't know anything about Jesus until you teach them about Jesus. So that's the case if Jesus is all in all and the end all to be all, then why is Jesus not everywhere at all times? It doesn't make sense to me. So if the baby in the womb has not been introduced to Jesus and the Aborigines doesn't know Jesus, then why don't they? Where is Jesus then? And I am not saying that Jesus didn't exist because there is plenty of evidence that He did. But I don't necessarily believe He is the ruler of all. I believe He was a great teacher of many, but I don't believe He was the ruler of all. We can make this as simple as the sun. The sun rises every single day and it touches everybody's lives no matter what. The Aborigines get up the sun is up. When the baby is in or out of the womb, the sun is up. I get up the sun is up. Someone in Alaska gets up the sun is up. That is the end all to be all that is something we all can relate to. That is something constant, intangible and relatable, and it touches everything in everybody. Jesus and religion on the other hand, not so much. He and other religions are a corner of teaching and a valid one. So I embrace the value of the teaching, but I don't believe that if I don't know Jesus or a particular religion that I am doomed.

TracyMac: Who are you to say these things?

NiCo: After being coached and having a lot of thought, our conversations and word pulling, I know I am freedom. I am a free spirit, I am a free thinker, I'm a free writer. I'm a free mother, lover, and just about everything I choose. That experience for me, to discover I was freedom, was difficult and scary, it was daunting. And it still feels that way on occasion. Yet it's been liberating, fun, sexy, exciting, and disturbing.

TracyMac: You would say sexy. So now realizing through our coaching experience that your spiritual identity is freedom, what do you look forward to doing from here? Where do you grow from here?

NiCo: I'm learning more and more that I want to help people find their freedom. Whatever that looks like. I'm learning how to touch people in their lives in a different way, to be less aggressive and more like the wind. Where they are caressed a little bit more and makes it easier to help them feel what they're supposed to be versus shoving them. I want to help people who feel they need to be or want them to be. So I'm looking forward to possibly doing coaching and training in the areas of sexuality and enlightenment. It feels like home when I talk about it and read about it. I am trying to figure how to delicately incorporate that because I do run an organization for youth. And that could be a little bit touchy. And I have to consider that.

TracyMac: Nicole, I appreciate your honesty. I appreciate the boldness about your honesty, at the risk of people thinking differently about me because of this conversation. But I know who I am and I know what I believe. It is because I know who I am and I know myself that no one or their beliefs are a threat. I believe that if people were more honest and forthright about their beliefs we would all be much freer. We would all experience relationships in a greater way. So I appreciate who you are. And I am grateful we can have the conversation and thank you for allowing me to experience your reality. This is your truth. If people agree with it, it is enlightening and if they don't agree with it, it is enlightening because that is what truth is. That is what truth does. And I as a coach and one who has coached you at one time, I know I am good at being non-judgmental and have the ability to accept people for who they are. I love you. I am grateful to know you exist in the world I'm grateful to know you as NiCo. I am grateful to know you as freedom, because it invites me to enjoy my own, unapologetically.

Implementation Guides: How do you define friendship? Do you only befriend those with the same beliefs? Why? Why not? What is your truth? How can someone be polygamous and not be polysexual? How do you express your freedoms? What do you believe about Jesus? What about religion? How can someone be spiritual without religious influence?

Chapter Twenty-Five

Relationships to Ponder—Music & Laughter

Dear Music:

I have loved you since the first time I remember hearing you. You played into my life and spoke to me like a sister, brother and best friend. Do you realize you were my friend before I had any others? I met you, you met me, and we hit it off from the start and have been connected— spirit, soul and body—ever since! Not only did you teach me to listen, but it was because of you that I could hear my own voice. I sang through a microphone before I ever used one to speak. You know half…okay, more than half the reason I used to enjoy going to church so much was because of you. As a little girl, I'd lay on the floor in front of the faux wood Panasonic speakers and listen to you all day. My mom played her gospel albums: James Cleveland, Walter and Tramaine Hawkins, Andre Crouch and so many others. My dad played his jazz and I'd hear songs like "My Funny Valentine," singers like Ella Fitzgerald, instrumentalists like Miles Davis and Herbie Hancock. I learned how to sing three and four-part harmonies at six and seven years old. I listened to songs over and over just to pick out the different instruments and stay with each one throughout the entire song and then do again for the next. I'd lay there and my imagination would allow me to see Daryl Coley, The Clark Sisters, B. B. King and Louis Armstrong in the light on the speaker. They all would be rockin' the house!

I remember during some of the most awkward times as a teenager, you were my bestie! I'd listen to radio show host Burke Johnson and "Inspirations Across America" every Sunday morning. I loved it. You came to me through Fred Hammond, Commissioned, The Winans, Take Six, Special Gift and so many others I patterned my love for you after. I'd lean my cassette tape recorder against the speaker of my boom box to make my weekly mix tape. Yep, that was the only mix tape I was going to get because we couldn't listen to secular music. Well, we weren't supposed to. But I would put my clock radio in my bed with me, cover my head, turn the volume down really low and lay the side of my face on the speaker and listen to Q97 FM out of Kinston, North Carolina. There I heard Cool Moe Dee, MC Lyte, Slick Rick, and Queen Latifah. I fell in love with songs like "Let's Wait A While" and "Control" by Janet Jackson. I woke up most mornings with lines on the side of my face because of you. I danced a little, but not too much because I wasn't supposed to be doing that either, other than the "charismatic bunny hop" or my "shout" and I practiced that – in heels. But dancing was overrated, why dance when you could hum along or as Musiq Soulchild would write much later, "Juslisen." I would just listen. Then, in the late '80s, you let me start writing about how I felt and I was able to create you, teach you and sing your lyrics a little. That was so empowering. I don't write lyrics or sing as often or as well as I used to, and I never did get back to playing that old stinkin' piano. But I don't think there's a genre of you I can't appreciate, but I do like some much more than others. Thank you for not taking that as prejudice by my way to express Music Appreciation.

You have so many people I love and appreciate who do you, oh so well, like: Snarky Puppy (every band member is over the moon!), Ledisi, India.Aire, Kim Burrell, Goapele, Raheem Devaughn, Nikki Ross, Lalah Hathaway (that chick can sing a freakin' chord!!!), Isaac Carree, Tori Kelly, Norman Brown, Jill Scott and so many, many others. And I have friends who are some of the best musicians and singers in the world!! I sing and play through them because I found another way to teach the world to sing, and that's through relationships. I help people write the music for their own lives, listen to and help them connect their parts, play their heart strings in concert so others who want to can sing along! Music, I thank God for you, all of you.

LAUGHTER

Dear Laughter:

Without you, I know I would be sick. You are a good medicine indeed. There have been times I've overdosed on you and the side effects were tears, loss of voice, back of the head aches, windedness, receiving dirty looks and the inability to speak to explain why. I blame myself, my family and friends. Sometimes I can't let out like I want because it's not appropriate to and my smile gets stuck trying to quiet you and my cheeks hurt so badly. Some of the craziest times I've had with you were caused by my brother and sister, my parents, my aunts, uncles and cousins. No one can beat our sense of humor and the jacked up, yet true stories, that create it. If we got paid for real-life comedy and laughter, we'd shut the World Bank down! I promise, they have used you so skillfully at times, I have almost passed out! Take it easy on me, please. I enjoy when you allow me to use you to help people not be so hard on themselves or take life too seriously. I know life is not a joke, but being able to include you during some of the most traumatic times makes it so sweet. I thank God for creating you; God's got a way and it is mighty sweet and it has a whole lot to do with you. I've gotten mad with you because you've gotten me into trouble. My mother, teachers and an employer have had to kindly ask me to leave the area because they knew you were about to erupt. I've gotten much better. I love how you let our teeth escape from behind the prison of our lips and it beautifies better than any plastic surgery or make-up. There was a time I didn't know you like I know you now. I didn't trust you, but somebody messed around and we got together for too long and now we've become one. We's married now! When I come around you show up. Thanks! I love you. LOL

Chapter Twenty-Six

Relationships to Ponder—We Are Family

"The great enemy of the truth is very often not the lie, deliberate, contrived and dishonest, but the myth, persistent, persuasive and unrealistic."

—John F. Kennedy

When Owen retired from the military, we decided to move from Japan back to North Carolina. He initially wanted to move to the Havelock area and I wanted to move to Raleigh. We moved to the Havelock area with intentions of staying, but because of family situations and neither of us were able to find adequate employment there, we set our sights on Raleigh. That was a very rough patch in our lives; although I found employment Owen was still on terminal leave and had not yet gotten hired. Jayda was in kindergarten and she was so excited about school. She liked her teachers, we liked her teachers. She loved going to school and telling us all about it when we all got home! She made new friends and she was enjoying living at her new house. That was all she knew, and it mattered to us because that was all she needed to know. She did not need to know we were making less income, stressed from moving, family transitions were draining, uncertain and crazy as hell! Not only that, our marriage had gone through infidelities. I had become very ill in 2007. I had missed work so much in 2007 and 2008 that I was on leave without pay.

I was working for the state of North Carolina and my employment situation was far from ideal; it sucked actually. I wasn't coaching much because I had not built a clientele in this area and I had not completed a level of certification I felt I needed. I was also going to school full-time. Some days if it weren't for knowing my purpose, being laser focused on my mission and having Owen's support, I would have wound my head and scratched my watch. We were living in an apartment and once Owen started working, we started looking for a home. With everything that was going on, looking for a home was a way to give us the assurance that our little family of three was going to be okay. We were going to be okay as individuals, we were going to be okay as a married couple, and as parents we were going to be okay as a family. My family had grown apart, and because Owen moved away from South Carolina over twenty years prior, his relationship with his family had grown distant due to distance. I didn't have any family in Raleigh and the way I felt at that time I questioned everything about marriage and family anyway.

While we were in the process of looking at homes, Owen had to attend a training class in Roanoke, Virginia. I was browsing the Internet one day, and I saw the pictures of a house. I just had to go see it. I wasn't at all familiar with the area it was in and I don't remember if I had GPS on my Blackberry back then. But, I printed a copy of the directions off MapQuest and one day on my lunch break I just had to go see this house. It was a new subdivision and I wasn't sure if it was going to be affordable, but I went anyway. I drove up to the model home and the realtor was returning from lunch. We talked briefly and she showed me around the model. I knew instantly, the look, lot and location was what I wanted. I couldn't wait for him to get back! As soon as he got back into town, I immediately took him to go see the model. He liked it just as much as I did, if not more. He liked it so much he and Jayda drove past the house almost every day. I couldn't do it. It's hard for me to visualize a finished work while it was still under construction. I can do that with people's lives, but I can't do that with wood and concrete. So after about six months our home was complete and Macfamily3 moved in December 23, 2008.

It was more than just another move. I moved twenty-two times in my life. Between my father being a Marine, my moving about and Owen being in the Navy, moving had become old hat. But this was different. I knew that it was giving our little family a fresh start. I knew that it was going to give Jayda a sense of geographical stability. Owen knew that after spending twenty years in the Navy and having left Charleston at the age of eighteen that this would be home. We wanted Jayda to be able to play safely, so we chose a lot in a cul-de-sac. And we prayed that we would have great neighbors and that the neighbors would have children who she could grow up with and play with. That meant a lot to us. She is an only child and there won't be anymore. We agreed with the doctors on that.

MEET THE NEIGHBORS

We enjoyed such a peaceful, yet exciting Christmas that year. My health began to change for the better. We were even closer to Jayda's school. Owen had gotten promoted. I had gotten control of my schedule of going to work from eight to five, maintaining a 3.5 GPA, seeing clients and enjoying time with myself as well as being a mother and wife. And though everything was going quite well I still wanted to be able see Jayda play outside with friends, in the spring, and not have to ride her bike alone. There were only three other homes in the cul-de-sac at the time and from what we could tell there were no children. But a new construction was going up directly across the street.

One day I was in the kitchen cooking, and Owen came in the house and said, "I saw some people across the street and they have two little girls with them."

"Really!? Go back out there and tell me what they look like."

"No! They just saw me."

"Go act like you're checking in the mail box."

He, being just as nosy as I was, went outside and casually acted like he was checking the mailbox. He waved to them and they eagerly waved back. Owen is not one who takes to new folks too readily, but the next thing I know he was walking them through our front door. I almost didn't have time to put the blind down and run back to the couch!

They were a very friendly looking family. They introduced themselves as Bridggette and Richard Campbell. They had to little girls: Ashley, who is the same age as Jayda, and Amber, who is two years younger. I knew immediately that they were the answers to our prayers. When God answers prayers they show up as people. As soon as Jayda, Ashley and Amber were introduced they didn't hesitate becoming acquainted. Jayda said, "You want to come up and play in my room?!" I don't even remember them answering. I just remember the three of them disappearing up the stairs and hearing lots of soprano laughter. Two to three hours later, Owen, Ricky, Bridggette and I were still talking. In that conversation we realized that not only were they the answer to our prayers, we were the answer to their prayers, too. They started out as people you would want to go peek at from the mailbox to our friends. Now, they are our family and as I like to say "framily."

Chapter Twenty-Seven

Parenting and Family

"In every conceivable manner, the family is the link to our past and the bridge to our future."

—Alex Haley

THE TRUTH ACCORDING TO BRIDGGETTE & RICHARD CAMPBELL

Though things changed for the better with my immediate family and there is consistent connection with Owen's family, the Campbells are now our framily, too (friends who have become family). We hit it off from the start. We enjoy good times together. We have introduced them to our family and they have introduced us to theirs. We have traveled together and we enjoy fun times at one another's homes, having old school house parties. But what impacts Owen and I the most about the Campbells is that they embrace Jayda as if she is one of their own. It sometimes brings me to tears. Our daughter does not have many close-knit relationships with relatives, but it's something about her Uncle Roy and Aunt Jackie Smalls that she adores and the love expressed through reciprocated and consistent action is undeniable. Roy and Jackie are a beautiful couple and they effortlessly balance being down to earth, yet are pillars in their families and community. Jayda is also tightly connected with some of our cousins and God knows I love that. She doesn't have blood sisters, yet her cousins—Cameron and Kendall—behave like blood brothers. We have also have been blessed with friends who have filled voids that were in relationships. They are framily! Jayda has known her friend, Bineta Deme, since first grade and her mother, Ndeye Ndické Seck, aka Nikki, is one of the sisters in my tribe. Jayda enjoyed vacationing with them in Palm Springs this summer and had a ball! Not only the Campbells, but we have other framily members as well. But with them living across the street, there is a convenience, and our connection that their daughters are ours, too. I thank God for our relationship. I thank God for who they are, how they are and where they live!

MEET THE NEIGHBORS

Richard: You know, where we lived before we didn't know any of our neighbors. We wanted to be around families. You were the first family we met. And the way things clicked, I told Bridggette, 'We have found people we can relate to right off the bat. We are supposed to be here!'

Bridggette: You know, when we were standing outside talking to Owen, he said, "You all come on in the house," and I knew this was going to work out just fine because for us to be perfect strangers, and he invited us into your home, I knew that we were going to be all right. We came in and started talking, and I remember you were still in school at that time; you were sitting on the couch doing homework. And our relationship started that night and I knew that it would last for a long time.

TracyMac: I didn't have any skepticism like I normally do. Normally, after checking someone out, DEEP, especially when it comes to my child, I have to find out about them. One thing I admire is that you have a wonderful sense of family. My family can be distant. Even on my dad's side of the family there are relatives I had not seen since the '70s, and I didn't see them again until June 2014. I see that changing for the better and look forward to seeing them a lot more often! There are relatives in Portsmouth, Virginia I've not seen since I was a child. Now some of that has to do with the fact that my parents moved to North Carolina when I was about three years old. Other than one in 2011, I haven't known about or attended a family reunion since the O'Jays released "A Family Reunion" (1975). Ricky, I see you family has reunions, you are connected to your parents, Ms.

Lavern O'Neal and Mr. Richard Campbell, your school friends, and your church friends. I really admire that. What gives you such a connection of being with family?

Richard: Neither one of us had a normal upbringing. My mom raised me on her own and my dad was in and out of my life. Bridggette was raised by her grandmother, Mrs. Irene Perry. Her mom was there, but it her grandmother was really the key to her upbringing. So when we got together, we knew we both missed out on having a mother and father in the house, and we made an unspoken commitment to each other that we didn't want our children to come up the way we did. That has been the driving factor of our relationship: let's try to show our children the right way that family can be. I have friends who are like family, like with you. When I invite someone into my home, I have a connection with them. When we first met you, we started out cool at the very beginning, and that's never happened with another couple before. Both of us were able to befriend both of you. I have a strong bond with you and with Owen. We hang out as a family.

Bridggette: I have a strong commitment and sense of relationship with my family because my dad wasn't there and my mom had to work. She was a single mom who provided for me to make life better for me. At some point, my mom, Mrs. Nancy Brown, was working three jobs. So it was just me and my grandmother. With my mom working all the time, and my father wasn't there, I chose to make the best of those bonds. And I have a love for people and I'm a loving, caring and giving person. I am drawn to people and I love building a relationship, especially if they mean something to me in my life.

TracyMac: So many people didn't grow up with two parents in a home, maybe the parent was around but not consistently. Both of you have had that experience. So how did you make this decision? You had the awareness that you didn't have the example. How did you meet and how did you decide that you could pull it off and not know how?

Richard: Tracy, I'm going to tell the story because I'm going to tell the truth. I don't know if Bridggette will. We met back in 1992; I was in a singing group. And we were at this concert and the guys in my group were trying to sneak backstage. These two ladies came out of the bathroom and saw us plotting to sneak backstage. We talked to them and exchange names. But there was really no connection made at that point. About three months later, I was at a club here in Raleigh, and one of the guys who was in the group with me said, 'Hey man, do you remember that girl?' But, alcohol was involved and I really didn't remember, and I didn't want to hurt her feelings. So we exchanged numbers, but we never really got a chance to talk. So another month went by and I was back at the same club again, and I had the thought in my head, I wonder what happened to that girl. No sooner than I had that thought, I looked up and there she was standing in my face. I'm not a superstitious person, but I do pay attention to signs. Now, to answer the second part of your question: How do we decide how we will conduct our family? I don't think we ever sat down and said, 'This is how we're going to do it.' I think situations and scenarios popped up along the way, and we handled it not knowing that it was the proper road to go down. We took things from her childhood and my childhood and evolved them into what we have now.

Bridget: I know we didn't live in a two-parent home, but we felt that was a right way to live. I remembered The Cosby Show, and seeing the dad was a doctor and the mom was a lawyer. I wanted that. I wanted that love surrounding me and a sense of family on a daily basis. What played out on television was very influential for me.

TracyMac: Now the girls are growing up so fast. Ashley is in the eighth grade and Amber is starting the sixth grade. Tell me about parenting.

Bridggette: Parenting can be difficult. Ashley asked me the other day if she could get a Facebook page. And, I have this fear that I want to hold on to her as tightly as possible so she's not exposed to some of these things that could corrupt her. Then I thought about it, she's thirteen years old and though we do have to protect her, I know I can't hold the reins so tight because she's growing up. She's going to have to experience life and begin to make choices. I didn't answer her because I said we're going to have to talk to your dad about it. And that's what's important to me, that the two of us make decisions together that affect our children. We have to be on the same page and not going into different directions. We want them to go out in the world and be independent young women, so we have to work together and do a lot of praying!

Richard: Having daughters is different; it was just me and my mom growing up, so I know what it was like to live with a woman. But now, I have three women in my house. (Pray!) I know that there are some things I can't teach my daughters about being women. So issues that involve that, I leave that to Bridggette. But when it comes to discipline and other areas, I want them to know right from wrong. We are constantly being told how well-mannered and well-behaved our children are. And that lets me know that I'm doing something right. When a situation comes up sometimes I say, 'What would my mother have done?' And I find myself doing what my mom did. I think I turned out okay. Now I am not perfect. But if her method of parenting worked then that's what I draw from. When I asked her about things she told me she would talk to her mother and asked her mother questions about raising me. I hope that when my daughters become parents they will call me and Bridggette. I think a lot of the problems we have today is lack of parenting or bad parenting.

GOT BOTH PARENTS? NOPE!

TracyMac: Sometimes people use the excuse that they didn't have both parents as a reason not to be good parents.

Richard: I think Bridggette and I are examples to blow that out of the water.

TracyMac: But what about someone who may need encouragement, who came from a single-parent home? Talk to someone who may want to use being raised by a single-parent as a reason why they act out, or why they ended up in jail, or why they have dysfunction.

Richard: I think it has a lot to do with what you want to do in life. If you want to be good at something you will be good at it. If you want to be bad at something you will be bad at it. I didn't have my father in my life. Now I'm not saying he wasn't around because there was time for him to have weekend visits and he would pick me up. But if you want to be a good mother or father, you will take the negatives and turn them into positives and if you had positives in your passion will turn them into incentives.

TracyMac: What made you act on the positive and the incentives?

Richard: My mother encouraged me to do my best.

Bridggette: I think it has a lot to do with your morals and values. If you don't place the value in being the best mother that you could be…

TracyMac: *B*ut, Bridget, your mom worked when you were younger. You were raised by your grandmother in rural North Carolina and your father was not in your life. Can you really overcome that? Can morals and values really do all of that?

Bridggette: Of course they can! I knew in my heart that my morals and values helped me because even though my dad wasn't there, I couldn't just cry about it and have a pity party. I had to move on and live for Bridggette. I could not use that as an excuse. Once I graduated from high school and went to college, I wanted my family to be proud of me. I wanted my mother and my grandmother to be proud of me. So, I made that decision that this was what I wanted to do! As a matter of fact, I went back to school to get my master's degree because you were my inspiration. At forty years old, I knew this was what I wanted for myself. I made that determination and had the passion, the drive and my morals and values. You have to pick up the pieces and keep moving.

TracyMac: You both had "parental figures" in your lives. Where was the majority of your mentorship for your coaching when it came to those values?

Richard: When I finally got out on my own, I talked a lot to my dad. For a long time I had a lot of hostility toward him in my younger years. But as I got closer to manhood, I wanted to know my father more. I'm supposed to be able to go to my father for advice. He has given me good advice, and he has given me some not so good advice. I have used him as an example of what to do and what not to do. I told Bridggette on several occasions, as far as being a parent, I want to be almost the opposite of what my father was to me and to my brother and sister. My dad worked a lot and even though he would pick me up on his visitation weekends, I didn't see him. I was at his house, but he wasn't there because he was working. One time I asked him, 'Dad why you always working? I never get to spend any time with you.' My dad's philosophy, when I was younger, was, 'I work hard now so my children don't have to take care of me when I get older.' And that made sense to me back then. He didn't want to be a financial burden to his children. But it has backfired because my brother and sister don't want anything to do with him. He never formed a bond with them when they were younger. I work every day, but my children are going to see me and I am going to spend time with them! They may have to say, we may not have him right this moment, but he's definitely going to make up for it quick! I see how that line of thinking turned out and I don't do that. I don't want anyone to ask me how my children are doing and my answer be, 'I haven't seen them in a few years.' I have forgiven my dad. I had let a lot of stuff to let go. He wasn't around when I needed him. I don't need him now, I want him now.

TracyMac: You know, sometimes I think we forget our parents are people, too. They made decisions and did things we didn't understand. But I like the way you said you 'Use him as an example of what to do and what not to do.' So, he mentored you in a way that was positive and negative shaping. And that's wise. Not only to know that, but to deliberately be conscious of it and do it or not do it.

Bridggette: My mom was a mentor to me. When I was

younger our relationship wasn't as tight, but as I got older our bond grew a little tighter and I was able to talk with her. When I was in college, I remember her telling me, 'Bridggette, you have got to get out here and be successful and make it on your own.' I went to college and goofed off and acted a fool, I wasted her money. I ended up graduating and I wanted to follow in her footsteps. She was a hard worker, she was dedicated to her family and she was dedicated to the church and her children. When she had a relationship with my dad she was steadily trying to hold on and he didn't want to be committed. He wasn't ready to settle down and be a father. I saw how that devastated her because she tried for years until she decided to move on. Shortly after that, she met and married a man she thought she could save. He was a drug addict and she was in an abusive relationship with him. I watched her have to deal with that. She had to sneak out of the house to leave him. Early one morning my mom got her brothers to come over to help her move. She walked away that day and never looked back. Before she left him, he bankrupted her. Prior to meeting him she had a nice little bank account and she had something to show for all of her hard work. After that, I saw her pull herself up by her bootstraps and keep on kicking! My grandmother helped her and she was able to recover from that. But bless her heart, after recovering from all of that she was diagnosed with breast cancer. Even after being diagnosed with breast cancer I heard her oncologist say to her, 'Ms. Brown, you're going to have to take about six months off from work because you're going to have to have chemo and the radiation.' And she said, 'No, I'm going to work!' And sure enough, she did not miss any days of work. She would do her chemo treatments on Friday so she would have the weekend to recuperate and be back to work on Monday. I was able to have the verbal conversations with her and just watch her life. She was my mentor, teaching me that you could overcome anything. I knew that her footsteps were the ones I wanted to follow in.

TracyMac: You both have the positive situations and the challenges as examples with both of your parents. So what would encouragement would you give a parent, within a single-parent or two-parent household, or blended family who may read or listen to this?

Richard: You are going to make mistakes. Don't be afraid to make mistakes and be able to learn from them and move on. Realize that you are raising someone who is going to be a part of society, so you have to be conscious of the product that you are producing.

Bridggette: You also have to value your family. My mother was fifty-two years old when she passed. And, family is so important and not only biological family but those who you develop these tight bonds with. You have got to value those relationships. Because tomorrow is not promised to any of us so make the best of every day that you have with that person. There may be some ups and downs, but do what you can to foster success in that person. Be there for that person because we need each other. I firmly believe that is why God put us here, to serve one another and to be there for each other.

TracyMac: If a family member were to pick up this book ten years from now, what would you want them to read about what you have to say about family?

Richard: I want them to send me some money.

TracyMac: Lord, have mercy. Let me rephrase. If this book were put into a time capsule and someone had to come back and read what you said about parenting and family, what would you want them to know?

Bridggette: Family, blood or not, is the most important relationship you can have. I want to be there for my family as much as I can. Now, we should not be a doormat for abusive situations. But just being there to show love and support is what I would want them to know. Because our time with one another is so precious and we want to do what we can to make a positive impact on one another. We also need to make memories. We want to offer our children something to reflect on.

Richard: Ditto. People always say life is short. No, it's not. Life is long and you need to do as much as you can to enjoy it.

As far as parenting goes, have fun with your children. Sit around and laugh and joke and try to be everything your child needs in life. Because there is going to come a time when your child is going to have to choose between their family and their friends or someone outside of your control. And maybe that one instance, based on that time spent, they may say what would my mother or father want me to do? If you can get that, and they do it, then I think you've done a good job.

My relationship with the Campbells and other friends who have become family to me can be summed up like this: I know some people say blood is thicker than water, but framily are those who choose to be blood and the thickening comes from anyone who consistently lives the definition through being and doing.

Implementation Guides: Who are those who have become your framily? How well do we know our neighbors? What are some things you don't do that your parents did? Who do you go to for parenting advice? How can you overcome excuses society may allow you to have? How can you create memories with your loved ones?

Chapter Twenty-Eight

Spirituality Within Health and Wellness

"The first wealth is health."
—Ralph Waldo Emerson

THE TRUTH ACCORDING TO ERIC THORNTON

I don't know if it was because of his career in law enforcement, or his natural bent to be somewhat skeptical, but Eric was hesitant, asked a truckload of questions, researched and searched before he hired me to be his life coach. I can appreciate that as I'm the same way when it comes to the matters of my heart and decisions about my life. But, as a young boy, when Eric would wake up every morning, no matter what day of the week, which side of the bed or which window he looked out of, he knew he was waking up on the rough side of town. And though he had the love of his mother and his sisters, Eric learned at a young age what it meant to see his mother struggle to take care of her family. She did her best. His young heart was hard enough to survive that side of town, yet tender enough to understand and express compassion. He learned to balance the two extreme experiences of the heart wrenching and the heartwarming, but not without his share of heart aching. Eric was a good student, but his existence, especially on the wrong side of the tracks, would be short lived had there not been for a sanctuary to rescue him from becoming a statistic and a product of that environment. By that I mean a literal sanctuary, the church. Eric was able to find a way of escape through a relationship with God and music.

CHURCH FAMILY

As a musician, he was able to experience a sense of belonging, be a part of an extended family, and cultivate relationships with his pastor and other godly men who mentored him. Not having a father at home, those relationships meant a lot to him. But, most of all, Eric was able to come to know God through having a relationship with Jesus Christ. Now when he woke up in the morning, no matter what side of the bed, no matter what day of the week and no matter which window he looked out of, he had a relationship with God, a relationship with an extended family, a relationship with music and a relationship with church and religion. Eric was finishing up high school, and his initial desire was to join the military. Because of the closeness of mentoring and family relationships he had formed, he chose not to. There was something in him that wanted to help, protect and serve. There was something in him that wanted to become what he needed as a young man from the rough side of town. So to maintain the sense of family and to live in close proximity of his family, Eric decided to pursue a career in law enforcement.

Eric: Law enforcement was another avenue to help those in need. It played a role and was another way to express my compassion for humanity and another way to be a positive role model. I wanted to be of service to society. I am able to draw from the pressures and experience I had growing up. Some of the temptations and peer pressure I had in various situations helped me to be able to be understanding. I carry out the law, and I don't always have to approach it from the letter of the law, but I also use the spirit of the law to see a need, give a word of encouragement, talk to people on a personal level and establish relationships. I am a mirror, and we reflect one another through relationships.

Eric learned and saw a lot about relationships and the more he experienced the more questions he had. He started asking his questions to those he had the closest relationships with, which were his church leaders and mentors. Some of his questions were answered with great positivity, others were met with skepticism. Some of his questions were welcomed by a collective rejection, leaving him wanting and with more questions. Not knowing who else he could ask, Eric began to entertain the questions within himself, and initially, the answers eluded him there, too. He wasn't looking for answers to agree with him, as he didn't know what the answers would be; he was desperate for answers to satisfy the questions.

Dissatisfaction welcomed him to look at people and things outside the box, outside of his religious context and outside of a dogmatic approach. He began to accept those who were not accepted, and embrace and love those who may have been rejected, including himself. He was able to accept himself and others for who they were without pretense or judgment. His compassion for humanity, life, health, wellness and humanity intensified even though he was filled with questions and short on answers. In his early twenties, he had questions like: If God loves us all the same, why do we treat "them" differently? If we are to love our neighbors as ourselves, why do we judge them for sins that God has already forgiven? Long before Joan Osborne sang, "What If God Was One of Us?" Eric asked questions like that as well as, what if God is *all* of us? This awareness of these questions shifted his entire relationship with God and himself. He had even more questions, and he began to read and study. He shut down distracting relationships, spent more time in prayer and meditation, and writing. He decided to focus on himself and his spirituality, and that an awareness of God within himself. The more he became aware of another experience of spirituality, the greater the distance became between the relationships he had with the church, his church family and religion.

Eric: I so appreciate and value my foundational relationship with the church and religion. It is because of the lives of those who mentored me and helped me foster a relationship with Jesus Christ that I can stand firm with what I believe about God today. It was the gateway to what I know and understand about spirituality today. I love them dearly and am grateful to God for them.

Eric began to become more aware of the hopes and dreams and aspirations that he had for his life. He began to experience the answers that had once eluded him through self-discovery. He began to feed on a more inclusive relationship with God, which brought about a major lifestyle change of how he chose to enjoy a more holistic approach to nutrition spiritually, emotionally and naturally. Just like with spiritual food, it was becoming a matter of life and death for Eric to change his natural diet.

Growing up on the rough side of town and in the church, soul food was not only celebratory but an economic and budgetary necessity. Fried pork chops, fried chicken, homemade macaroni and cheese, rice and gravy, collard greens seasoned with fatback or ham hocks, candied yams, fried cabbage, fried corn, Jiffy cornbread, yeast rolls, homemade pound cake, peach cobbler and vanilla ice cream, sweet potato pie and top it off with a tall glass of red Kool-Aid or sweet tea. Some kitchens wouldn't be complete without a can of bacon grease nestled beside the stove. And just to set the record straight, soul food is not only a black thing and can be found anywhere, especially down south or in the country, white folks, too. It has so much charm, comfort and hospitality; it can exist anywhere and be enjoyed by anybody. It knows no prejudice and is very welcoming to everybody. Cookies, cakes, candy, sodas, chips and fast food have perfect attendance in many mouths and bodies. They enter the mouth like family and give the tongue a traitor's hug on the way down.

Once they pass the taste buds, palate and uvula, without moderation, they can wreak deadly havoc on the body. I know them all too well. Eric did too. Eric knew that one of the other ways he was to protect and serve was for the body. It isn't because he came up with some whimsical idea; he had to learn to live a healthier lifestyle from the things he suffered. He could see that his body was experiencing his past thoughts and actions. During his spiritual awakening, he also had a rude awakening to the fact that he had become overweight, had hypertension, was borderline diabetic, and had a severe case of sleep apnea, stress and depression. He realized his eating habits and his body were out of order.

HELP? POLICE?!

Eric: I knew I needed help. I knew I needed a lifestyle change. I had to make changes, food wise in nutrition and my mentality. It was a journey of trial and error. You have to know what works for you. I was dealing with stress on the job as well as in my personal life. I had to change how I dealt with challenges in life. There was a time I was so stressed out, I began having panic attacks. I had to get therapy. I know it's not common within the black culture; we generally don't believe in getting help. In some cases, a psychiatrist, psychotherapist, or a therapist or even a life coach is taboo, especially among black men. We may be okay getting a mentor, but the other avenues of help aren't as accepted. I needed to talk my problems out, and I had some hidden things I needed to deal with. I know people may think I'm supposed to be a strong black man, I am a police officer and I went to get help?! I am also a seeker of truth and whatever that truth is, if I need help with finding truth or getting help, I am going to find it. I had to get help, so I did! Initially, there was some shame and embarrassment, so I don't want anyone to think getting help was easy, it wasn't like I just had the courage. It was a challenge and I had to deal with those "taboo" thoughts about getting help for myself. When I had panic attacks, my heart rate would get so fast, I felt like I was going to die. That wasn't the reality. Getting therapy helped me differentiate between mind and body and also helped me understand how they are connected as well. I would have thoughts or have arguments with people in my head and it would trigger my emotions. The therapy helped me understand what the anxiety was all about.

Hey! Don't just look at Eric. You know, it's not on the lips on our faces we have to contend with, it is the mouth of our minds that set the tone for our lives, through our bodies. According to the truth of Eric, health has to be experienced from a holistic approach. He has taken the ability to successfully deal with stress, health, confidence, low self-esteem, to get out of the normal cultural mind conditioning of diet and thought. Our behaviors are learned. Some folks have the behavior of eating an unhealthy Sunday dinner, watching football and catching a nap. A similar scenario plays out other days of the week. It may not be so much about what we weigh, but are we healthy? Are we well enough to carry out our purpose and mission? I don't have to quote statistics. Some of our foods are filled with toxins, as are some medications. Not only do you have to recover from an illness, you have to recover from the medicine you took to recover from the illness. I am a witness. Have mercy!

What we eat and everything centered on being well thrives in all aspects of life. Health and wellness affect how you carry out and relate to your personal and professional life, family, financial, emotional, spiritual, how you express yourself. It affects knowing who you are, your purpose, and it can determine how well we are able to overcome or even prevent challenges.

Eric: As a wellness coach and a certified physical trainer, it's not about how many pushups my clients can do and how many miles they can run nor is it only about diet. But I offer a deliberate conditioning for the body to express the mind and the spirit. Just like poor health, disease and death cross lines, health and wellness cross gender lines, racial lines, geographical lines and segregation fostered by religion and economic status—your spirit, soul and body are created to work together in tandem. You have to go beyond the place where you've always had a struggle. So as a wellness coach, I integrate spiritual awareness that does not take on the characteristics of any religion, church or denomination, but I support each person's unique consciousness of who God is and use that to positively shift their physical wellness. God has given you power to speak to your body and tell it what to do, and when you are spiritually aligned and follow through with physical action and proper healthy habits, a lifestyle of wellness is inevitable and will be evident. Relaxation, prayer, stillness and meditation are just as important as consistent movement and nutrition. Health and wellness can save your life. It's not only what we feed our bodies, because we have many gates: ears, eyes, mouth and mind. What are we hearing, seeing, saying and thinking? What negative energies are you still allowing yourself to entertain?

Implementation Guides: How can your career be used to express compassion for humanity and be of service for community and society? How do feel about a law enforcement officers? Who protects and serves them? Why would a black man need therapy? What do you know about life coaching vs. therapy? What is your relationship with your health, holistically? How can you tell your body what to do? How can you take better care of yourself—spirit, soul and body?

Chapter Twenty-Nine

Relationships to Ponder—Abuse

Dear Abuse:

The first thing that comes to mind when I think about you is someone being sexually or physically abused, and I don't know a damn thing about that. Some of my friends do and "WOW" is the best way I can describe their experiences. They are truly heroes and SHEroes in my book! Not because they were abused, but because they've gone beyond it. They maturely speak about their pasts with you. Because I didn't know about you from a sexual or physical experience, I figured I didn't know you at all. Then I had to get real with myself and see how I knew you every time I allowed aspects of collective interpretations of religious perceptions to abuse me, or when I used to beat myself up and allow my negative self-talk to treat my mind so badly that it wanted to seek out shelter. Every time it tried to take cover I'd show up there, too. The beauty of my mind was afraid to be alone with me but I was everywhere I was. It's something we've all done or do and it can be difficult to stop. But it can be stopped. One of the arresting officers of self-abuse is self-discovery. The incriminating witnesses are purpose, mission and passion. The judge, jury and verdict are accountability, healthy relationships and implementation. Abuse, I also knew you in the name of dependability because when people knew I was dependable, for some reason they felt they didn't have to be. There's just an innate part of me that wants to help and support people I know; if they need me, I will be there. But that can also be a character flaw.

I would sacrifice myself to show up for people and when it came to me, they thought I had it, or assumed someone else was supporting me. Most never asked and I would tell them no different. I taught them to treat me that way and gave them permission to abuse the relationship, by not requiring reciprocation from them. Their support didn't have to be equal giving, but at least attempt to make an equal sacrifice. Purpose taught me how to filter my relationships, personally and professionally and to stop creating dysfunction for you to ride in on. It only took one question and a statement for me to stop being taken for granted and taken advantage of. The question I ask is: How can I serve or be of help to you? And the statement I make is: What I need from you is…

Abuse, it's something how you go away whenever self-discovery is present, especially when I ask that question and complete that statement to myself.

Implementation Guides: What is your relationship with abuse? Ask three to five of your closest, personal and professional relationships: How can I serve or be of help to you? Then, make the statement: What I need from you is… Don't be so hard on them or yourself, if this is new. Maybe you can use it as a catalyst to spark a depth of conversation. If you really want to fortify the relationship, do it often and be creative.

Chapter Thirty

Beyond Survival

"Faith is about trusting God when you have unanswered questions."
—Joel Osteen

THE TRUTH ACCORDING TO ROBIN WHITE

I can't remember the exact date, but I do recall checking my Facebook page and there was a message from Lavender Rose, inquiring about my coaching services. "LavendeRose" was Robin White, and after being in a relationship with Robin, if anyone ever asked me about her, the first thing that would come to mind is that she is a woman of faith. There is no doubt she loves the Lord and has no shame about living a Christian lifestyle, and will offer to help you live one, too, if you would like. I'll tell you, she lives her life as if she's got God in her back pocket.

A native of Goldsboro, North Carolina, she is a licensed minister and a certified life coach. She is never "preachy," yet she is always ready to be a faithful witness to the glory of God in her life. She has such a calming and tranquil spirit, and her gift and ability to encourage and motivate is effortless and is second to none. I have witnessed Robin go through things with her head up and a smile on her face that would have knocked some people down to their knees. But wait, she has been knocked down to her knees several times throughout her life and had bounced right back up. Her lifestyle as an intercessor makes being on her knees in prayer, figuratively and literally, a most powerful posture to live from.

Robin: I am a minister and a certified life coach. I have come to the realization that I really have a genuine love for people. I really enjoy working with and talking to people from all different walks of life. I'm a mother of two young women, Chanel and

Chantel, and I have a grandson whose name is Greyson. My coaching practice is called "Beyond Survival Life Coaching." I'm also involved in direct sales and I work with Wake Tech Community College here in Raleigh, North Carolina. When I think about coaching, and I think about Avon, and being a mom and a grandmother and a minister, I like to say you helped me, through coaching, that purpose meets my passion and they shook hands and hooked up. My passion is helping people. As a life coach working with women who have survived abuse and can live beyond it beautifies women from the inside and Avon allows me to help women beautify on the outside. So I help beautify women from the inside out. I help work on the whole woman. But it wasn't always this way…

IN THE FACE

At seventeen years old she became a single mom. At twenty-one she married an abusive boyfriend, whom she thought she could change if they got married. As a boyfriend, the abuse was verbal and eventually became physical. The abuse didn't happen all at one time, it was very gradual. As a boyfriend, he was very controlling—she liked the attention—and then he started picking her friends. "I don't want you going out." "I don't want you going to the club." "I don't want you to go out with your friends." He would check up on her and ask, "Where are you and what are you doing?" Then it became very verbal; not so much as him degrading her, but always fussing. The way he saw it, she couldn't do anything right. Wherever she would go, he would have said, "You should have done this" or "You should've told me that."

Robin had been invited to a party and her boyfriend told her not to go. And she didn't go. She did go, however, with her cousin real quick to get something to eat. And when she returned his car was parked in front of her parents' house. She was very excited to see him and as he approached her—without saying a word, without asking any questions—he hit her right in the face. That was the start of it. Robin didn't have a clue what had just happened to her, let alone why. As a young girl, she had witnessed her mom and dad fight, but she didn't understand why her boyfriend, whom she loved, had hit her. So that night she followed him. She followed him because she wanted to know why.

"Why did you hit me?" she asked.

He said, "I was angry because you went to the party."

Robin apologized. "I should have let you know where I was going. I didn't go to the party."

She went into a very apologetic episode on her part, even though she never went to the party. He accepted her apology. He promised her he would never hit her again.

He said, "I love you."

She believed him.

That's how the cycle started. Should she have asked for help? Robin didn't know she needed help, as her cousins were in the car with her that day but they didn't do anything and they didn't tell their parents. Robin didn't tell her parents. She wasn't a fighter; she never liked confrontation. As common with the cycle of abuse, getting hit didn't stop with his promises. She would go home sometimes with the physical evidence of having been hit or abused.

Her mom would ask, "What happened?"

Robin would say, "Oh, I got into a fight."

There wasn't a second question and there was never anything else said or done about it. Did her mom know?

He promised every time he would never do it again and she believed him. Repeatedly, he would make his promise and he would break it. Everything in Robin hoped that he would keep his promise and every time he broke it she would give him another opportunity to keep it. After all, it was a promise, right? They dated for about a year and he asked her to marry him and she said yes. Yes, she loved him and wanted to be with him, but one of the reasons why she said yes is because with him being in the Air Force, he had gotten orders to Korea. She couldn't fathom living the rest of her life in Goldsboro, North Carolina with her daughter. They married while he was on leave from Korea. Robin was so ready to get out of Goldsboro, fleeing other familiar dysfunctions; she hopped on a train to follow him, went across country to live with his family in California while he was away. The abuse continued.

Of course it paused when he was in Korea, as far as the physical part goes, but he became more controlling through his family. He told them, "Don't let Robin go here, don't let Robin do that." And for whatever reason, his family heeded his instruction and enforced his orders. Robin didn't go here. Robin didn't do that. Living with the hope that he would keep his promises, she thought that if they married and she became his wife, the abuse would stop. But when they got married, it worsened. But after two years of marriage, and only six months of living together as a couple, she was fed up. She was not only fed up with being abused, she was exhausted from having the thoughts of how to get out of it and worn out from fearing for her life.

BLEACH AND GRAPEFRUIT JUICE

One day she was doing the laundry, and things had gotten much worse instead of better. Her daughter, Chanel, was three and her daughter, Chantelle, was a few months old. While he was at work, the thought came to her mind, as she was pouring bleach into the wash machine with the white clothes, *What if I poison his food? What if I pour some of this bleach into his grapefruit juice?* She did it. She got the container, twisted off the cap and carefully, but quickly, poured bleach into his grapefruit juice. She put the cap back on. She looked at it. She nervously shook it up. She smelled it. The smell of the bleach in the grapefruit juice was too strong. The stronger the smell, the weaker her plan. That was not going to work. She thought, *If this man comes home and smells bleach in his grapefruit juice he is going to beat my tail even worse.* She poured that mixed drink out! The plan was quickly aborted.

Her husband had gone out that night, which was not too much different than other nights, considering she believed was having an affair. And though she felt powerless when it came to his extramarital activities as well as the abuse, she viewed this moment to make one empowering call for survival. She called her parents. By this time she was living in New Mexico, and Robin made her parents aware of several instances of abuse, but there was not an offering for her to come back home, or suggestions that she leave. When she called home, she asked her dad to come get her. She knew for her temperament this was a desperate move to ask for help, and she also knew that her life depended on it. She had gotten into the habit of asking God her prayers not let him come home and it was okay if God allowed something to happen to him.

She knew she had to leave and was anxious to leave because it was becoming a matter of life or death, hers or his. It became a matter of survival. At twenty-two years old, kill or be killed was imminent. When she called her parents, they made a plan to come get her and her two little girls in two weeks. She was attending a church in New Mexico and some friends allowed her to start moving some of her things into their house, to make a swift departure. But within the first week, things began to escalate and after an abusive situation, she called her cousin, and her cousin came through! Her cousin called her parents in Goldsboro, North Carolina, and told them what was going on. Her dad left on a Sunday evening and was in New Mexico by 7:00 a.m. Tuesday morning.

Her husband had come home just after her dad showed up and realized she was leaving. And he immediately began to apologize, cry, begged her to stay and began to manipulate her emotions. If her dad hadn't shown up would she have left? Had it not been for her dad she may have stayed. But when she looked at her dad, she said, "Ain't no way I'm going to let my dad drive from North Carolina to get me and I not go back with him. I have to go. I can't stay here with you." She left!

Now even though it was an abusive marriage, because of Robin's beliefs and her love for him, she still wanted her marriage. Sometime later, she chose to make a trip out to New Mexico so that her youngest daughter could see her father for her first birthday. She wanted to see if there was any hope in making it work. If there was any question, she got her answer upon arrival. The young woman who she believed he had been having an affair with had moved in with him as soon as Robin left. That was it. She never went back again. They divorced. He eventually married the young woman and his cycle continued. The young woman once asked Robin how to stop the abuse and Robin said, "You're going to have to get out." The last time Robin had any contact with an ex-in-law, her ex was on his fifth marriage.

DOMESTIC ABUSE STARTS WHERE?

Everyone, whatever their sex and age, can benefit from Robin's story. It doesn't matter if the abuse is physical, sexual, or emotional. And, some people are even experiencing financial abuse. That's when one person doesn't make the other person aware of financial status when the state of both parties' finances is involved, usually to hide destructive habits or to be manipulative or controlling. Or when one spouse or partner controls the finances and does not allow the other to have access or fair knowledge. But no matter what kind of abuse it is, you have to rescue yourself and get out. There are some relationships where correction and reconciliation can take place and the abuse can cease, and if that be the case, great. But you still have to get out, even if it's temporary. If the getting out does not mean a physical or geographical getting out, it always has to be a spiritual, mental and emotional exit. Get out or you will be out!

Robin: Domestic abuse does not just happen in marriages. It can happen during dating stages, at schools. It looks like caring and attention, then their friendships is controlled. Demands like 'You need to meet me here after school.' He/she may even say 'You don't need to sit with them you can only sit with me.' It starts out as an acceptable possession and a lot of times they don't see it, and as parents we don't see it because there's nothing really wrong. We see it as them just wanting to be together, but a form of control is being built. Some of the other signs that control is being built and could lead to abuse starts with and saying things like, 'I'm going to call you at 10:00 PM and you better answer your phone.' Or 'I called you last night, why didn't you answer your phone?!' To some people it would sound like he is caring and loving the person, and that may be. They make movies about it, but the potential for abusive behavior is real. When I was in college, I did my thesis paper on it and I learned that accepting abusive behavior actually starts in elementary school and kindergarten. When a little boy hits a little girl or a little girl hits a little boy, and parents say 'Oh, that's just a love tap." The little girl says, 'Mommy, he pulled my hair,' and her mom says, 'It's okay he's just being playful." A little boy may say, 'She punched me,' and the adult says, "It's okay she just likes you, she didn't mean to hurt you." That teaches children that it's okay to hit if you like someone. They grow up with that in their mind so when they're hit and tugged on it becomes acceptable behavior. When that behavior is mixed with "I love you" something has already registered that it's okay. Or 'I must have made him angry and I'm sorry. I shouldn't have made him angry,' and the responsibility falls on the person who is being abused while the abuser gets away with it.

Parents have to handle that aggressively without going to the extreme. One thing we have to teach our young girls is that it's not okay to hit and it's not okay to be hit. And if someone hits you or does something to you, you have to let someone know! Tell kids where those safe places are. It is unacceptable for someone to hit you and turn around and apologize to you and never tell and nothing ever be done about it. Even as a grandmother, I've talked to my grandson about hitting. We don't use violence to express how we feel. Growing up, violence was a solution. If he gets in your face, hit 'em. If they say something to you, hit 'em. That was considered tough. If somebody does this, you do that.

TracyMac: Some of our upbringings perpetuated violence and the gender lines get blurred, especially if the woman could hold her own. Even now days some young girls rile up at these young boys ready to fight; they are in their faces. Statistically, the female is more likely to be a victim of physical abuse, but young boys are being verbally abused and hit and you don't know how much more they can take. Who do they tell? Do we expect them to "take it like a man"? We have to strongly encourage our children, no matter the gender to tell, talk and walk! Tell someone who can do something about it, talk about it with someone who can help and walk away from that relationship! We see these things in the movies and because most movies are fictional, we take a fictional approach and don't deal with it, and in real life especially when most movies have a "happy" ending. And speaking of happy ending, I'm glad that relationship ended on a positive note for you. I am glad you got out! I know those two years or so of your young life are only part of your story. Let's fast-forward to where you are now in life. How have relationships affected who you are now?

Robin: I walked away and healed from that situation and it didn't take me long. My girls are grown and my grandson is eight and now I am divorced for the second time. I am much stronger. I am like a palm tree; I bend but I don't break. I always sway and I love that about myself. A lot of it has to do with everything that I've gone through. Whatever I have gone through are not tools to feel sorry for myself or make someone else feel sorry for me. I survived that and should there be another storm, I can survive that, too. I learned to live beyond survival! Because of who I am, I have to keep going. I love people; it is my privilege and responsibility to help them keep going as well. I have gone through so many things, and if I can do it, they can do it.

MY DADDY

Robin: At twenty-nine years old I found out that my dad was not my biological father and I met my biological father. My dad is the biological father of all of my siblings. When I found out, I handled it without being angry. As a matter fact, I never got angry with anybody. I just dealt with it. That is when I understood my relationship with my dad. I understood the man my daddy is. The man that drove to New Mexico to get me was not my biological father, he is my daddy! Since then I have gotten to know my biological father and I love him just as much. Sometimes I have to remind him that I did not have an awful childhood, I was not deprived. Most of the things in my life that happened to me happened in adulthood. I raised both of my girls, and my first ex-husband was still trying to control me through child support and through my youngest daughter. And I decided in 1999 to relieve him of his parental rights, and during that time I was getting well over $800 in child support. That was the bulk of my income back then. But I had to make a choice whether to be controlled and get his money, or be free from him and be happy. I had people to ask me, 'Girl, do you know what you're doing? Are you really going to do that?' I didn't get a lot of support on this decision. But I didn't need it. What I needed was to be free, completely free from his control. I did not have to deal with him anymore and my daughter wouldn't have to deal with him anymore either.

TracyMac: Robin, I have never been in an abusive relationship or a child support situation like this, and I will not try to compare myself to your incredible triumphs. But, as it pertains to money, one of my coaches at the time, Dr. Undrai Fizer, asked me a question. I was contemplating my financial situation when I kept procrastinating about leaving my state job and coaching full-time. I had the complete support of my husband, and I knew the mission of my life consisted of coaching full-time, but I was concerned about taking a financial leap. My husband, Owen, didn't seem to be concerned at all. He's always had this optimistic outlook that if you pursue your purpose and mission, things will always work out. But I didn't want to let him down and I wanted to be sure we would be okay financially and coaching full-time would be the right move at the right time. One day Undrai asked me, "Mac, how much are you selling yourself for by not leaving? Who's buying you and how much are they paying you not to live your truth?" I knew I had to prepare financially because that's what a good business woman does. But it almost sickened me when I realized that my mission and the business of my life was being bought to die with every check by people I no longer wanted to be with, while those I wanted to serve in a greater capacity were held hostage because I didn't have time. I didn't like the answer, so I changed it. I made my answer match my mission. I resigned and hired myself. Mind you, it was low budget pay, but I did. Had I not, I wouldn't have had the time to serve you and so many others since then. You acted on those questions without ever having to be asked and that is commendable, that's BOSS!! You were saying I'd rather have my peace. I'd rather have my freedom. I'd rather have my babies have peace and freedom than to be bought for $800 a month. And that was before coaching, that was before being a licensed minister and that was before Avon.

THE TESTS IN THE TESTIMONY

In 2010, Robin met her second husband and they married. During that time, Robin had been working with a company for fourteen years and got word in 2010 that they were going to be shutting down. But she wasn't too worried because she had been with them for fourteen years and she knew she would get a nice severance package and could collect her 401(K) and look for another job. Her then husband said, "You don't have to worry about working right now."

Robin: We had a plan. I knew we had a plan, but for some reason I knew I had to have my plan, too. Little did I know that six months into the marriage he would say, 'I don't want this anymore. I don't want this marriage anymore.' He never said why. He just left. No reason. Gone. Now I still had money, but I did not know I was going to have to go through my finances as quickly as I did. He left. I managed to stay afloat and got a contract job in 2012. February 2013, I was rear ended and the car I was driving was almost paid off, and it was totaled. I had to get a new car while working a contract job. That contract job ended in June of 2013 and as of May 2014, I have not had a job since. I got unemployment for six months, and that was it. What I had in savings and what I had in my checking account began to dwindle. But last year when I was laid off, I became proactive and was able to use the North Carolina foreclosure prevention program and it is by the grace of God that I still have my home. So when people say the government doesn't do anything, they do, they helped. That program has worked for me. I am thankful for it. They have helped pay my mortgage and my homeowners association dues.

TracyMac: Robin, one reason why I wanted you to be included in this project is because I know your story. I don't know everything about it, but I know enough that proves you are beyond a survivor! I wanted you to be included because so many times when people tell their stories they only tell the ending, or the bright side. But, your story is still in progress. Even though you are out of the bad relationship, you overcame being controlled and abused, and even abandoned by your second marriage. You lost a job after fourteen years, you lose a second job and then you get rear ended and you're still saying, 'But God.' You know your journey is not over, and you are still in the testing part of your testimony. I admire you for that. You always have a genuine and beautiful smile on your face. When we get together you love to laugh and we talk and have a good time. Where does all of this come from? And you want to be somebody's life coach? You are still in the thick of it, so why do you feel you can coach or help someone now? How are you going to coach someone or minister to someone when you still have issues and challenges? What can you do, Robin? How is all this going to work?

Robin: Tracy, you already said it, you said, 'But God.' To be truthful, I have been coaching and ministering all of my adult life throughout all of my issues, and that is because I am transparent. I may not have had the formal training or the right tools to be as successful as I am now. But people want to know how you can help them and they want to see your walk. And if I'm walking what I'm talking people are watching more than they are listening. They are encouraged by seeing me get through it more so than talking about it. I give God the glory for my life and I make sure He gets all the glory out of my life. I am able to coach and minister to women and take them beyond survival. I can listen to them, I can hear them and I understand where they are. I can minister to them and share with them the Word of God and the testimony of my life and at the same time I can help them discover who they are so their story can become a testimony in their lives. They help me because once I hear them, what I'm going through is minimized. I am becoming an even better coach now that I have the right tools from going to coach certification and even being a licensed minister. I am called to help and now I'm qualified to help. The woman I am here to help looks like I did. She realizes there is more to her life and what she's been through, what she's going through but she doesn't know how to get there. She needs to know what it is to live life beyond survival. As a life coach, I appreciate you for coaching me. I am now able to help women of all ages and from all walks of life.

TracyMac: Robin, I just want to thank God for you, and thank you for doing the work, becoming what it takes and making this sacrifice to be certified and trained as a coach and going through the training it took for you to become a licensed minister. You are so equipped to serve, help and assist women to experience survival and beyond because with you they can go and grow beyond survival. You have become what you needed. You are now ready to help that young lady who may have become a single parent at seventeen, who may be dealing with an abusive relationship with her boyfriend or husband, who may be a young wife or young military wife who wants out of an abusive marriage. For that single parent that has to raise two children and can't depend on child support and you are able to be there for that woman whose husband may have abandoned her for a reason that was never communicated. You are able to be there for that person who has had a stable job for years and has been let go. You are able to assist that woman who has experienced unemployment. I'm thankful that because of you, I know motivation, organization, resilience, hope, faith and love. Thank you for going beyond survival, spiritually, physically, emotionally, financially and now professionally.

Implementation Guides: How have you been experienced or been exposed to abuse? What are some of the first signs teenagers should suspect about abuse? How can parents teach their children to recognize abuse? How has your ex attempted to control you/ your children? Do you know where to go to for help? Domestic Violence hotline 1(800)799-7233—website: www.thehotline.org. What if he/she leaves? What test of your testimony are you in? How do you live beyond survival?

Chapter Thirty-One

Relationships to Ponder—Money, Debt and Credit

"So you think money is the root of all evil. Have you ever asked what is the root of all money?"

—Ayn Rand

Dear Money and Associates:

I feel like we have a beef or something. Of all the types of relationships my friends and I talk about, you and I know the least about one another. That's not because we don't know of one another, but until recently, I didn't know how we communicated. I didn't know your language. What I was taught about you as a child was not only was the love of you evil, but people who loved you were evil, too. I was conditioned to believe that if I had you beyond what it took to survive from month-to-month, that you could sneakily make me evil, too. Most of my thoughts about you come from my Christian upbringing. When I was a little girl, your name came up most during church at offering time. I would hear pastors, trustees, deacons or anyone else who was taking up an offering quote Malachi 3:8 and 1Timothy 6:10. You made people robbers, and loving you was evil, just evil! That's how it was interpreted. Maybe you have never read it for yourself, so I'll read it to you just like it was read to me repeatedly, with the vibe of Martin Luther King, Jr's I have a dream speech: *"Will a man rob God? Yet you have robbed Me! But you say, 'In what way have we robbed You? In tithes and offerings." "The Love of money is the root of all evil."*

Do you hear that? How'd you get such a bad rep? What did you do? You came to church in people's wallets and they read those verses to get you out! To keep from being a robber, I would always ask my parents for at least a quarter or a dollar. I didn't have an income because I was too young to be required to tithe, but I could give an offering. But as soon as I got my first babysitting job at eleven years old, and my first "real" job at Hardee's at fourteen, you know I gave 10% to make sure I wouldn't love you. I didn't know if simply loving you was evil or if you made people evil. So I didn't want to take my chances at being a sanctified felon. I remember cashing my check and as soon as I would unseal the bank envelope, verify the bank teller gave me the correct cash, I would count out 10% as if it were hot potato. I rather enjoyed being able to give. I wanted to give. Giving had become habit, but at that age it's common to question everything, and I did.

I didn't begin to question the Scripture, per se, but I did begin to question how it was being interpreted. If the love of you was the root of all evil why did they want you so much and ask so often? And if I gave you to the church, so there could be food in God's house, how come when my family was hungry we couldn't get any? And how come my tithe, my 10%, never seemed to be enough? When I was a little girl, how come once people gave their 10%, I'd hear them ask for offering, then benevolence giving, then alms giving, then auxiliary giving, then pastor's anniversary giving, missionary and let's not forget the building fund? As I got older, those were questions I dared not ask at church. I thought loving you was so evil that asking about you, or simply having a conversation may make you and the saints think we were dating. I couldn't have that because I was a virgin in every way and you were going to be the first one to screw me. All I knew was that you and I would not be accomplices when it came to robbing God.

EVIL: LACK OR LOVE

Then I remember in the early '90s hearing how much God wanted His people to prosper and be blessed. I had the question: Who weren't God's people? But that's a whole other topic.

Hearing how much God wanted His people to be blessed, and have things, houses, cars, savings accounts… Wait! Savings is accounts?! What about the saints who believed it in the rapture? Why would they have a savings account? Why would they save for a rainy day when they wouldn't need money on judgment day? But those who talk about financial blessings were labeled as preaching a "prosperity gospel." It seemed too over the top to talk about you in church that way and the denominational argument was a match made in hell.

Now, you know that was foundational, but that is not my complete story about you and I, you know that. I just wanted to remind you how our relationship started. I will say that in the mid to late '80s my dad would preach about you differently. There weren't all of these funds and auxiliaries and anniversaries to give to, but there was emphasis on the tithe and offering. And the discipleship classes and different seminars and workshops our church offered back then, you know the subject of you was included. I don't know if it was because of the initial way we met or because the conversations had been so negative, or maybe because I only heard about you in church. I didn't know how you worked anywhere else. When it came to you I had only heard that the love of money was the root of all evil. But one day I read a quote by Mark Twain, which said, "The lack of money is the root of all evil." I know one is Bible, the other is truth, too. I believe both statements equally. But no matter what I believe, what I know is you and I have to do so much better about our relationship. I've never been completely without you, thank God. Yet, there have been close calls and some pretty shady dealings between us.

THREE JOBS, MAN

You see, I don't know how to have a relationship without loving who and/or what I'm having a relationship with, so I kept my distance. Especially when I allowed people to make me feel guilty when I had you and, well... I will admit, I have felt used by you because of your friend debt, or should I say credit, because the use of one invites the other. I remember when I turned twenty and I went to buy a car. I got turned down because I didn't have enough credit. In other words, I didn't have any debt.

I wasn't spendthrift, and I have never been one who liked to shop nor spend money frivolously. I began to save my money and help others. At twenty years old, I had over $5,000 in my savings account, but the car dealership didn't want to hear it without a co-signer. I asked but couldn't get one. The finance manager recommended that I get a credit card.

I remember going to Twin Rivers Mall in New Bern, North Carolina. I didn't know which store would give me credit, which store I wanted credit from or what credit was really all about. I wasn't really into clothes, but when I walked through the main entrance of the mall, to the right was my answer! There it was: Kay's Jewelers. They had a lot of nice, little, shiny things in their cases. I liked rings, necklaces and bracelets. I thought I had hit the jackpot when the salesman told me I was approved for a $1,000 line of credit! Woo hoo! I hit the jackpot! Little did I know that meant I was simultaneously being introduced to debt and the jackpot hit me. I was approved for a temporary account the same day, but I couldn't believe it so I didn't make a purchase that day. I wanted to wait until I got the credit card in the mail. I needed proof that I had credit.

I picked out a watch, ring and necklace and they placed it on hold for me. Once my credit card came in the mail I was so excited! I had gotten paid from all three of my jobs. I took 15% of you out for my tithe and offering. I paid my rent and utilities. I had given my parents the agreed amount for the use of my mom's car until I could buy my own. I went to the grocery store and bought my food for the next few weeks and I put money in my savings account. Because now, you see, at this time I was making a lot of you, but it took three jobs to do it, like the dad on *Everybody Hates Chris.*

THE SYSTEM

I still couldn't figure out this credit thing because I had money, I had my jobs and they still wouldn't let me buy a car. But I went to the mall. My excitement that day wasn't so much about the jewelry. It was because the car salesman and the jewelry salesman told me that once I got credit and paid my account, within three to six months I could come back and apply for a car loan. So the jewelry was my path to a car. I stopped by the bank to get cash because I didn't want to put all of the pieces I wanted on my charge account. Once I got to the mall, I was disappointed because they sold the items I asked them to hold. I picked out a Citizen watch, a fourteen-karat gold herringbone necklace and a wideband gold ring instead.

"I want to pay cash for some this," I told the salesman.

"Well," he said, "you get a 20% discount if you use your card."

Now I didn't know enough about your friend credit to understand how it worked, but I did know your friend math enough to know 20% off meant I would pay less. They didn't tell me about the fine, microscopic print, which brought your associate "interest" into our relationship. (He introduced himself to me about thirty days later. His last name was 18%.) That day, I put my cash back in my wallet, pulled out my credit card and felt all grown up as he placed my credit card down onto the machine, put the rectangle shaped, tricolor (white, pink and yellow) receipt on top and pulled the embosser across, twice. I saw TRACY A. JONES and this long ass account number impressed from the bottom copy to the top.

My heart was beating so fast when I asked the salesman, "May I pay part of my balance now, after you charge the card?"

"No, you have to wait for them to generate a bill for you, or it will mess up the system."

I believed him and tucked my hard earned cash back into my wallet again. I wore my watch and ring out the store. He boxed up my necklace, placed it in the bag along with my receipt and I walked away. I had you in my wallet, but your associates—credit, debt and interest—were now in my bag and I felt no heavier. I had all four of you all by myself.

I wanted a new pair of black shoes and I needed a new black dress for church, so I walked down to Belk. Since I still had you, I used you to pay for the dress and shoes. But before I did, wouldn't you know it…they offered me a credit application. But as Nancy Reagan said back then, I just said "No." I didn't say no because I didn't want the credit, I said no because I didn't understand it. Plus, I liked how simply you worked as cash and you multiplied in the bank for me, but I still didn't want to love you. Did I? I didn't understand why anybody wouldn't want you, in the form of my cash, and I didn't understand why not paying my bill before it came due could mess up a system. It wasn't until much later that system was messing mine up.

Cash was easy to understand. All I had to be able to do was add and subtract, spend less of you than I was earning and give my tithes and offerings. I didn't understand why credit had to prove my ability to handle you when my checking and savings account, my ability to pay my rent and utilities on time, every single time, for the past eighteen months wouldn't suffice. Both salesman ended up being right because after about four months of paying my Kay Jeweler's credit card bill, I was able to finance my first car all-by-my-self and credit and debt have been with me ever since. They came along in the form of other credit cards, several other vehicles, mortgages, medical expenses, and student loans. Now, student loans have got to be another root of all evil, sheesh! The more I have of them there have been less of you in my wallet and my savings account. Is it because I didn't love you? Did you disown me? Is it because we have used one another so much so and ignorantly over the years, that not only do we not love one another, but for some reason it seemed that we didn't like one another?

I know credit and debt aren't bad, but when you mix it with how I was conditioned to feel, and not feel about you, with the way they showed up in my life without a translator, I didn't having a clue. I was satisfied as long as I could pay my bills from month to month. Oh, bills—those are the love letters that come in the mail every month from debt and credit reminding me of how "interested" they are to make sure I use you to pay them. My relationship with them has been very intense at times. I remember when Owen and I seriously considered bankruptcy. Do you know bankruptcy? You all act like you don't know one another because when people use it, it's because you've left or decided not to show up the way they once thought you would. Is that evil, too? But we overcame that situation. We got help. And it didn't hurt that we worked to make more of you. But we didn't know about our value. There is still a relationship with you I don't know how to have. I resented you because somebody thought it was a great idea to put credit and debt between us.

IF LOVING YOU IS WRONG

I had no idea that I would get sick and have to be hospitalized not too long after I bought my first car and though I had those three jobs, none of them offered health insurance, making debt show up in the worst way. There have been numerous instances of medical debt since then and I learned how to be healed through it and use you to take care of it, too. Even as I write you this letter I can see how my misunderstanding of you is, in part, because of how evil I thought loving you could be. But I realize loving you and having you are two different things. Loving and lacking you may be the same evil. Even though I'm much more open to a relationship with you because I heard that you were spiritual, I began to investigate. But it wasn't until 2011 when I started coaching full-time that I realized my only knowledge and association with you was based on a church or nonprofit mentality, but I was starting a for-profit business and didn't know my worth. I wanted your help when funding things for my vision, but I didn't want you to get the big head and act like you dictated it or controlled me. I had to learn, and am still having to learn, how you work, non-offensive ways of how to get you and use you without being perceived as evil to myself. I had seen good people have you, but I couldn't understand how they could have you and be in a relationship with you and not love you, but most of all not be evil. "If Loving You Is Wrong..." how could they be right? I only knew a few of them personally, until recently.

Implementation Guides: What is your history with money, credit and debt? What is your relationships with money like now? Where did you get your financial education? What are you teaching your children about money? What is your greatest financial lesson?

Chapter Thirty-Two

Changing My Money Mindset

I attended the "Speak and Write To Make Millions" conference with transformational speaker, international coach, mind-blowing entrepreneur, business mogul, motivational master and breakthrough specialist, Lisa Nichols. Attending that conference gave my breakthroughs, breakthroughs! I had already written my first book and was working on my second when I heard of the conference. I had only heard of Lisa Nichols in November 2013 when I had three different people on three separate occasions to tell me that something about me reminded them of her. So of course I set out to find out who she was and what the similarities were. I went to YouTube, and from the very first video through the fourth, all I could do was cry. Not being one to cry often, I wasn't quite sure what my tears were all about, and it had nothing to do with whatever those people may have felt the similarities were. But hearing her speak and watching her show her story, I was able to see a potential I didn't know I had. I went to her website to sign up to start getting her updates and newsletters. The busyness of the New Year made sure that was all I did.

But in March 2014, I became aware of the "Speak and Write to Make Millions" conference. *"No matter what"* my business bottom line was, no matter how much the conference cost, I knew it was part of my mission to be there. I have to admit, I could get with the speaking part and the writing part because I knew the language of those worlds and I could be better and do better at both. But the part about making millions was equally exciting and intimidating because millions meant they were going to talk about you and I didn't know how to have that conversation. It was worse than remedial, it was rejecting and foreign. I didn't know how to have a relationship with you that didn't require me to love you in a way that would introduce me to an evil I did not need in my life. Not only did I know it was meant for me to attend, but I invited my cousin. I knew from the way we were raised, she had a beef with you, too. And as a fellow business owner, I knew that both of our successes depended on changing our relationship with you and ASAP was not soon enough.

In all the thousands of church services, conferences, workshops and symposiums I attended, taught, served and sang at, I had never experienced being emptied and filled simultaneously with such intensity. It was transformational. And though I will never have the words to describe the impact that experience had on my life and the relationships and friendships that it allowed me to build, my main take away from those life-changing moments was not only the quote, but the evidence that "Good people make good money." I didn't have to love you, but I work so well, in purpose and mission, you couldn't help but love me! Wow!!! Breakthrough!!

NEW PEOPLE AND INFLUENCE

There is where I met Jewel. She's in this book and we have become wonderful friends. She's proof that friendship is not about longevity but vibrations and connectivity. I met Margaret Packer there, too. I'd spoken with her over the phone just before the conference. She is Lisa Nichols' assistant and the executive manager at Motivating the Masses and her gift of encouragement is genuine, fierce and impeccable. Margret spoke words to me between one of the sessions that caused me to go into the ugly cry in public! She said, "Do you realize who you are? Do you understand how powerful you are? You are amazing and you have every tool you need to be financially successful, but you have got to change your money mindset. Because, as influential as you are to so many people, you do not want to taint them with an unhealthy money mindset…" I don't care if that was a script she told everyone she met or not, it was created for me. Her spirit was loving, healing and genuine. She demonstrated "genshai" and I received. Yet, it was such a painful pill to swallow, especially because I didn't know how to change my money mindset. I didn't know I had one. When I discovered how unhealthy my money mindset was, I decided to change it. I am reaching out. I am learning more and more every day because I used the strength of vulnerability to ask for help, not once, but often. I realize it is a process and the process counts. I have my complete cooperation and permission to continue to evolve, unapologetically.

During the conference, there was another shift other than with Lisa, Margret, Susie Carder, CeCe Clark, Allyson Byrd, Jennifer Kem, Nicole Roberts Jones and the entire *Motivating the Masses* tribe. I met my incredible "Earth Angel," Dineen Merriweather and we have the most beautiful time together when we meet for lunch. We only live minutes from one another and she is amazing!

Before "Speak & Write To Make Millions," I met Dr. Towanna Freeman of Black Life Coaches Network (BLC). Dr. Freeman is doing an outstanding job of providing a platform and a viable network, while maintaining a premium level of professionalism among black life coaches. When I became a contributor and member BLC, Dr. Freeman helped to sharpen my clarity as it pertains to being laser focused on my coaching niche and clientele. For that, I am forever grateful to her.

I saw Dr. Towanna interviewing a coach on the topic about black women millionaires, of which I didn't know any personally—"No Not One" *(hymn - Oatman & Hugg)*. Not only was I intrigued by the topic, but that particular conversation revealed my own fear and ignorance to me. During the interview, I wondered what in the hell had I been thinking about you, money. How did I get from believing loving you was the root of all evil to thinking I didn't deserve to have you, and that my work would make you love me? How could I allow a lack of you to convolute our relationship because of resenting my relationship with credit and debt? How come no one ever told me how evil they could be or teach me the proper way to use them for my good? In the course of listening, I heard and saw an educated, professional, black woman business owner who had an awareness about money, debt, credit and prosperity that I didn't have a clue about. This interview was proof, before "Speak and Write to Make Millions," that if she could, why couldn't I? I could, too, if I wanted to. Did I? But how?

MY WORTH

I was so overwhelmed, realizing what I didn't know and how much of my worth I wasn't aware of or knew how to properly monetize, I had to breathe, and take one step at a time. One person in my life who is helping me with understanding my brand value and financial worth is my friend, colleague and fellow coach, Deanna Hamilton. Deanna has such an authoritative and spontaneous mindset when it comes to money, her business names are "The Money Making Mom" and "Success Coaching Systems." Deanna and I have created a co-coaching friendship and she is exactly one of the people I needed to help me shift and be held accountable ensure its continuance! Her attitude about money is admirable and contagious. I've never been broke, per se, and felt I was doing okay, but she has a way about her that makes me feel both scared and comfortable. She said to me once, "You are too good at what you do not to make the money that shows it. When we coach people we are touching and affecting generations three to four times removed. And people who don't understand and appreciate the value of that temporary investment don't deserve the quality of your service." Part of that felt intimidating and the other part felt like, hell yeah! I tell people that, but I hadn't turned the mirror on myself.

Implementation Guides: How can you shift your money mindset? What ways can you ask for help? Who are your mentors (in your face or in your head), colleagues, and accountability partners who can help you? Who can you express the strength in vulnerability with? What is your worth and value, and how does that show up, including financially?

Chapter Thirty-Three

Acceptance Without Excuses

"Assumptions are the termites of relationships."
—Henry Winkler

THE TRUTH ACCORDING TO JEWEL CARTER

Jewel and I met at the "Speak and Write to Make Millions" workshop sponsored by Motivating the Masses that was held in San Diego in April 2014. We met the last night of the conference and sat in the lobby talking from midnight until after 3:00 AM, and I had a 6:00 AM flight to catch. Both of us were in the process of writing a book. We shared some of the same experiences and both of us are quick witted and have daring sense of humors. Why not?! We argued over who was the shortest. This is my book so, I say she is. We discovered so many similarities that made us hit it off right away. But the three that stood out was we both don't like to wear heels, no matter how short we are, or a lot of makeup and we don't like to go shopping! Yes! I finally met another woman whose husband shops for her more than she does!

SOUL TWIN POWER

We say we're soul twins! Even though we had to go all the way to San Diego to meet and only lived two-and-half hours away from one another. Jewel is in broadcasting and has been doing that since college. She has been working in radio most of her life, as a radio personality and in promotions. She also hosts a radio show called "Jewel's Soul Therapy."

Jewel: It's more than just a show to me. It's a way of thought and life. I don't do gossip. I do real stories and things that mean something to me. It's something about being on the air and being real with people and they feel like they know you because you are genuine. I didn't realize how many people don't have someone ask them, how is your day? I also do quotes and thoughts of inspiration because some people don't get that. I took it for granted because my mother told me every single day of my life, until she passed, that she loved me. I thought everybody had that. I'm a mother and a wife and even though both of my parents are deceased I'm still a daughter. I'm a self-proclaimed soul therapist. My life story is the one that I'm living right now; it's a story of rebirth. It's the story of reaching a certain age. I will be fifty soon and you asked the question what's next?

First, let me go back. Getting married was about the relationship with my man, having children; it was about the relationship of being a mom. But now I am rediscovering my passions and taking all those things off the shelf that I put away—being a wife a mother and a daughter. I make no apologies and have no regrets, but it is time now for me to take care of myself in a way that I've never done before. Everything I have ever asked for has been given to me or either I worked for it, and yet, I still felt like that was not enough. I looked at myself and said what's wrong with you? I wasn't filling my life with those things that really had meaning. So, I began to ask myself what has meaning to me. It was traveling, helping people, showing up for people and overcoming my excuses and fears of why I was continuing to allow myself to play small. And the biggest part of my story is that I stayed small even though I had this huge voice and this big presence, I played small.

RELATIONSHIPS DO WHAT?

Jewel has a way of bringing people together and she has a way of nurturing people. People are able to identify with her because she's authentic and she's able to meet them where ever they are. We share those same qualities about people and relationships. I know we aren't exactly the same, so I asked her, "What are your strongest beliefs about relationships?"

Jewel: They change. If you can understand that, you will be less likely to hold on longer than you should or try to make relationship something they're not. You won't feel bad if you feel like relationships aren't what they used to be.

But the most important relationship is the one you have with yourself. The first relationship that comes to mind that changed was the relationship I had with my mother. When I was growing up she took care of me, but as she got older I ended up taking care of her before she passed. The other relationship that comes to mind is a relationship I have with my husband. We just celebrated our fourteenth anniversary. When we first met, our relationship was very intense and I felt that if I never saw him again I was grateful and I still feel that way. When we first got married it changed, again we went from just being cool to him having to become a responsible father and having to provide. Our relationship also changed because I was once a very possessive person. I would say he's my man and now I say he's a man I choose to be with and he chooses to be with me.

Our relationship is very organic; it grows and it moves and has ups and downs. But I no longer look at him as my possession. He has feelings and he has thoughts. As much as I love him, I have to be honest that there are times that he may think about being with someone else, and yes I mean sexually and intimately. The way I perceive marriage has changed. I see my marriage differently. It feels like me. It's not textbook. We don't have traditional opinions and views. You hear couples say if he or she stepped out on me, that's a deal breaker. At one time I thought being cheated on was the worst thing that could ever happen. But it happened, and I survived. It happened more than once. Someone cheating on me is not a reflection of me or them needing something I wasn't giving them. It is really about what their needs and desires are. I won't even say it is from lack. I don't believe they're looking for something that they are missing from home or within, or that they lack confidence. I believe we're really true to who we are; we do have feelings. I don't want to bring church in it and for a lot of people they choose to be monogamous and forsake all others. And if that really shines with you and is organic and how you feel, that works for you. But, if you're forcing it on someone, that's not fair. Don't get me wrong; I don't have an open marriage. But I get it. And I believe

I don't lean toward having an open marriage because of my belief system that marriage is one man one woman.

TracyMac: If marriage is not one man, one woman, why did you get married?

Jewel: I got married because I was in love with this man. I wanted to be with him and I wanted him to be the man to help me raise my children. For all legal purposes, it made sense. I wanted him to be on my bank account with me, or if I was in the hospital or injured he could make decisions. And aside from that, no matter what or who comes in or out of our lives, this was the man I wanted to wake up and see every morning. As I am allowed to wake up, I want to see him. If I was to go out of town or out of the country, I want to come back home to him. So for me, that was why I got married. Some people get married for comfort, some people get married for security and some people get married to show someone off as a trophy.

I believe you get married because you love someone. And if he chose to be with someone else, that does not mean he loves me any less. In choosing to be with someone else sexually does not take anything away from me. Now don't get me wrong, I know my body is my temple. It is not a visitor's center. I love it and I cherish it and I appreciate it. I never have or never will invite any and everybody to partake of it, and I hold true to that. I jokingly say my lesbian friends have been with more men than I have.

TracyMac: But, Jewel, what about society and the religious frame work, common morals and values?

Jewel: I know people want to throw the biblical implications and rules, but sometimes sex is just sex. Sometimes you may just want to be held or enjoy a sexual expression with another person. It is just a belief. I don't believe that my husband having sex with another woman means that he doesn't love me. I just believe it means that he wanted to have sex. I wasn't there and he was physically attracted to somebody. At the end of the day, he and I are fine, we communicate well. My relationship with him is my relationship with him. We provide for this household, my children are taken care of. We still hold hands, we still date and talk. We still make good love. And that doesn't change unless I say that it does and that's my power. Now trust and believe I have not always felt this way or thought this way.

THE TROLLEY

Jewel: *I*t wasn't until I began to understand what it meant not to be attached to things and possess people. And not being attached allows people to evolve and change and be free. If there are places in me that are jealous about him or other things, it always goes back to me: Why am I feeling this way? But that question also has to be resolved in my knowing that I am happy. And I am happy! I do not put my happiness as a burden on someone else through my expectations. My purpose is to be who I am, and not what other people think I should be. It's not what they want for me. I am responsible to be on my journey and the quest for why I am. There's a Wayne Dyer story that I love. He talks about your life being like a trolley and you're driving it. Some people get on for the entire journey and others get on and get off. And it's not your responsibility to say, "Hey! Why are you getting on and why you get off?" But they've got their own lives and their own purposes to pursue. My purpose now is to also amplify my voice, as I had been whispering for a long time.

TracyMac: Why did you feel you had to whisper?

Jewel: I whispered because I felt like my story was not as important as anyone else's. I felt like it had already been told or that it had been said. I could tell you things that happened to me as a child; they've happened to someone else or may have happened to you or someone you know. I am not defined by the tragedies that happened in my life. I am defined by how I overcame them and what I am doing today in spite and despite the things that happened. I didn't just jump into this state of being; it's been a journey of connecting with people really being open to different experiences, times of prayer and meditation.

TracyMac: Why do you meditate and what does that have to do with not whispering?

Jewel: Meditation helps me to be able to hear my own voice and flush out the chatter of everyone else's voices. I was able to take confidence in that and get back to writing short stories as well as poetry. Those writings and thoughts are ways in which I hear my own voice. I went to live in Bali for month. I went there to be at a place that I wasn't familiar with, to meet people that I didn't know. I wanted to confirm who I was born to be and in the process of becoming. I was with people I never met before for those thirty days. It was a women's event and I had always said my entire life that I did not like women. It was amazing; the relationships I was able to build. Being with all women for thirty days helped me to see that my issue wasn't with women it was with me. Looking at them, I could see the things within myself when I looked at their weaknesses. If I were with guys I wouldn't have to deal with those things. I'm not a girly girl and I don't care for wearing heels and makeup or shopping.

WAKE UP CALL IN BALI

Jewel: I wouldn't have to face those things when I hung out with guys. I was living small because I did not want attention. I wanted to be in the room and you not know I was there. But people have never allowed me to play small. No matter how much I dressed down, people still would come to me. I know I've always been different. And when I was in Bali, we were required to go around the room and say something positive about one another. The program had eight specific definitions that we were to use to describe one another. When it was my turn to be defined using one of the eight, the facilitator said, 'Jewel you are the ninth.' They confirmed the positive things people had said to me all of my life. They would say I was unique and attractive, too. I didn't believe them because they knew me and they were supposed to love me. This time, I was hearing it from strangers.

TracyMac: What did that mean to you?

Jewel: It confirmed that what I have to say does matter and has an impact and meaning. Knowing who you are and being happy about your life starts with the desire. When you wake up and realize that you're close to fifty, having to be open and honest that your life has been about everyone else, is a wakeup call!

TracyMac: How can someone else experience this kind of wakeup call?

Jewel: You don't have to go to Bali. You can go in your bathroom or you can sit in the time and just be still and quiet. Get in touch with your desires. And as easy as it sounds, it's just as hard to do it. In this day and time, it can be hard to be still and just listen, but we can make the choice to be brave enough to do it regardless of what other people think, even if it requires us to reach out for help. You can't live your life being who everyone else wants you to be. This is your life. You may have to have that conversation with your mate that says I love you, but this is what I want for my life. Is this something you can understand, or is this something you can get with? You have to decide what works for you.

WHEN A MAN HURTS

TracyMac: Does what works for you always works for your husband and vice versa?

Jewel: Some of the ways my husband feels I don't feel, and that's okay. I understand it. I don't have to agree with him. What I do appreciate is his him being honest with me. That's the most important thing. You never know how those closest to you really feel until you have the conversation. Just yesterday I had an amazing conversation with my husband where I was able to tell him that I appreciated him for always trying to put on that suit and that cape to take care of the family and go through the things a man chooses to go through. There are times that a man may just want to be held, be still, be quiet or not have to be responsible.

TracyMac: You're right, Jewel! Men don't have that space and society isn't readily giving it to them. I don't' think all men feel the same way, nor do all women, But I have successfully coached a number of men and have several close male friends, most happen to be black. Who listens to him, his thoughts, fears, dreams, ideas and desires in life? Who gives him a judgment-free zone and a safe place to be listened to? Me. I am one, but we need more "Peace Places" for our brothers. Not to skew the demographic, men of other races need that, too.

Jewel: He can't just sit down and cry, or bellyache to his friends or even read them a poem that he's written. Men don't have that space, especially black man. It is difficult; they still have to keep it moving. When we sit down and cry in front of anybody they say aww, what's wrong? But what happens when a man sits down and cries in front of everybody. Yes! When a man says how he feels and he sensitive and strong about it people perceive that as weakness. He has feelings. I think the way me and my husband perceive relationships and marriage is more popular. I just think we are willing to talk about it and be honest. It may have to knock down the walls of tradition habit personal expectations. People have to revisit why and how do I love you. Is it because you show up the way as only I want you to? In the way society wants you to apply love? Or can you show up being you? Do I provide a safe space for you to be honest, be organic and be authentic and who you are? Am I going to love you? And even greater am I going to love me? You being you is what attracts people because it invites them to be themselves. Whether I agree or not, I always appreciate people who say what other people are afraid to admit and say. Or even if they disagree, be confident enough in themselves to have the conversation.

F.E.A.R., F&%*! EXCUSES

TracyMac: So you've stopped whispering, you've had a depth of conversation with your husband, with me and the reader where most people won't. You've asked one another in the words of The Dells, "Where do we go from here?" You all decided to keep going on together, your way. What are you looking forward to doing with your authenticity?

Jewel: As I evolve and continue to show up authentically for myself and others, I am looking forward to really enhancing my show "Jewel's Soul Therapy" It's a personal development resolution. It's designed to inspire elevate and transform the "why" in you. Why'd you get up, why you love, why'd you get mad? If you don't know your "why," you're only going through the motions. Once you understand the purpose behind something you know why you're doing it. It makes so many things make sense. I look forward to hearing other people's stories and listening to them telling their stories. And we're able to exchange and learn from one another's lessons. I look forward to developing and discovering the parts of me that I don't know exist. I look forward to loving myself more. The more I love me the more I am capable of loving other people. I love people for who they are and where they are right now. Not for what they're going to be what they used to be. Don't be afraid to ask for help! Don't be afraid to figure it out. I'm looking forward to releasing my new book F.E.A.R., F&%*! Excuses and Act Revolutionary. I know what it's like to use excuses to live small and I wanted to help other people overcome that as well.

Implementation Guides: What's wrong with me if it seems I already have enough? Why do I keep choosing to play small? What if my marital relationship changes? What are some of the ways a marriage or long-term relationship can change? What if I see marriage/relationship differently while I'm in it? What if my spouse or partner cheats? Why get married? Why get married if infidelity isn't a deal breaker? Is sex just sex? What do you believe about sex? What about marital entitlements?

Chapter Thirty-Four

A Tribute to Relationships

"If civilization is to survive, we must cultivate the science of human relationships—the ability of all peoples, of all kinds, to live together, in the same world at peace."

—Franklin D. Roosevelt

Dear Relationships:

I love you. I hear you and I listen to you. I love the way you show up in and around my life. I appreciate the people, places and things you have revealed yourself through that allow me to enjoy life even more abundantly. There are so many things about you I have learned because you have allowed me to experience who you are. Yet, there are numerous things about you I know nothing about, and I understand that is a way to keep me addicted to you, and I don't mind being your love slave, junkie or allowing you to pimp me at all. I will wear your T-shirt: CALM DOWN—I LOVE RELATIONSHIPS, and use your hashtag (#Relationships) because I "real-eyes" being a love slave for you only binds me to create my freedoms. Being your junkie has me strung out on love for self and others. Is there really a difference? The hits and the highs far outweigh the blows and the lows. You pimp me out, too, for my own pleasures of love and acceptance. I don't have to turn tricks to take turns with my three favorites: Purpose, Mission and Passion, and they don't get jealous. You showed them how to treat me and we share. They work to please me all at the same time.

Do you remember the day you met me? I don't remember the day I met you, nor do I ever remember us being introduced. You make me feel like you've known me before I met myself, which makes me believe you know more about me than I do.

You show up in all ways always. I don't want to deceive you with compliments because all our experiences didn't feel so good. Through you, my heart knows what it is to be broken, feel aches and shed tears. Yet, it knows much more about how it feels to be filled to overflowing with various depths of love, causing it to expand and I don't know how you give it legs, as there are times it leaps for joy! It has a hearty laugh, no matter how it hears something funny, even if the joke has been on me.

I love how you thread and intertwine my strengths and weaknesses into the universal tapestry of all there is. I love how you allowed my uniqueness and oddities to add vibrant color and a velvety texture to the people, places and things where I am interwoven. Even if they can't see me, they feel me. Even if they don't know it's me, they know the peace, wisdom, abundance, laughter, success and wealth that I AM. The way you allow their lives to blend and be interconnected to mine, reveals your expressions of love to and for me, without shame, hesitation or judgment. You let me see there is not a being in God's great Universe who doesn't want to be found attractive, have their "flaws"; not just overlooked, but accepted, and still be loved, liked, listened to, valued and understood. Acceptance is bliss! I am one of them as they are all of me. I love how you don't force me to prioritize God or divide God Almighty into a separate category, because there are none that could contain. But you have allowed me to see and understand that everywhere you or anything else is God is. The way you are personified through purpose, mission and passion makes me continually long for you, your touch, to mold and massage me and woo me into the life of another. And I simply can't get enough of your divine hands. If it weren't for God using you, I wouldn't know God, myself or anyone else. I love how God is using you to show me how God is with me, works through me, is for me and shows up as me—and that takes nothing away from the omnipotence of who and how God is. I couldn't take anything away from the "Omni" of God, even if I tried. You have helped me see the only distance between me and God are your ears and eyes, and that is only so God can view the soul of my humanity to see me as God is. After all, there is no degree of separation.

You know, there are times where situations and circumstances caused me to feel you had forgotten about me, but now I know that's when you wanted me to have me all to myself. The times when I am alone, you created the space of stillness for me to love, discover and appreciate who I AM. You have shown up in every area of my life in a way that doesn't make God a priority, but allows God to be everything, anywhere and all the time. You've shown me how God is masterfully finessed into all the ways you befriend me: me, family, friends, marriage, sexuality, health, parenting, money, career, and time, and among them you require me to have no favorites, preventing me from having to divide my heart. I absolutely love you for that.

Relationships, you are my confidant and lover because you have looked upon my nakedness, seen my flaws and you love me right along with every last one of them. There is no threat to share you with others. I understand that's what you want anyway because you wouldn't survive without me, us and we that way. You've done so much for me as if I am the only cause you champion, as if my life matters, as if I am worthy to love and be loved through you and I believe you and I know I do! I know you. I trust you. I understand more about you now than I ever have before because we are friends and lovers, making music together, playing in symphony. God writes the lyrics on my heart and living through you helps me sing in harmony with those whom I am connected.

Thank you for being the life in my music and teaching me to read your notes, so you can conduct the orchestra that makes the sound of my life. Now I know you believe in me. You know me. You trust me. To show you how much I love you, I wanted to write letters about how I feel, think and know you in so many ways. But no way could I do that alone, as I am not alone. But I knew I could get by with a little help from my friends, family and colleagues. I called them and they answered, and boy did we have some things to share about how each one of us experience you and question you, too. After all, the many ways you exist has conditioned you to be the answer and the solution to every question the world has. The things we have discussed I am forever grateful for. You and your ways have allowed me, and those whom I am blessed to share my life with, to unite. We arise in chorus so others can also sing in their unique way: "Relationships: Nothing But The Truth." Namaste.

Chapter Thirty-Five

Relationships: Discovery and Implementation

"Maybe our stories are just data with a soul."

—Brene Brown

The subject of relationships and the perceptions of truth are ever evolving and inexhaustible. The truth of our individual stories and experiences are requiring us to lose the fairy tales and Jurassic mentalities to allow our God-given purpose to construct the architectural definitions of our unique relationships. No matter the longevity or how precious the hand-me-down information or sacred the God-inspired stories and texts written by other human beings, will you continue to allow them to override the truth of your equally sacred experiences you have with you and yours right now?!

Relationships only teach wisdom to students who choose to be wise. Stories are memories that we attach beliefs to, based on the perception of whomever is experiencing it. The value of the relationship is only as good as the investment and truth ensures a high-yielding ROI. This resource offered many different aspects, perceptions and experiences. So there is no one aspect of truth being promoted, because experience gifts everyone with a portion and there's much more to discover and realize. The perception of truth is as unique as the fingerprint of the person seeing, believing, thinking or feeling it. The way to get to a person's truth about relationships is to ask questions and boy, did they answer. I did too. Did you?

Use the Implementation Guides to discover, develop and live your wisdom and truth. Know your answers and shift from information to implementation. Close the divide between knowing and doing, you're worth intelligent action. Some of these stories you may have agreed with, some may have ticked you off, others may have caused you to think, change or engage in conversation about your truth. Like you, these seemingly ordinary people whose stories and experiences and perceptions are no less than brilliant.

A lot about how we exchange lives and form relationships has a lot to do with history, but I believe it can have more to do with, the relationship with ourselves now through self-discovery, purpose, mission and passion - What's the difference? I want to share an excerpt from my first book, "The Book of Purpose: The YOU Testament".

PURPOSE, MISSION AND PASSION

Some believe purpose, mission and passion are one and the same and that may be the truth of their experience. I really needed to see them separately, so I could more successfully understand, strategize and implement. No matter how great the purpose, plan or high the goals you have the responsibility to execute. It's torturous to think and re-think about your purpose and not give it an assignment or lack the energy to bring it to life. Seeing the difference between purpose, mission and passion could very well be the ticket to advance from thought to achievement! *Purpose is who you are and why you are here. Mission is what you are here to do and the means by which you function. Passion is the energy and level of intensity by which you successfully carry it out, consistently.* They are your why, what and how.

You can change your mission or complete it. Some missions automatically progress to another. Your profession or career path, social connectivity, functions, titles and duties are assignments that are subject to change. Therefore, since your assignments can be changed; it is dangerous to substitute them for purpose. You may be offered a job, you may earn a promotion, get laid off, fired or retire. They can come and go, but who you are is not controlled by your missions. That is why your missions may very well be many, but your purpose remains constant and you consciously bring who you are into everything you do. *I believe that purpose is who you are and why you are here, mission is the common thread of, and the means by which you carry out your purpose; the vehicle. Passion is the level of power of the emotion, willingness to sacrifice and boundless enthusiasm and intensity used to do it.* The passion is the fuel. It's not always 100%. You have decisions to make, there are responsibilities to time, the cooperation of others, spiritual maturation, human limitations, needful rest and quiet and finances are just some of the things that can affect your mission and the intensity or your level of passion.

Your passion is turned on by purpose regardless of the mission. Passion will fuel the mission as long as purpose says so. Passion is in love with purpose no matter what the mission looks like. It's your spiritual heart rate. Passion is the personal trainer for each mission and keeps it in shape for purpose sake! It's what gives you the enthusiasm to make a career change in spite of opinion and the economy or the drive, go back to school to freshen up skills or develop a new talent for purpose. It is also the strength you need to sit down when stress says keep going, as well as the power to abandon fear by keeping your head up, eyes focused and mouth shut during a challenge. It's the zeal that establishes the exercise regimen for the mission. Passion is the driving force for having joy and being happy about your assignment and it gets the opportunity to demonstrate the work ethic of the *shower you.* It's energizing the most excellent you there is to do what comes natural and it is on fire, but not burned out! Being passionate is enjoying the mission, having the energy and intensity for it. Passion can show up for work even if the direct deposit has yet to make it to the bank because passion isn't in it just for the pay, it's in it for the pleasure. You love to do it and to be sure, it loves you too!

Implementation Guide: What is your relationship with purpose, mission and passion?

References

Living Epistles
Diane Hamilton – Revitalize Coaching Systems
Website: http://www.revitalizecoachingsystems.com/
Email: diane@revitalizecoachingsystems.com
Dr. Undrai Fizer – KAIROS Institute of Personal Discovery
Website: www.undraifizer.com
Email: drundraifizer@mac.com
Duane & Sharon Reynolds
Email: aspire2b1@gmail.com
Eric Thornton – Thornton Wellness Center
Website: www.thorntonwellnesscenter.com
Email: center4lifewellness@gmail.com
Frandrea Madden
Email: flmadden@ncsu.edu
Jewel Carter – Jewel's Voice Works
Website: www.jewelsvoiceworks.com
Email: jewel@jewelsvoicworks.com
Kisha Lee – Purpose TV, Production & Photography
Website: www.purposeproductionsandphotography.com
Email: kishallee@yahoo.com
Latonia Talley
Email: lftalley@yahoo.com
Margaret Packer – Motivating the Masses
Website: http://motivatingthemasses.com
Email: margaret@motivatingthemasses.com
Marquis Hunt – The LifeXChange
Email: marquis.hunt@gmail.com
Nicole Winstead – Full Swing Golf Academy
Email: winsteadnicole@yahoo.com
Richard & Bridggette Campbell
Email: bridggettec@gmail.com
Email: richcamp1973@gmail.com

Robin White – "LavendeRose" Beyond Survival Coaching Services –
Website: www.lavenderoselifecoaching.com
Email: robinawhite92610@aol.com
Timothy Watson – Tim Watson Music –
Website: www.timwatsonmusic.com
Email: talk2timwatson@gmail.com
Walter E. Jones & Thomasine Rawls Jones
Email: liltwin9445@gmail.com
Email: wejones1944@gmail.com

About the Author

As a result of working with Tracy McNeil (Coach TracyMac), small business owners, leaders and change agents save time to consistently enjoy healthy relationships, increase influence and boost revenue. They transform their hard work into "heart work" and experience accelerated wins in every area! Coach TracyMac is a motivational listener, "The Relationship Broker," a personal development strategist and as many of her clients will attest, she is also known as "The Purpose Whisper."

As founder of Peace Place LLC, TracyMac Coaching Services, TracyMac Publishing and Strategic Alliances, Coach TracyMac has been coaching since 2004 and is also the author of *The Book of Purpose: The You Testament*, a thought-provoking book that assists the reader in discovering the answers to two of life's most intriguing questions: Who am I? Why am I here? Their purpose! Serving in many leadership capacities, her twenty-seven years of experience include the private sector, non-profits and state and federal government, which gives her the skill to connect with people from diverse cultures and economic levels. She attended Winston Salem State University and later earned her Bachelor of Arts Degree in Behavioral Science from Western International University. She graduated Magna Cum Laude and is a member of the Golden Key International Honor Society. Additionally, she is a graduate of Coach Training Alliance and a Certified Master Life Strategist with The Kairos Institute of Personal Discovery.

Her purpose, mission, life experience, sense of humor and heartwarming spirit empowers Coach TracyMac with the ability to assist others in discovering relevant results and practical solutions. Through individual and group coaching, workshops, seminars and keynote speeches, her knowledge and flexibility paves a way to support her clients through their challenges, and she demonstrates the prevailing excellence to help them overcome.

She thrives on seeing her clients have breakthrough moments that are life-changing and evident in their success. She currently lives in Raleigh, North Carolina with her husband Owen, of twenty-one years, and their beautiful daughter Jayda. Coach TracyMac has proven to be a powerful investment in the success and overall quality of life, by helping others discover, evolve, create, implement and achieve!

It's all about relationships. On Purpose. Through Mission. With Passion.

www.lifecoachttracymac.com

Dear Reader...

Hi!

Either you read this book or you're flipping through, maybe even straight to the back of it. If you've read it, I hope you really enjoyed these unique truths about relationships and embrace your own even greater! Feel free to contact me and let me know about your reading experience. I'd love to hear from you.

If you came straight to the back of the book, I do that, that's how I knew you may be here, too. I know you may be asking, *TracyMac, why should I read your book and what's in it for me? What am I going to get out of all of this relationship stuff?* What's in it for you? Let me ask you, what are your truths about your relationships, especially the one you're having with yourself? What truths have you experienced that can't be overridden by an opinion, book or even a sacred text? How are your relationships evolving, or are you stuck in an archaic mentality that doesn't match the desires of the truth of your reality? What do you want? How are your relationships working for you and how are you working for them?

I wanted to offer a reality check by letting you in on some of my relationships to illuminate the truth of yours. This book is written to offer you relationships from various perspectives, with people, places and things and motivate you. When was the last time you've seen a book representing women and men, ages thirty-five to seventy—unmarried, married, divorced—especially within the African American community, talking openly about relationships of all kinds?

When was the last time you've read a book about relationships and it wasn't some know-it-all trying to tell you what to do about your life, especially when they don't know a thing about who you are or what you do? I couldn't think of one either, so I asked the experts, the best references I knew...everyday people like me and you. They told me the truth, just like we needed to hear it and addressed questions like:

- What do you do if you wanted to belong, but didn't want to be forced to fit in?
- What if you and God are good, but you're tired of church and religion as usual?
- How can you heal after incest, rape or abuse?
- How can you change your money mindset when what you know is all know?
- What if what you feel about marriage changes after you say "I do"?
- How can you parent well if your parents weren't there?
- What if you have always felt different, weird or strange all of your life?
- What if reaping what you sow means something even greater?
- What if you are attracted to someone who is totally opposite from you?
- What if you love more than one person?
- What if you need help having an awkward or potentially controversial conversation with your spouse, a family member or friend about love, marriage, God, church, sex, dating, money, religion?
- And more

These are some of the questions we offer our truths to answer. Yet, the practical solutions to these questions are laid out, your way, in *Relationships: Nothing But The Truth*. We don't tell you what to do, we tell you the TRUTH of what we did and do.

You need this book!

Your relationships would love for you to experience this book!

It is an incredible read for book clubs and discussion groups, too, that will incite great conversation!

See how we connect with one another, enjoy this experience and share in it with me, as I share the various forms of relationships. They are encouraging, heart-felt, and thought-provoking, funny stories interjecting principles, valuable lessons, and intriguing testimonies.

Whatever you need and how you choose to see it is what you will get—*Relationships: Nothing But The Truth!*

In service and on purpose,
Tracy McNeil
(TracyMac)

*A portion of our book sales will be donated to support Multiple Sclerosis and Bi Polar Disorder, as a token of love and consideration of dear friends whose children are affected.

CPSIA information can be obtained at www.ICGtesting.com
Printed in the USA
BVOW05s1356171214

379260BV00001B/1/P

9 780989 101301